Money and Free Speech

Money and Free Speech

Campaign Finance Reform and the Courts

Melvin I. Urofsky

UNIVERSITY PRESS OF KANSAS

Published by the University Press of Kansas (Lawrence, Kansas 66045),
which was organized by the Kansas Board of Regents and is operated and
funded by Emporia State University, Fort Hays State University, Kansas
State University, Pittsburg State University, the University of Kansas, and
Wichita State University

Library of Congress Cataloging-in-Publication Data

Urofsky, Melvin I.
Money and speech : campaign finance reform and the courts /
Melvin I. Urofsky.
p. cm.
Includes bibliographical references and index.
ISBN 0-7006-1403-6 (cloth : alk. paper)
1. Campaign funds—Law and legislation—United States—History.
2. Law reform—United States.   I. Title.
KF4920.U76 2005
342.73'078—dc22
2005009168

British Library Cataloguing-in-Publication Data is available.

Printed in the United States of America

10 9 8 7 6 5 4 3 2 1

The paper used in this publication meets the minimum requirements of
the American National Standard for Permanence of Paper for Printed
Library Materials Z39.48-1984.

For my grandson
Aaron Beckett Urofsky,
"Little friend to all the world"

Contents

Preface

> If there be time to expose through discussion
> the falsehood and fallacies, to avert the evil by
> the processes of education, the remedy to be
> applied is more speech, not enforced silence.
> —Justice Louis D. Brandeis, *Whitney v.*
> *California* (1927)

In some ways, this book began at lunch in Williamsburg with a dear and now departed friend, Eric Tachau of Louisville, Kentucky. We were talking about the recently passed McCain-Feingold law, more formally known as the Bipartisan Campaign Finance Reform Act (BCRA) of 2002. Eric asked me what I thought of it, and I confessed I did not know all of the details. But, I noted that after the campaign excesses of the 1990s, the sale of sleepovers in the Lincoln Bedroom, and the obscene amounts that George W. Bush had raised in 2000 from wealthy interests, it seemed to me that preventing corruption in the campaign finance system just might qualify as the type of compelling governmental interest that courts have demanded in order for the government to regulate speech.

Eric, a true believer in the sacredness of free speech, disagreed. One could not regulate speech, especially political speech, no matter how perverted it seemingly had become. Then, as befitted a man who was a grandnephew of Louis Brandeis, he reminded me that Brandeis had always said that the cure for bad speech was not its restriction, but more speech. Eric, as those who knew him can well testify, was no knee-jerk theorist of free speech. This was a man who had put his body and his livelihood on the line when he stood up for civil rights in his home city, long before it became fashionable for whites to do so. He and his wife Mary K. had not just talked about civil rights and civil liberties; they had fought for them.

In the weeks and months that followed, our conversation gnawed at me until I decided to do something about it. I determined to research the topic, and then when I had reached some conclusion, write it out. At the start, I fully expected that I would continue to hold my original view: that corruption through large-dollar, soft-money contributions threatened the integrity of a free electoral system. But the more I learned, the more I began to doubt—not necessarily the premise—but the means that had been chosen in BCRA. The more I spoke with other people, including civil libertarians, lawyers, and scholars who study this issue, the more aware I became of the nuances in campaign finance, the problem of trying to regulate what nearly all jurists and scholars believe is the core value of the First Amendment Speech Clause—political speech—and the ingenuity that candidates and donors can conjure up to provide the political system with the fuel it needs—namely, money.

A number of scholars have tried to come up with alternative systems of running political campaigns, and I am aware of the work of people like Bruce Ackerman and Elizabeth Garrett, to name only two, as well as the economic interpretations of the Chicago school. But in the end my interest focused on the efforts of reluctant Congresses to "fix" the system and the responses of the courts to those efforts. Therefore this is not a book about campaign finance and its reform in all of its many-splendored apparitions. I have no interest in engaging in a theoretical debate over alternative systems of looking at campaigns or of financing them. As an historian, I wanted to know what had happened; at the same time, I did not think readers would appreciate it if I digressed from the main story into each of the dozens of hearings that have been held on the subject. The road from the Tillman Act of 1907 to the BCRA of 2002 is full of curves and dead-end side roads; the story here is focused on the main path, because it is that path, and the laws of it, to which the courts have responded.

The Supreme Court's responses are easier to chart; it hands down far fewer decisions than Congress passes laws, and holds no committee hearings. Although the negotiations and preliminary drafts of opinions often form interesting stories, in the end the law is what the Court announces in the pages of *U.S. Reports*.

In the debates in Congress, the arguments made to the courts, and ultimately the majority and dissenting opinions of the Supreme Court, two themes emerged; the same two themes run through this book. On the one hand there is the appeal to basic First Amendment jurisprudence, and the belief that political speech, more than any other kind, ought to be shielded from any form of governmental intrusion. This is a more abstract way of saying that we are not really interested in who gives money to whom, or how much, or why. The grossest forms of corruption can be handled by precise laws, so leave the speech that is at the heart of political campaigns alone. In the end, the people will decide which views they agree with and can, by their votes, punish those whom they believe have abused or exploited the system. To quote Justice Brennan, political speech should be "wide open and robust."

On the other hand there is an appeal to facts and common sense. Yes, speech is important, but if we allow large sums of money to influence who can talk, who can gain access to candidates and officeholders, then the speech will be meaningless. Clean up the system, remove the worst abuses, so that the candidates can compete on a more or less even playing field. If this involves some relatively minor regulation of speech, then the prevention of corruption or even of its appearance is the compelling governmental interest necessary to justify that limitation.

The courts have adopted neither of these arguments in full, and their opinions often seem to walk a very narrow path between the Scylla of potential corruption on the one side and the Charybdis of regulating political speech, with the dangers that implies, on the other.

For purposes of truth in advertising, the reader should know that I started on one side, but in the course of my research and writing gradually moved to the other. I have tried to be fair to both, and still feel great sympathy for those who (legitimately) worry about the impact of large wealth on our political system. But as I explain in the Epilogue, not only is money essential to the political system, it is in fact a form of speech, and although the authors of the McCain-Feingold law had idealistic and praiseworthy goals, they failed to take into account realities other than abuses—the realities of how U.S. politics is financed, how it has operated for many years, and above all, how many factors go into each person's decision on how to vote. The work of the reformers, and the response of the courts, is a classic case of U.S. democracy in action, and a number of important lessons emerge as the story is told.

The organization of this book is also designed to help the reader follow the main issues. Clearly the courts did not wait until the passage of McCain-Feingold to start hearing cases on regulation of campaign finance and its relation to First Amendment strictures. In many ways, there is a certain dance going on. Congress passes a law; the courts make certain judgments; Congress takes those decisions into account in its next effort at reform. I have not ignored the steps of that dance, but as I have done in other works, I've chosen the more straightforward approach of concentrating first on the legislative aspects (noting, of course, responses to judicial interpretations), and then on the court cases.

Over the years I have been very fortunate to have had friends and colleagues on whom I could impose to read and comment on my manuscripts. In every instance the final product has been better for their suggestions. Much of whatever merit this book may have resulted from their suggestions; I alone am responsible for the final work and its defects. Among those who agreed to read this manuscript, I owe thanks to Beth Garrett, Jill Norgren, David O'Brien, Scot Powe, Bill Wiecek, and Chuck Zelden. Above all, I am grateful to my longtime friend and coeditor of the *Brandeis Letters,* David W. Levy, whose eye for prose and insistence on grammatical correctness are unparalleled. As usual, David took far more time out of his work schedule than I had any right to ask, so he can be sure that I will ask him again.

The University Press of Kansas is one of the best presses to work with, academic or commercial, and Mike Briggs, the editor in chief, is, to put it mildly, a mensch. Others who worked so hard to turn the manuscript into the book you are holding include production manager Larisa Martin, senior production editor Susan McRory, and the general factotum in charge of publicity and other things, Susan K. Schott. It was a pleasure working with Melanie Stafford again; she is an author's ideal copy editor. Thanks to all of them.

This book is dedicated to our newest grandchild, Aaron Beckett Urofsky, or "the boy" as his cousins Emma and Chloe initially called him. Like them, he is a great time-spender, and one of the joys of writing this book was that he and his family lived with us for three months before his father, my son Robert, took up his teaching position at Clemson University. I no doubt would have finished the manuscript sooner had Aaron not been there, but I would not for anything have missed watching him learn to crawl and walk and splash in the pool.

PART I
CAMPAIGN FINANCE REFORM

1 / Campaign Finance Reform before 1971

> There are two things that are important in
> politics. The first is money, and I can't
> remember what the second is.
> —Mark Hanna

THE STORY is told that Samuel Gompers, the president of the American Federation of Labor, once approached his friend, Senator Boies Penrose, the Republican boss of Pennsylvania, seeking support for legislation—then pending in Congress—to abolish child labor. Penrose supposedly replied, "But Sam, you know as damn well as I do that I can't stand for a bill like that. Why those fellows this bill is aimed at—those mill owners—are good for two hundred thousand dollars a year to the party. You can't afford to monkey with business that friendly."[1]

Money is the mother's milk of politics, and this is as true in the twenty-first century as it was in the nineteenth. Both a presidential candidate trying to get his message to 280 million people spread out over 6 million square miles and a soccer parent running for town supervisor in a metropolitan suburb need money to pay for billboards, posters, mailings, television and radio time, and the full-time workers who staff the campaigns. To ignore this truth is to avoid the central issue in campaign finance reform—money is the fuel of political campaigns. So what rules, if any, can be adopted to ensure fairness, and how do we keep those who have access to large amounts of money from corrupting the political process in which money is a critical necessity? Moreover, does limiting money—who gives it, how much they give, and how it can be spent—actually accomplish what the reformers seek, namely, a political arena in which all candidates vie for office on a level playing field? Beyond that is an even larger question: Do limits on fund-raising and expenditures violate the most fundamental of all rights guaranteed by the Constitution, the First Amendment's protection of free speech? As in most public policy debates in a democratic society, the issues are rarely simple, and "truth," if it exists, is not easily seen in stark terms of black and white. In trying to understand where we are at this point in our history, and how we have reached the current state of both legislative efforts at reform and the ensuing judicial responses, we need to turn to our past.

★ ★ ★ ★ ★

It has always cost money to run for office, although the amount of money spent, as well as the type of expenditures made, has changed considerably over the years. In colonial days and the early years of the republic, campaign finance was not an issue, nor would it be seen as a problem for the better part of the nation's first century. When George Washington first ran for office, a seat in the Virginia House of Burgesses in 1757, he appealed to a rather limited constituency. In the Mount Vernon area, there were 391 eligible voters, all of whom were white, male, and owned property. Washington personally knew most of them, and he ran not on a platform of issues but on one of character, reflecting the older British tradition of "standing for office." He also spent money, some £39, to buy refreshments for the voters including 160 gallons of rum and other alcoholic beverages, or more than a quart for each eligible voter. The purchase of food and drink remained a staple in U.S. politics well into the twentieth century, and in Washington's time and later, the candidate usually bore the costs himself. This, of course, limited access to office to the affluent, but that did not seem to bother anyone.[2]

Although a few states passed laws attempting to limit food and drink provided to voters, candidates apparently largely ignored these restrictions. The voters expected such treatment, and there is no evidence that in a time when all candidates set out buffets, people cast their votes on the basis of who had the best caterer. (They did expect the buffet, however, and in 1777 James Madison lost his race for reelection to the Virginia legislature because he refused to provide liquor at his rallies.) Aside from these few, ineffective laws, states pretty much left candidates alone in terms of how much they spent and how they spent it.

In 1776, the year Americans declared their independence from

Great Britain, of the approximately 2.5 million men, women, and children—the free and the slaves, only one in five adult white males met the property requirements needed to cast a ballot. Election campaigns themselves remained fairly simple exercises—some rallies where food and drink would be served, some speeches presented, and perhaps some printed handbills distributed. There appears to have been no vote-buying or other fraud, and although this is not to say that election fraud did not exist, it would have been very limited, since the elections involved a relatively small voter base. Moreover, not until Washington's second term in office did the first political parties appear, and they changed the face of U.S. politics forever. Whether one supported the Federalist Party of Washington, Hamilton, and Adams, or the Democratic-Republican Party of Jefferson and Madison, one now cast a ballot for issues as well as for the character of the candidate. In fact, as time went on, in some races the person running became less important than the party label he carried.

The existence of parties based on viewpoint changed the nature of politics. Both parties needed ways to get their message across to the people, not only during the actual election campaigns but at other times too. Both the Federalist and Democratic-Republican parties as well as their successors turned to newspapers as a means of broadcasting their beliefs, and since newspapers reflected the views of the owner-editor, this meant subsidizing him throughout the year. In 1791 Thomas Jefferson asked Philip Freneau to take up residence in Philadelphia, gave him a part-time job as a translator in the State Department, and made him the editor of the *National Gazette*.[3] The Federalists, with money provided by Alexander Hamilton, Rufus King, and others, had already begun subsidizing a paper of their own, the *Gazette of the United States*. At both the national and state levels, whatever party held power could also provide lucrative contracts for government printing work to friendly newspapers. The newspaper owners responded with alacrity, extravagantly praising the candidates and positions of their benefactors, and vilifying with equal fervor those of their opponents. Much of the campaigning before the Civil War relied on newspapers, and as late as 1850, a wealthy supporter who wanted to further the political ambitions of James Buchanan gave $10,000 to help start a newspaper to trumpet Buchanan's virtues. In 1860 Abraham Lincoln secretly bought a small

German-language weekly in Illinois for $400, and then gave it to an editor who agreed to support the policies of Lincoln and the Republican Party and to publish in both German and English.[4]

John Quincy Adams, the sixth president of the United States, believed, as did his father, that the presidency should be neither sought nor declined, and "to pay money for securing it directly or indirectly [was] incorrect in principle."[5] A noble sentiment, but aside from the possible exception of Washington's first election, it had never been true. There had always been expenses, whether for food and drink or printed matter or later for torchlight parades and "illuminations." The first professional campaign managers—and the costs attendant to them—appeared on the scene around 1828, and within a decade the country witnessed the first documented case of outright vote-buying in the 1838 mayoral race in New York City.[6]

The era of mass politicking began in earnest with Andrew Jackson and the organization of the Democratic Party—the successor to Jefferson's Democratic-Republicans—in the late 1820s. Much of the credit goes to Jackson's lieutenant and successor, Martin Van Buren of New York, who organized the first popular mass campaign around the hero of the battle of New Orleans. By 1829 the electorate had expanded due to immigration into the United States as well as the removal of property and religious qualifications for voting. Van Buren built upon the older base of newspapers with rallies, pamphlets, and the appearance of the candidate himself at certain gatherings. Van Buren also oversaw the organization of the Democrats as a mass party, with organizations at the national, state, and local level. Although the quadrennial campaign for the presidency remained the chief goal of the party, the faithful could now be called upon to support candidates in state and local elections as well as for the House of Representatives. By the late 1830s nearly every political office in the country involved a contest between the two chief parties, the Democrats and the Whigs (a party that arose in opposition to Andrew Jackson). By then congressional races cost $3,000 to $4,000 (approximately $79,000 in 2003 dollars), and the 1830 gubernatorial race in Kentucky cost between $10,000 and $15,000, or over $247,000 in 2003 dollars.[7]

By 1840 parties utilized more than just newspapers and pamphlets to woo the voters. Pictures, banners, buttons, and other novelty items appeared. In the presidential campaign of that year, the

Whig Party supporters of William Henry Harrison utilized "conventions and mass meetings, parades and processions with banners and floats, long speeches on the log-cabin theme, log-cabin songbooks and log-cabin newspapers, Harrison pictures, and Tippecanoe handkerchiefs and badges."[8] None of this, of course, came cheaply.

Initially money for these races came from either the candidate's pockets (if he had the resources) or from small contributions by the party faithful. But as the costs rose, party leaders began looking for donors who could make significant gifts to the cause. Prominent New York Whigs such as Philip Hone and Thurlow Weed raised thousands of dollars from fellow merchants, bankers, and well-heeled friends.[9] The Democrats also had their wealthy donors, such as the banker August Belmont. In a development that worried many people, banks and corporations began making donations to one party or the other in an effort to affect policy. Jackson, who understood a great deal about politics but little about banking and finance, declared himself an enemy of the Bank of the United States, the largest corporation in the country at the time, vowing to revoke its charter. The president of the bank, Nicholas Biddle, chose not to sit idly by, and between 1830 and 1832 spent $42,000—an enormous sum in those days—on literature and advertisements in an effort to defeat Jackson in 1832. Although Old Hickory won, and did in fact kill off the bank, the campaign of that year saw what might well be called the first example of issue advocacy, the spending of money not for or against any particular candidate, but in favor of a policy. By influencing how people felt on that issue, its sponsors hoped that the voters would then favor candidates supporting that view.[10]

During the Civil War, corporations became an integral part of campaign financing, since government contracts provided so large a source of their income. Abraham Lincoln predicted in 1864 that "as a result of the war, corporations have become enthroned, and an era of corruption in high places will follow. The money power of the country will endeavor to prolong its rule by preying upon the prejudices of the people until all wealth is concentrated in a few hands and the Republic is destroyed."[11]

Although there is certainly some hyperbole in Lincoln's comment, he understood that with the growth of large government capable of rewarding its friends with great bounty, U.S. business owners would pour money into politics in order to ensure that they would get their share. In the election of 1864, the Republicans spent over $125,000 to get Lincoln reelected. That amount doubled by 1872 when the GOP spent $250,000 to reelect Ulysses S. Grant; four years later the two parties spent almost $900,000 apiece in the bitterly contested race between Rutherford B. Hayes and Samuel J. Tilden.[12] Over the next decades, business owners sought land grants to build railroads, tariffs to keep out foreign competition, a sound currency, and freedom from regulatory legislation. To achieve these goals, they freely supplied campaign funds, and in some instances fees and investment opportunities, to ensure friendly government.

Critics of the growing and, as they saw it, pernicious influence of business in politics pointed to the excesses of the Grant adminis-tration, especially the Crédit Mobilier scandal, in which members of Congress lined their pockets with stock from a company building the transcontinental railway; and the Whiskey Ring, whose mem-bers skimmed off revenue from liquor taxes for the benefit of both parties. But although corruption captured the public attention, in fact the majority of party funds came not from big corporations, but from assessments on officeholders and contractors. Andrew Jackson had famously said, "To the victor belong the spoils," by which he meant government offices should be in the hands of the party faith-ful. Typically the postmaster general, from Jackson's time through the administration of Harry Truman, handled the awarding of gov-ernment jobs, and the officeholders showed their loyalty by return-ing a percentage—usually 2 percent—of their salaries (or in the case of contractors, a percentage of their price) to the party.[13] This assessment system, first used in the 1830s by the Jacksonian Democ-rats, grew so much that by 1878 approximately $9 out of every $10 of the Republican Party's congressional campaign committees' income came from kickbacks from officeholders.[14] Not until a disgruntled office-seeker assassinated James A. Garfield in 1881 did Congress finally put an end to this practice; and it later approved the Pendle-ton Act creating the civil service system.[15]

The passage of the Pendleton Act and similar laws at the state level, although sometimes hailed as the first efforts at campaign finance reform, actually sought to protect government employees from party officials. But reliance upon the assessment system meant that no one donor had disproportionate influence within the party or upon elected officials because of the amount of money he or she gave. In essence, assessments ensured that parties would be free from big money by relying on a large group of small givers. The parties had never, of course, abandoned wealthy backers, but with their main source of revenue at both the federal and state levels now eliminated, both the Democrats and the Republicans had to look elsewhere to cover the costs of ever more expensive campaigns.

★ ★ ★ ★ ★

The growing industrialization of the country as well as economic expansion across the continent made a closer relationship between business and government inevitable. The building of the transcontinental railroad, for example, could not have taken place without the federal government financing it through a series of land grants. Sponsors of regional railroads and canals looked to state and local government for needed subsidies. The tariff schedules passed by Congress gave infant U.S. industries protection from European competitors, although the protection continued long after the companies needed it. Wealthy men like August Belmont and his son, August Belmont, Jr., Samuel Tilden, John Wanamaker, and Jay Gould continued to be important contributors to the two parties. Gradually, however, the amount collected from corporations, primarily by Republicans but by Democrats as well, became the chief source of funding for political campaigns. In the campaign of 1888, for example, Philadelphia department store magnate John Wanamaker contributed $50,000 to the presidential campaign of Republican Benjamin Harrison. Moreover, 40 percent of the party's national campaign expenditures (totaling $1.35 million) came from manufacturing and corporate interests in Pennsylvania alone, collected by that state's party boss, Matthew Quay, who had just assumed the post of national party chair.[16]

By the 1890s campaign costs had risen across the entire political spectrum. The 1892 contest between Republican Benjamin Harrison and Democrat Grover Cleveland cost more than $4 million, with the victorious Cleveland outspending his opponent by almost three to two. That same year Carter Henry Harrison spent $500,000 to become mayor of Chicago, and "Hinky Dink" Kenna raised $100,000 in his race for alderman. Kenna lost, however, when someone stole his campaign funds.[17] No one, however, had a greater gift for getting corporations to give money to politics than Marcus Alonzo Hanna of Ohio.

Hanna had made his fortune in coal, iron, and oil, and from the 1880s on had dabbled in Ohio Republican politics. He retired from business completely in 1895 to devote himself to the election to the presidency of his good friend William McKinley. He financed McKinley's primary campaign practically out of his own pocket with a donation of $100,000, and then, as national chair of the Republican Party, turned to the greater task of raising money for the presidential campaign. The Democrats and the Populists nominated William Jennings Bryan on a platform of silver currency and other "radical" ideas, all of which played directly into Hanna's plan.

He contacted bankers and businessmen all over the country with a simple message—election of the radical Bryan would be bad for business, but the victory of McKinley would assure the continuation of the gold standard in currency and prosperity for big industries. He then went on to tell them how much they should give. He assessed banks one-quarter of 1 percent of their capital, and assigned other businesses flat amounts based on their ability to pay.[18] He reportedly raised $3,350,000 for McKinley's campaign, twice the amount spent by Harrison in 1892. No presidential hopeful had ever spent that much, and the sum would not be exceeded until the Harding campaign of 1920.[19] Unofficial estimates, however, put the amount at well over $10 million. Hanna collected $250,000 from Standard Oil alone, an amount almost as large as Bryan's entire campaign fund, and a similar amount from J. P. Morgan. The Chicago meat-packing houses combined to give $400,000.[20]

Interestingly, Hanna made it quite clear to those whom he tapped that the only thing they could expect would be a probusiness attitude from a Republican administration. He insulated McKinley from donors, and returned money from contributors who in any way implied that they expected special favors. He even refunded money to corporations who, for one reason or another, sent in more than their assessed rate. Hanna had no difficulty raising money, because the nation's business community, including well-to-do Democrats, feared the consequences of a Bryan victory. The fact that the depression that had begun in 1893 lifted soon after McKinley took office—an event that had nothing to do with the Republican victory—helped to embed the idea in the minds of business leaders that the Republicans stood for prosperity and the interests of the banking and corporate community. That idea, in large part, has survived to this day.

Although Hanna passed from the scene not long after the death of McKinley in 1901, the banks and corporations he had cultivated in 1896 continued to provide the financial base for the Republican Party. McKinley's successor, Theodore Roosevelt, shook the faith of many businessmen with attacks on corporate greed and his efforts to break up some of the larger monopolies. Nonetheless, corporate support provided 73 percent of Roosevelt's 1904 campaign chest, which amounted to a little over $2 million. In fact, four men alone—J. P. Morgan, John D. Archbold of Standard Oil, George Gould of the Missouri Pacific Railroad, and Chauncey Depew of the New York Central Railroad—either personally or through their companies, provided one-fourth of Roosevelt's expenses.[21]

The Democrats, although often outspent by the Republicans, also had their corporate sponsors and deep pockets.[22] In 1896 the owners of silver mines in the western states contributed a hefty part of Bryan's campaign chest, and both parties relied upon wealthy donors. In the 1904 election, for example, the Democratic candidate, Alton B. Parker, received more than $700,000 from August Belmont, Jr., and Thomas Fortune Ryan. The Democratic vice-presidential candidate, Henry Davis, owned silver mines and made a large contribution. Although the parties continued to solicit money from small donors, in fact the amount of money raised this way did little more than augment the crucial contributions of large givers. As late as 1928, both parties relied on contributors of $1,000 or more for 70 percent of their expenses; to put that figure in some perspective, that year a new car cost $500.[23]

* * * * *

Around the turn of the century some states began, for the first time, to regulate campaign finance. In 1897 Nebraska, Missouri, Tennessee, and Florida banned corporate contributions. All four states had voted for Bryan the year before, and the statutes were enacted in retaliation against the corporate sponsors of McKinley. These laws, passed partly out of political pique and partly out of democratic idealism, foreshadowed a problem to which we will return again and again in this study. Corporations gave money to advance positions they believed would be of benefit to them, the same reason that individual donors made contributions. These donations constituted then, as now, a form of expression, or of speech. Moreover, this speech, either by a company or a person, involved political issues, and political speech has always been considered that form of expression most protected by the First Amendment to the Constitution. By 1897 the courts had already determined that a corporation had some of those rights accruing to "persons" mentioned in the Fourteenth Amendment.[24] If natural persons could make contributions to further their interests, then could corporate persons be denied their rights of expression? This basic issue—whether some expression can be silenced in the name of reform—will arise over and over again in the debate on campaign finance.

One should not think that only populists feared what large concentrations of money could do to corrupt the political process. In 1894, the conservative New York lawyer Elihu Root saw the need for more effective legislation and urged the Constitutional Convention of the State of New York to prohibit political contributions by corporations:

> The idea is to prevent . . . the great railroad companies, the great insurance companies, the great telephone companies, the great aggregations of wealth from using their corporate funds, directly or indirectly, to send members of the legislature to these halls in order to vote for their protection and the advancement of their interests as against those of the public. It strikes at a constantly growing evil which has done more to shake the confidence of the plain people of small means of this country in our political institutions than any other practice which has ever obtained since the foundation of our Government. And I believe that the time has come when something ought to be done to put a check to the giving of $50,000 or $100,000 by a great corporation toward political purposes upon the understanding that a debt is created from a political party to it.[25]

On the federal level, Congress did not act until a major scandal revealed the extent to which corporations had become involved in the political process. In 1905, the big three life insurance companies—the

New York, the Mutual, and the Equitable—came under investigation by the State of New York. The Armstrong Committee and its counsel, Charles Evans Hughes, relentlessly exposed how officers of the companies had abused their trust by using assets belonging to the policyholders as their private piggy banks, which they raided for a variety of personal purposes. On September 15, Hughes called to the stand the treasurer of New York Life, and asked him to explain a nonledger check for $48,702.50 issued at the order of the company's president, John A. McCall. The treasurer confessed that he knew nothing about it. Hughes then called George W. Perkins, a partner of J. P. Morgan, a power in the Republican Party, and a vice president of New York Life. Perkins quite openly acknowledged that the check represented money paid to the Republican National Committee. He added that the company had paid similar amounts to the Republican presidential campaigns of 1896 and 1900, and defended the payments as "an absolutely legitimate thing for us to do to protect the securities of these hundreds and thousands of [policyholders] everywhere."[26]

Although everyone knew that corporations gave money to political campaigns, the investigation detailed how much had gone to the Republican Party, and suddenly the idea of corporate contributions became scandalous and a menace to democracy. The *New York Tribune*, one of the nation's leading Republican newspapers, reported the following day that the testimony "caused a profound sensation as it furnished the first tangible evidence of connections between the insurance company and a political party." In fact, the committee members knew about where the money had gone the night before, and efforts had been made to dissuade them from following up that line of investigation. Perkins himself had taken Hughes aside during the lunch break before he took the stand, and told the counsel that he was fooling around with dynamite. "That $48,000 was a contribution to President Roosevelt's campaign fund. You want to think very carefully before you put that in evidence. You can't tell what may become of it."[27]

A week later Roosevelt met with some of his leading advisors at his home at Sagamore Hill on Long Island. Although the meeting had been planned before the Perkins testimony, there is little question that the Republican leaders discussed ways to control the damage. Two of those present, Secretary of State Elihu Root and former ambassador Joseph H. Choate, had previously suggested prohibiting the use of corporate funds for political purposes. Although nothing had come of the earlier proposal, it now reappeared in December 1905 in Roosevelt's annual message to Congress. After repeating an earlier call for greater publicity about campaign finance, he declared, "All contributions by corporations to any political committee or for any political purpose should be forbidden by law; directors should not be permitted to use stockholders' money for such purposes; and, moreover, a prohibition of this kind would be, as far as it went, an effective method of stopping the evils aimed at in corrupt practices acts."[28]

In fact, a bill to that effect had been introduced into Congress five years earlier by one of the founders of the Republican Party, Senator William E. Chandler of New Hampshire. In a single page he proposed two provisions: no federally chartered corporations and no corporations engaged in interstate commerce could contribute to any election campaign at any level—state, national, or local; and all corporations, no matter their size, could not contribute to congressional campaigns. At the time no one paid any attention to the Chandler bill, but the revelations of the Armstrong Committee and Roosevelt's message to Congress breathed new life into the measure. Chandler by then had retired from the Senate, but he did try to get another Republican senator to sponsor it. When that endeavor failed, he turned to Senator Benjamin R. Tillman, the populist and racist Democrat from South Carolina. The onetime radical Republican from the North and the unreconstructed Confederate had become friends nearly a decade earlier, when Tillman had backed Chandler in a battle over the cost of armor plating for navy vessels.[29]

It took Tillman the better part of two years to move the bill through Congress. He managed to get the Senate to pass it without debate in June 1906, a result many attributed to fear that the GOP would be branded as a party of corporate corruption in the upcoming midterm election. Then the bill went to the House of Representatives, where it died when the House adjourned without bringing it to the floor. The Republicans kept control of Congress and decided that they could afford to appease public opinion. The House passed the bill in its original form, but the Senate Elections Committee weakened it, because the chair, Joseph Foraker of Ohio, did not believe that Congress had the power to regulate state-chartered corporations. Chandler's original proposal rested primarily on congressional authority to regulate interstate commerce, and only secondarily on the power to regulate elections to the House, and he would have barred political contributions from all corporations but the smallest.

In the eyes of many, the final version of the Tillman Act was but a pale shadow of the original proposal.[30] It banned contributions only by federally chartered corporations, a group that represented only a small percentage of companies. How effective it proved is hard to determine. According to one analysis, although it dried up actual cash, the companies soon found ways around it by donating other items, such as office space, typewriters, and even travel (many of the federally chartered companies were railroads). Another way around the law involved keeping company officers on the payroll even when they devoted all of their time to working for a candidate. Since enforcement proved nonexistent, within a few years money from corporate coffers again flowed into campaigns.[31] A half-century after passage of the Tillman Act, one board chair, Duncan Norton Taylor, told a reporter that "a lot of corporate presidents just reach in the till and get $25,000 to contribute to political campaigns."[32] The first federal effort at campaign finance reform, in short, had little practical effect.

A second bill passed a few years later had a more lasting effect. In 1910 Congress passed the Publicity Act (sometimes called the first Federal Corrupt Practices Act) that Theodore Roosevelt had requested five years earlier.[33] The new law required the postelection disclosure in House races of each donor of more than $100, a sum equal to $1,667 in 2000 dollars. The following year Congress passed amendments also requiring disclosure to be made 10 days before the election, and extended the coverage to include Senate races. Although at that time state legislators still chose senators, a great deal of politicking went on that in most ways resembled political campaigns. The amendments also limited the amount that could be spent in Senate races to $10,000, and in House races to $5,000.

Like the Tillman Act, the new law failed to do what its sponsors had hoped for: to shine a bright light on campaign financing. Although it did set a precedent for making contributor lists public, the bill failed for four reasons. First, Congress doubted its constitutional power to regulate state and local committees, so the disclosure rules applied only to party committees operating in two or more states, or, in other words, only to the national committees, which at that time played a minor role in congressional elections. Second, the law on its face seemed to apply only to candidates, so committees, nominally without the candidate's knowledge or involvement, soon sprouted to assist in the campaigns, and they completely ignored the reporting rules. (The role of so-called independent committees would be another issue that would recur in the debate over campaign finance reform.) Third, a decade later the Supreme Court held that Congress had no power to regulate primaries,[34] and in practically the entire South, whoever won the Democratic primary faced only token opposition in the general election. Finally, the bill had no enforcement provisions, and did not assign responsibility for monitoring and enforcement to any federal agency. Although the disclosure requirements would later be expanded and would become an important part of campaign finance reform, in the short term the Publicity Act and its amendments, like the Tillman Act before it, did little to curb abuses in campaign fund-raising.[35]

★ ★ ★ ★ ★

Truman Newberry had spent some $100,000 in the Michigan primaries against Henry Ford before going on to win election to the U.S. Senate in 1918. A federal court then indicted Newberry for excessive campaign expenditures in violation of not only the 1910 law, but also a Michigan statute that limited senatorial campaign expenses to $3,750. He appealed his conviction to the Supreme Court, which in 1921, by a 5–4 vote, struck down those parts of the 1910 law as they applied to Senate races. The opinion by Justice McKenna rested primarily on federalism grounds, since at the time the law had been passed, state legislatures still chose senators. But McKenna's opinion said nothing about the provisions regulating House races, and four members of the Court believed the law completely constitutional. According to one interpretation, now that the Seventeenth Amendment had been ratified, providing for direct election of senators, Congress merely had to reenact the 1911 amendments for the bill to meet constitutional requirements.

When members of the House sought Attorney General Harry Daugherty's opinion, however, he informed them that in light of the *Newberry* decision, all the provisions of the bill had been invalidated, and candidates for neither the House nor the Senate had to file reports on their campaign contributors or expenditures.[36] Although both Democrats and Republicans disagreed with this interpretation, they did nothing until the country once again reacted to a major political scandal, the Teapot Dome affair.

Technically, Teapot Dome had nothing to do with campaign contributions; it involved, instead, simple old-fashioned bribery of public officials, especially Secretary of the Interior Albert B. Fall, who awarded oil leases on federal land in return for kickbacks from the oil companies.[37] Harding himself had not been the choice of the big corporations, and the majority of his money in both the primaries and the campaign came from small contributors or from wealthy friends. But in the investigation it emerged that oil magnate Harry Sinclair had made large, albeit legal, contributions to the Republican Party in nonelection years, thus escaping the provisions of the Publicity Act, which required disclosure of money received only in an election year. During the debate over campaign finance regulation, Senator Joseph Robinson (D-Ark.) declared: "We all know . . . that one of the great political evils of the time is the apparent hold on political parties which business interests and certain organizations seek and sometimes obtain by reason of liberal campaign contributions."[38] Moreover, Robinson declared, many people assumed that donors to winning campaigns then expected, and sometimes demanded, some form of "consideration" as a token of gratitude.

Congress, after dithering about for more than a year, finally passed the Federal Corrupt Practices Act of 1925, and President Coolidge promptly signed it into law.[39] The new measure closed the loophole Sinclair had exploited by requiring disclosures regardless of when donors gave their money. It raised the spending ceiling for Senate races to $25,000 and required disclosure of all receipts by candidates for either the House or the Senate and by political committees acting in two or more states.

The bill had a number of flaws. It required reporting only those expenditures made with a candidate's "knowledge or consent," and most office-seekers interpreted this as applying only to their own personal outlays. As a result, they did not report expenditures made by committees. As political scientist Louise Overacker commented, evasion of the law only required that "the astute candidate be discreetly ignorant of what his friends are doing."[40] Passed on the eve of the great expansion of radio in the 1920s, leading to the purchase of air time for political advertisements, the act's spending limits were out-of-date before Coolidge even signed the bill. As a result, nearly all payments for air time went through committees, which routinely ignored both the limit and the reporting provisions. National party committees, the only ones affected by the measure, evaded the provisions applying to them by routing funds through state or local groups. The reports they did file tended to be vague and incomplete. Other committees claimed the law did not apply to them, and House Clerk William Tyler Page, the officer designated in the law to receive the reports, could do little about it. "It is not for me to say," he said, "whether an organization, politically active, comes within the purview of the law or not. That was for the officers of such associations [themselves] to determine."[41] If any other sign were needed that Congress really did not intend this bill to be very effective, one merely had to note that it lacked any enforcement provisions. There would not be a single successful prosecution under the act for the 46 years that it remained on the statute books.[42]

In addition, Congress did not challenge the Supreme Court's ruling that it had no authority over primaries, even though many in the legislature believed that *Newberry* did not provide a clear precedent. Even after the Supreme Court rejected this holding and held that Congress had authority over primaries in *United States v. Classic* (1941), Congress did not act.[43] A coalition of Republicans and southern Democrats opposed federal regulation of primaries, and although Congress attempted further regulation of elections in the two decades following World War II, it did not reassert the authority first claimed in 1911 until the Federal Election Campaign Act of 1971 (see Chapter 2).

★ ★ ★ ★ ★

Franklin Roosevelt once complained that when he took office, capitalism was like a drowning man. He and the New Deal rescued the fellow, only to be reproved a few years later for failing to save his hat as well. Certainly big business did not see Roosevelt and the Democrats as its friends in the 1930s and continued to direct most corporate contributions to the assistance of the Republican Party and its candidates. In fact, in all four of his victorious presidential campaigns, Roosevelt found himself outspent by his Republican opponents. So the Democrats turned to some creative fund-raising and also uncovered a new and potent ally in the labor unions that benefited so greatly from New Deal measures.

Since the law prohibited corporations from donating money to presidential campaigns, the Democrats produced a souvenir book for the 1936 national convention. In it they had pictures and articles about their candidates, interspersed with many pages of advertisements, with full-page ads costing $2,500. Nothing in the law prohibited a company from taking out an ad, even in a political publication. The Democratic National Committee sold the books to corporations and others; cheap editions sold at $2.50 apiece, deluxe copies autographed by the president himself went for $100. The party raised $250,000 that year as a result of the book, easily covering the cost of the convention. The souvenir book became a staple of the national and even state conventions of both parties for the next 35 years.[44]

The souvenir book might defray the costs of the national convention, but it played a relatively small role in paying for increasingly expensive political campaigns. In the bitterly fought 1928 election between Herbert Hoover and Alfred E. Smith, the Republican National Committee officially spent $6,256,110, and its Democratic counterpart expended $5,342,350. Although these numbers by themselves would have made the campaign the most expensive in U.S. history up to that time, the actual costs of the campaign, including amounts spent by state and local committees, probably exceeded $20 million. Moreover, the donation patterns again showed party reliance on big givers. More than 90,000 people contributed to Smith's campaign, and 140,000 gave to Hoover's. One percent of the givers to both parties gave half of the total amount raised. Small contributors, identified as those giving less than $100, accounted for only one-eighth of the sums raised by the Democrats, and for 8 percent of the Republican war chest.[45]

The 1928 campaign took place at the height of the decade's prosperity; four years later both parties spent far less—a total of $5.1 million by the national committees—but they still relied on large givers, who in each case gave more than 40 percent of the totals raised. By 1936, though, the amount contributed by donors of $5,000 or more had shrunk to 26 percent for the Democrats and 24.2 percent for the Republicans.[46] Although the GOP continued to rely upon business contributions, the Democrats had successfully tapped into a new source not only of revenue, but of campaign workers—the labor unions.

The Republicans had been no friends of labor unions, and conservative judges—usually Republicans—had consistently struck down laws that helped workers and had issued injunctions preventing strikes or pickets.[47] With the New Deal, labor for the first time found an administration in Washington sympathetic to its goals. The National Industrial Recovery Act of 1933 guaranteed labor unions' right to bargain collectively, required industrial codes to adopt fair labor standards of minimum wages and maximum hours, and appropriated $3.3 billion to put unemployed workers on the payrolls of federal projects. After the Supreme Court invalidated the act, Congress passed the Wagner Labor Relations Act of 1935, reaffirming labor unions' right to organize and bargain collectively, and established the powerful National Labor Relations Board to enforce this policy. The 1935 Social Security Act created a fund to provide supplemental benefits to older Americans, and in 1938 Congress passed the Fair Labor Standards Act, establishing maximum hours, minimum wages, and safety conditions for workers employed in interstate commerce. Overseeing all these developments were prominent Democrats like Harold Ickes and Frances Perkins, whom organized labor recognized as friends.

Years earlier Samuel Gompers had established the political policy for the American Federation of Labor: it would reward its friends and punish its enemies, but it would neither take overt political stands nor endorse particular parties or candidates. All that changed in the 1930s as both the more conservative AFL as well as the newer and more liberal unions in the Congress of Industrial Organizations rushed to reward Roosevelt and the Democrats not only with their votes but with dollars. Although in 1936 Roosevelt rejected a $250,000 check hand-delivered by CIO president John L. Lewis because he feared being too closely associated with unions, the Democratic National Committee had no problem accepting the money and in fact got an additional half million from labor unions for that election.[48] Organized labor had contributed nothing to either party in 1928 or 1932, but roughly 10 percent of all Democratic campaign funds came from unions in 1936 and 16 percent in 1940.[49]

By the late 1930s, however, both Republicans and conservative southern Democrats suspected that Roosevelt was using New Deal programs—especially those benefiting labor—to build a powerful new political base for himself. The various government employment projects such as the Public Works Administration, the Civilian Conservation Corps, the Tennessee Valley Authority, and the Works Progress Administration had put millions of men and women to work on the government payroll, but outside the civil service restrictions of the Pendleton Act. After Roosevelt failed to purge the Democratic Party of its more conservative members in the 1938 election, a coalition of Republicans and conservative Democrats united to push through the Hatch Act in 1939.[50]

Named for its chief sponsor, Senator Carl Hatch of New Mexico, the measure extended the ban on political contributions and participation in campaigns beyond the civil service (covered under the Pendleton Act) to include all government employees. Although supposedly a reform measure, the bill had no other purpose than to strike at what its sponsors feared was Franklin Roosevelt's growing political power. The following year, Congress amended the Hatch Act to ban donations by federal contractors, or by employees of state agencies, financed in whole or in part by federal funds. The amendment also limited contributions to national committees to $5,000, and placed a spending limit on national committees of $3 million per campaign.[51] The Hatch Act amendments proved as futile as previous measures. The $5,000 limit on contributions only meant that people wishing to give more than that amount would funnel their money into other committees, a practice the act did not cover. Although neither national committee spent more than $3 million until the election of 1952, the total expenses easily surpassed that limit.

Then in the midst of World War II, Republicans capitalized on the negative reactions to a bitter strike by John L. Lewis's United Mine Workers to push through, over a presidential veto, the Smith-Connally Act, also known as the War Labor Disputes Act. Section 9 of the act prohibited labor unions from contributing to political campaigns for the duration of the war.[52] The unions circumvented §9 with a device that would come to play a key role in the debate over campaign finance reform a half-century later, the political action committee, or PAC. Union members contributed to labor-organized PACs through automatic payroll check-offs, and then the PACs, supposedly independent entities, contributed that money to candidates. Lawyers for the CIO also interpreted §9 as prohibiting donations going directly to candidates, but not for expenditures made independently. The CIO, therefore, freely engaged in a whole variety of activities and supported particular Democratic candidates. Once again, an effort at supposed campaign finance reform—although in truth an attack on the political activities of labor unions—produced results opposite to those intended. In the 1944 presidential campaign organized labor participated more fully than it had ever done before, and the CIO's PAC alone spent almost $2 million in support of Democratic candidates.[53]

★ ★ ★ ★ ★

Well before the end of the war, organized labor had become a major ally of the Democratic Party, and when the Republicans gained control of both houses of Congress in 1946, for the first time in 16 years, they wasted no time in going after the unions. The Taft-Hartley Act, passed over Harry Truman's veto, made permanent the Smith-Connally ban on union contributions. It also banned all union expenditures on political activity, including communications with union members that related to politics. As the House report accompanying the bill noted, the term "making any contribution" was to be interpreted broadly, to include not just direct contributions to candidates, but the indirect expenditure of funds to help candidates. Unions could not use money from their general treasury for political purposes, even, under §304, to fund a newsletter for members in which the union endorsed a candidate. Taft-Hartley not only attempted to regulate the use of money, but for the first time overtly tried to limit the political speech of a particular group.[54]

The unions immediately challenged this latter section, and the *CIO News* published an editorial backing a Democratic candidate in Maryland. The government brought suit, and eventually the case reached the Supreme Court, which, in a rather convoluted opinion by Justice Stanley Reed, totally twisted the legislative history of the act to hold that the ban did not apply to internal communications. None of the justices wanted to support a ban on union's communications with their members, but only Justice Wiley Rutledge, joined by Hugo Black, William O. Douglas, and Frank Murphy, believed that §304 violated the First Amendment because it limited free speech.[55]

In 1957 the Justice Department indicted the United Auto Workers for violating Taft-Hartley's ban on external communications—that is, sending political messages to the public at large. The union defended itself by claiming that this ban, like that on internal communications, violated the First Amendment. The Warren Court, under attack because of its rulings on segregation and the free speech rights of communists, ducked the issue on procedural grounds, and sent the case back to a district court, where a jury trial acquitted the union.[56] The case marked the first time that any group had been indicted for speaking to the public about political issues, and in some ways foreshadowed the debate of the 1990s about "issue advocacy," and whether groups can spend money that helps a candidate through "education" of the public about particular issues.

Despite this victory, unions for the most part did cease direct communications with the public, because they really had no need for it. Workers, at that time still heavily Democratic, continued to send money to the union PACs through payroll check-offs, and the PACs not only made contributions to candidates but also financed messages to the public. Moreover, internal communications through union newspapers and newsletters reached millions of members, urging them to support particular candidates, usually Democratic. Truman's surprise victory over Thomas Dewey in the 1948 election is often credited to the support he received from labor unions angry at the Republicans and grateful to Truman for his effort to block Taft-Hartley through a veto. Truman benefited not only from the money unions spent on his behalf, but also from the tens of thousands of union members who worked on campaigns, staffed phone banks, registered voters, and helped Democrats in a myriad of other ways.

Ironically, very few corporations at this time set up PACs to evade the restrictions placed on them by the Corrupt Practices Act. Commentators believe that in part corporations doubted that they could legally use company funds to establish a PAC. Moreover, company officials felt no need to do so. As noted earlier, well after the passage of the Tillman Act, corporate executives made large contributions for which their companies reimbursed them, or just simply ignored the ban by reaching into the corporate till and sending in money to a campaign committee. The lack of enforcement of the Tillman Law made chances of indictment practically nil.[57]

⋆ ⋆ ⋆ ⋆ ⋆

By the late 1950s, the United States financed its campaigns through a system that, according to Frank Sorauf, a political scientist at the University of Minnesota, had several features that would in effect determine the course of future campaign finance reform. To begin with, campaigns at the national level, including congressional races, depended primarily upon large contributors consisting of wealthy individuals, corporations (which funneled their money through their officers' supposedly "personal" donations), and labor unions. In 1952 about two-thirds of all money spent on federal elections came from donations of $500 or more ($2,300 in current dollars). In state and local politics, patronage and payments remained a significant source of funds, with large contributors often rewarded after a victorious campaign with plum appointments.[58]

Political parties also played an important role in campaigns as the intermediaries between contributors and candidates. Although federal rules may have limited expenditures by the national committees, members of the Democratic and Republican National Committees knew and, directly or indirectly, helped guide other committees and PACs in spending money beyond what federal law allowed. Very often the solicitations for funds, an important part of raising money for campaigns, came from party officials.

Finally, federal and state laws aimed at regulating campaign finance all added up to nothing more than an exercise in futility. Although some of the more blatant and corrupt practices had been eliminated or at least marginalized, no mechanism existed to enforce the laws, nor, if truth be told, did government officials really want to do so. Both Democrats and Republicans wanted and needed money to run their campaigns.[59]

All this began to change in the 1960s, with the development of new campaign technologies unlinked to print media, and a concomitant change in the nature of political parties. Although there had been public opinion polls since the 1930s, and politicians had begun using them in the 1940s, John F. Kennedy's campaign in 1960 used polls in a way that had not been done before, essentially relying upon them to shape campaign strategy. At the same time, radio and television became the new media, and the costs of buying air time and producing sophisticated commercials drove up the expenses of campaigning far beyond what they had been. In 1948 the Democratic National Committee spent $2.7 million on the Truman campaign. In the two races in which Dwight Eisenhower ran for president, the Republican National Committee spent $6.6 million in 1952 and $7.8 million in 1956. In 1960 the national Nixon campaign spent $10.1 million, and the Democrats paid out $9.8 million for Kennedy. When Nixon ran again in 1968, his campaign exceeded $25.4 million, and four years later the Nixon reelection campaign spent $61.4 million.[60] Although not all of this money went to radio and television, much of the increase can be attributed to the costs associated with these media. Later, new technologies such as direct mailing and the use of computers for a variety of purposes would add to the skyrocketing costs.

Related to this development, the nature of political parties and their relationships to candidates and campaigns changed. Through the 1940s and into the 1950s, there had been close ties between the candidate and party leaders. Originally, the parties had existed for the sole purpose of getting their candidates elected, and candidates in turn recognized their obligations to party officials and workers for their own success in attaining office. Franklin Roosevelt and Harry Truman worked hand in glove with the national Democratic leadership, not only during campaign years but between elections as well. Voters often went Democratic or Republican regardless of the candidate, because they understood that the candidates shared and represented the basic values of the party.[61]

The new technologies, however, placed greater emphasis on candidates than on their parties. In print advertising, campaign managers could spell out party platforms and positions. Television and radio demanded sound bites, and the former also required candidates who could project to the viewers. Many people credit John F. Kennedy's photogenic appearance, in his first debate with Richard Nixon, as the single most important factor that led to his eking out victory in 1960. Suddenly candidates had to have sex appeal and be able to use the new media. Throughout the nineteenth century it is likely that no more than a few thousand people at a time actually saw or heard the candidates. William Jennings Bryan's barnstorming candidacy in the 1896 election changed the model to some degree, but even with all the campaigning that Woodrow Wilson or Herbert Hoover or Franklin Roosevelt did, no more than 2 or 3 percent of the electorate—if that much—actually saw the men.

In 1960 nobody who owned a television set could avoid images and advertisements for Kennedy or Nixon, and that pattern has only intensified. As a result, political parties, although still important, became to some extent secondary in the crucial matter of raising funds. Candidates and their own advisors now did the soliciting, and in 1972 Richard Nixon had so little use for the Republican National Committee that he established his own group, the Committee to Re-elect the President (CREEP), that operated wholly independently from the RNC.

Few people welcomed this development. Fund-raising, which had been cyclical and tied to national races, now became constant. The results of an election had barely been certified before fund-raising began for the next one. The traditional start of the presidential campaign, Labor Day, disappeared as candidates began declaring their availability two or even three years earlier. Although some candidates, such as Barry Goldwater (who in 1964 stood far to the right of the mainstream Republican Party) and George McGovern (who in 1972 stood far to the left of the mainstream Democratic Party) raised a relatively high percentage of their campaign funds from small contributors, the role of the big givers—either directly to the candidates or to the national party committees, PACs, or other groups—became more and more important in funding campaigns.

A number of commissions sought to establish guidelines for campaign finance reform during the 1950s and 1960s, including one that President Kennedy set up, which unsuccessfully called for matching federal funds in presidential races. But little actually happened. In 1966 Congress passed the Long Act, designed to lessen the influence of wealthy contributors on presidential races.[62] The measure also called for public funding of political parties to pay for presidential campaigns, but ensuing acts of Congress permanently postponed implementation of that section.

Looking back, one needed only seven fingers to count the acts of Congress that tried to impose some order and reform on campaign finance practices—the Tillman Act (1907), the Publicity Act (1910), the Federal Corrupt Practices Act (1925), the Hatch Act (1939), the Smith-Connally Act (1943), the Taft-Hartley Act (1947), and the

Long Act (1966). In addition, by 1959, 43 states had some requirements for reporting campaign finance expenditures by candidates, their committees, or committees run by the parties; and 31 states had some limits on expenditures, although in most cases the limits applied only to the candidate or those expenditures made with his or her knowledge or consent. Only four states had limits on individual contributions, and these ranged from $1,000 to $5,000 a person, and could be easily bypassed through contributions to party committees.[63]

The effects of these laws, at both the federal and state levels, could be described as negligible at best. As quickly as legislatures enacted new laws and restrictions, candidates and parties found means around them. Moreover, as one commentator noted, "many state and federal laws are unenforced because they are unenforceable; the statutes themselves are vague and riddled with loopholes."[64] Then in 1971 Congress passed the first serious attempt to reform campaign finance. The law it enacted, subsequent amendments, and the judicial response to them form the next chapter in our story.

2 / Reform and Response: The Federal Election Campaign Act and Buckley

> In other words, the American system is absolutely powerless to prevent a Rockefeller from spending $4 million in family money to elect himself governor. . . . Does that make any sense? Does it make any constitutional sense? . . . Of course money is a lot more than "speech." We know that money talks; but that is the problem, not the answer.
> —Anthony Lewis

SHORTLY after John F. Kennedy became president in 1961, he appointed a commission on campaign costs in presidential elections. The total cost of the presidential campaign in 1960 had been nearly $20 million, almost twice as much as the $11.6 million spent in 1952.[1] Aside from the escalating costs involved in running for public office (even the 1960 figures would soon seem like small potatoes), there had been increasing concern that the injection of large sums of money from private donors would corrupt not only candidates and elected officials, but the integrity of the political process itself. The regulatory system then in effect had proven both ineffective and unworkable. Representative Jim Wright (D-Tex.) noted that "there is not a member of Congress, myself included, who has not knowingly evaded its purpose in one way or another."[2] Over the next decade Congress struggled fitfully with the issue, finally passing, in 1971, the first significant campaign finance reform measure in decades. Following the revelations of the Watergate scandal, Congress then toughened the law, only to see much of its work undone by the Supreme Court in the landmark decision of *Buckley v. Valeo* (1976).[3]

Both the provisions that the Court left standing, as well as the First Amendment rationale of *Buckley*, would color efforts at campaign finance reform for the next quarter-century.

★ ★ ★ ★ ★

With the exception of the limitation on unions written into the Taft-Hartley measure, Congress did little in the years following World War II to deal with the growing problem of campaign finances. Some committees did hold hearings, and in 1948 and again in 1951, special House committees on campaign expenditures reported that the existing laws needed significant revision. The 1951 committee stated flatly that it was "patently impossible for a candidate to conduct a Congressional or Senatorial campaign" within existing limits and that the laws' "present unrealistic limitations on campaign contributions and expenditures are an invitation to criminal violation."[4] The report, however, produced no legislation, and it would be 10 more years before another House committee showed any interest in the subject. Powerful Speaker of the House Sam Rayburn of Texas opposed any measure that would bring expenses for primary elections under scrutiny, as in those days, in Texas and most of the South, whoever won the Democratic primary would coast to victory in the general election.

Over on the Senate side of the capitol, the Election Subcommittee of the Committee on Rules and Administration proposed in 1953 that the spending limit on national political committees be raised from $3 million to $10 million a year, a proposal that reflected the reality of increasing costs in running an election. The full Senate ignored the proposal, but in 1955 Senator Thomas Hennings of Missouri, the new chair of the subcommittee, introduced a bill that required all political committees active in campaigns for federal office to file financial reports, even if they operated in only one state. In addition, the Hennings bill recommended raising the spending limits on congressional candidates and national committees; although the bill cleared the full committee it never reached the Senate floor for a vote.[5]

Then in February 1956, Senator Francis Case (R-S.Dak.) announced that he had been offered a $2,500 campaign gift (later revealed to have come from the president of the Superior Oil Company of

California) if he would vote for a bill to benefit the natural gas industry. Although both houses of Congress passed the measure, President Dwight Eisenhower found this effort at such overt bribery so discomforting that he vetoed the bill. The Case disclosure led to three separate congressional investigations, and suddenly the moribund drive to reform campaign finance appeared to gain new life. Lyndon Johnson (D-Tex.), the Senate majority leader, and William Knowland (R-Calif.), the minority leader, introduced a resolution that had 88 cosponsors. To no one's surprise, the bill never got out of committee, since as some wags figured, with so many cosponsors it might have passed if it ever actually came to the Senate floor. James Reston, a political reporter for the *New York Times*, wrote that Johnson and Knowland wanted "to block the investigation if possible, to limit it in any event, and to get it out of the control of the Senate Elections subcommittee."[6]

But although they managed to block any reform, the two could not stop the Senate Privileges and Elections Subcommittee, chaired by Albert H. Gore of Tennessee. Although prevented from looking into the allegations raised by the Case disclosure, the committee far surpassed previous efforts to examine and catalogue the financing of U.S. political campaigns at the national level. It assembled a large research staff under the direction of Alexander Heard, perhaps the country's leading expert on campaign finance. The report included a long list of major donors arranged alphabetically and by family group—such as the DuPonts, Rockefellers, and Mellons—as well as the top corporate donors. Heard and other scholars as well as some newspaper reporters also tried to examine the documents filed with the clerks of the House and Senate by members of Congress reporting what they had spent in their election campaigns. They found the materials to be of little value, varying greatly in format and detail, and practically inaccessible because of the uncooperative nature of the clerks' offices. Republicans screamed that the committee had distorted its findings in order to, according to Andrew F. Schoepel (R-Kan.), support the "New Dealer" thesis that "the Republican Party was the party of big business and that the Democrats were the party concerned with labor and the so-called little man." Although normally the Gore committee could have expected to see its report printed as a Senate document, which would have given it a relatively wide distribution, Schoepel prevailed on Senate leaders to withhold funds for printing; as a result the committee report appeared in a very limited edition as an unnumbered committee print, and received practically no notice by the press or the public.[7]

In the meantime Senator Hennings kept plugging away at his proposal, and after he became chair of the full Rules and Administration Committee in 1957 he managed to get his bill reported out of committee, only to see the leadership forestall any floor debate. Three years later he finally managed to secure floor debate, and realized that for all the lip service paid to campaign finance reform, very few members of the Senate had any interest in changing things. Hennings, in order to get his bill out of committee, had agreed to tone down some of the provisions, with the intention of adding back stronger measures during the floor debate. With the help of Senators Kenneth Keating (R-N.Y.) and Estes Kefauver (D-Tenn.), Hennings did in fact strengthen the bill. Candidates for federal office would have to report expenditures not only in the general elections but in the primaries as well; state and local committees would be required to report if they spent $2,500 or more in a campaign for federal office; no individual could contribute more than an aggregate of $10,000 to political campaigns in any one year; the ceilings on expenditures for House and Senate campaigns were raised significantly to reflect the actual costs of running for office; and candidates for president and vice president could spend up to 20 cents for each vote cast in any one of the three preceding presidential elections. The strengthened Hennings bill passed the Senate by a comfortable margin of 59 to 22. Sam Rayburn buried it in the House. Shortly after that Hennings died, and no one in the Senate stepped up to take his place as a champion of reform.[8]

The focus of reform then shifted to the White House. John Kennedy had been interested in campaign financing for a long time. While in the Senate he had been a member of the Special Committee to Investigate Political Activities, Lobbying, and Campaign Contributions, one of the groups formed after the Case disclosure in 1956. As a wealthy man, he knew the importance of money in politics, and had often heard accusations that his family fortune had bought public offices for him. But as the nominal leader of the Democratic Party, Kennedy also knew about the $3.8 million deficit from the 1960 campaign that the party now had to cover. Kennedy named Alexander Heard, the same man who had staffed the Gore investigation, to chair a presidential commission on campaign costs in presidential elections.

The committee submitted its report the following year, and made some limited, albeit innovative, recommendations. The proposals offered by the committee included the following:

- Individuals, businesses, labor unions, and private organizations should be encouraged to participate in and underwrite voluntary nonpartisan political activities such as voter registration and fund-raising drives, and expenses related to these activities should be tax deductible.
- Tax incentives should be tried for an experimental period, covering at least two presidential campaigns, allowing individual contributors to take a credit against their federal income taxes for a certain percentage of their donations, or to take a deduction of up to $1,000 in any given tax year.
- The unrealistic and unenforceable ceilings on individual contributions and on total expenditures by political committees should be abolished, and an effective system of public disclosure should be put into place.
- Congress should provide funds for the reasonable and necessary transition costs that a newly elected president would have in preparing to take over the office.
- Section 315 of the Federal Communications Act should be suspended, as it had been in 1960, to permit broadcasters to make the airwaves available to the nominees of the major political parties on an equal basis (such as for debates) without having to do so for the candidates of the dozens of fringe parties.[9]

The report, submitted in April 1962, received warm approval by President Kennedy at a news conference. The chairs of the Democratic and Republican National Committees endorsed it, as did former presidents Truman and Eisenhower, along with Richard Nixon, Adlai Stevenson, and Thomas E. Dewey—all the living presidential candidates of both major parties in the previous 25 years.

Frank Sorauf dismisses the report as inconsequential, claiming Kennedy gave it only perfunctory support, and Congress brushed it aside without any serious consideration.[10] Robert Mutch agrees that nothing happened in the remaining year and a half of the Kennedy administration, but points out that several of the proposals eventually became enacted into law or federal regulation.[11] Herbert Alexander, on the contrary, considers the report a success. It represented "a model and comprehensive program" for reforming campaign finance, and although most of the proposals had been aired before, especially by liberal Democrats, he sees the real impact of the report as generating debate and getting things moving by providing a complete and detailed analysis of the problems facing the system. "The report," he claims, "accomplished its purpose."[12]

In fact, only one of the commission's recommendations became effective during Kennedy's time. The Internal Revenue Service authorized taxpayers to deduct expenditures in connection with local, state, and federal elections, if the money went to advertising designed to encourage voter registration, the sponsorship of debates among candidates, or giving employees paid time off to register and vote. The IRS ruling remained in effect for many years, and few people realized that the costs associated with joint appearances of candidates on radio or television, or "battle pages" in newspapers could be sponsored by corporations and counted as business expenses.

Very little else happened for the rest of the decade. President Lyndon Johnson in his 1966 State of the Union message announced that campaign finance reform would be a high priority of his administration. He derided the laws then on the books: "Inadequate in their scope when enacted, they are now obsolete. More loophole than law, they invite evasion and circumvention."[13] He promised to send Congress comprehensive legislation, but it took Johnson four months before he sent a bill up to the capitol. The measure he recommended consisted primarily of proposals that reformers had been making for more than two decades—primary elections would be brought under the law, contribution limits would be tightened, there would be greater disclosure and publicity of campaign finances, and all restrictions on expenditures would be repealed.

The Republicans responded with a reform bill of their own, which embodied many of the president's proposals but also included the strengthening of disclosure requirements by establishing an independent Federal Election Commission. The Republicans also proposed drastically restricting the money spent by political action committees sponsored by unions representing employees of federal contractors. The resulting deadlock led to the demise of both proposals, and the only surprise came when both houses of Congress accepted Senator Russell Long's amendment to a tax bill providing for public funding of presidential elections, using a voluntary check-off on individual income tax forms.[14] (The proposal, although enacted, would not become operational for another decade.) Despite more hearings and other proposals, Congress failed to act on campaign finance reform for the rest of the decade.[15]

★ ★ ★ ★ ★

It would be easy to dismiss congressional—and presidential—inaction by cynically noting that the system of campaign finance regulation in place, if it can be called a system, apparently worked. Candidates could raise as much money as possible, they could rely on wealthy contributors (in 1968 Mrs. John D. Rockefeller spent $1.5 million on her stepson Nelson's bid for the Republican presidential nomination, and W. Clement Stone, a Chicago insurance magnate, gave the GOP $2.8 million, most of it to Richard M. Nixon's campaign), and the reporting requirements could best be described as meaningless.[16] When Richard Nixon became president in 1969, W. Pat Jennings, the clerk of the House of Representatives, sent to the Justice Department a list of 20 Nixon fund-raising committees that had failed to file a single report for the campaign, along with the names of 107 congressional candidates who had also violated the disclosure law. A year later the Justice Department announced that none of the violators would be prosecuted, because, given the history of the act and its enforcement, it would be unfair to do so. However, the department declared it would prosecute violators in the future.[17]

Although there is undoubtedly some truth in that response, the fact is that campaigning had become more and more expensive, and many House members and senators had come to believe that they spent far too much time chasing after political contributions. The biggest campaign, that for the presidency, cost the most and each four years the sums expended by both parties leaped upward. When Thomas Dewey had run against Harry Truman in 1948, their combined expenditures had been a little under $5 million, or about the same amount that had been spent in the 1944 race between Dewey and Franklin Roosevelt.[18] In Table 2.1 one can see nothing but an upward spiral.

Table 2.1. Comparative Party Expenditures in Presidential Campaigns, 1952–1968 (in $ millions)

	Democrats	Republicans	Total
1952	Stevenson ($5.03)	Eisenhower ($6.61)	$11.64
1956	Stevenson ($5.11)	Eisenhower ($7.78)	$12.89
1960	Kennedy ($9.80)	Nixon ($10.13)	$19.93
1964	Johnson ($8.76)	Goldwater ($16.03)	$24.79
1968	Humphrey (11.59)	Nixon ($25.40)	$36.99[1]

[1]These numbers are taken from Alexander, *Financing Politics*, Table 1-1, 5. Even holding dollars constant, between 1952 and 1968 campaign costs rose two and a half times.

These numbers would be eclipsed by the $91 million spent in the 1972 election, with Richard Nixon outspending George McGovern by a 2–1 margin.

Although both parties tried to appeal to all income levels, during the 1960s the Republicans actually had far more success attracting small, so-called nickel-and-dime givers. Republican fund drives in 1968 produced $6.6 million in gifts, averaging $15 from each of 450,000 individual contributors. Although Barry Goldwater in 1964 and George McGovern in 1972 raised large sums from a broad base of small donors, for the most part the GOP relied primarily on big givers, especially corporate donors, to finance their presidential campaigns; and the Democrats, who began to rebuild their small donor base at the end of the decade, looked primarily to labor unions and their political arms for money.[19] If one adds in the costs of primary campaigns, fought out in at least one party each year except 1956, the totals are significantly higher.

Nor did the costs of running for the House or Senate remain stable. According to a study by the Citizens' Research Foundation, shown in Table 2.2, the total cost of campaigning for all federal offices in presidential election years tripled between 1952 (the first year for which dependable figures are available) and 1972.

During this time, the cost of running for a seat in Congress—at least in California, where fairly reliable data could be found—more than tripled for the House, and went up fivefold for the Senate, as shown in Table 2.3.

The big change in the 1960s, of course, involved the growing use of television in campaigns. In 1952 the government freeze on new

Table 2.2. Expenditures in All Federal Campaigns, 1952–1972

1952	$140 million
1956	$155 million
1960	$175 million
1964	$200 million
1968	$300 million
1972	$425 million[2]

[2] Jacobson, *Money in Congressional Elections*, 166. Jacobson notes that the numbers for some of these years are "best guesses," given the poor reporting system in place. Even holding the dollar values constant, the costs doubled in the 20-year period.

stations ended, and in the following years television stations and, more importantly, household sets, proliferated. Television became an important—and expensive—part of campaigning. In 1952, the first year both parties used the new medium, they spent $3.7 million for purchasing time; 20 years later that number had tripled. Abraham Lincoln's entire campaign in 1860 had cost $100,000; in 1960 it took that much to buy 30 minutes of air time.[20]

Table 2.3. Expenditures in U.S. Congressional Races, 1958–1970 (in $ millions)

	House	Senate
1958	$1.0	$1.3
1960	$1.6	
1962	$2.4	$0.8
1964	$2.4	$3.2
1966	$2.6	
1968	$3.7	$5.3
1970	$3.6	$6.7[3]

[3] Ibid., 167. In constant dollars the cost of a Senate race quadrupled. In 1960 and 1966 there were no elections for the Senate, and in 1962 a popular incumbent faced only nominal opposition, resulting in the low expenditures that year. One can understand why it would cost more for a Senate race than for a House seat. House districts are fairly small and compact, while a senator represents—and must campaign in—the whole state. In geographically large states like California, New York, Texas, or Pennsylvania, travel costs associated with a Senate race easily outstrip those involved in one House district, where the candidate can usually get around by car or, in some urban areas, by public transportation.

The problem did not abate; if anything it worsened as the years passed. To give but one example, in 1988 former Florida governor Reuben Askew sought the Democratic nomination for the U.S. Senate. One of his aides recalled a primary campaign rally in northern Florida:

A hunched-over, withered dirt farmer approached the governor with a $100 check. "I want you to have this," said the man, trembling with awe. "I've supported you for years, and I'm behind you now." With a 30-second television spot in Tampa costing around $6,000, the farmer's contribution paid for about a half-second of television. I didn't have the heart to tell him.[21]

Television may have been the single greatest factor in increasing overall campaign costs by 50 percent between 1964 and 1968. As Senator Edward Kennedy (D-Mass.) later testified, "Like a colossus of the ancient world, television stands astride our political system, demanding tribute from every candidate for public office, incumbent or challenger. Its appetite is insatiable, its impact unique." Senator Albert Gore (D-Tenn.), who would go down to defeat in the 1974 election following a massive media blitz by his opponent, warned that "in the days of slogans, labels, image-making mass communications, monopolizing the time of the television that goes into the homes of the American people is a great danger to the democratic process."[22]

Although some studies indicate that television ads are not very effective in House district races, their impact grows in statewide Senate races, and of course, in the nationwide presidential campaign. A survey taken of 23 senators and 91 representatives after the 1968 election found that nearly three-fourths of the Senate candidates had used television extensively, 18 percent had used "some" television, and only 9 percent had used none. By contrast, only a quarter of the House races had depended heavily on television, and nearly half had not used the medium at all.[23] Politicians, and especially members of the Senate, began to look more favorably on spending and contribution restrictions as radio and television advertising became a bottomless pit soaking up millions of dollars.

The ever-increasing costs of campaigning, and the resulting reliance on corporate and union contributions, raised fears that the end result would be corruption not only of individuals, but of the entire political system and the faith of the citizenry in its integrity. Although there are plenty of stories about corporate donations leading to favorable legislation, many political analysts note that there are so many issues confronting members of Congress it would be almost impossible for them to pay back every contributor by voting for each one's interests, especially since some of those interests probably conflict.[24] Senators and representatives are keenly aware of what the main economic interests are in their home state or district, and realize that if they hope to keep their seats, they have to vote in a way that will benefit their constituents. If a senator comes from a dairy state, she will not require a contribution from the dairy industry in order to support legislation favoring dairy farmers. While one may not agree with Charles Wilson's aphorism, "What's good for General Motors is good for the country," a congressman from Detroit is certainly aware that a healthy GM means jobs for his constituents and prosperity for his district.

But many people worried about the impression that the money could corrupt the system. Senator Adlai E. Stevenson III (D-Ill.) put it quite succinctly when he testified that "even if all of the dollars were honestly contributed and honestly spent, they would still have a corrupting influence on our politics. For the vast sums now required for political campaigns raise the unholy specter that politics in the future will be an enterprise for rich people only, for rich candidates, or at the very least, candidates backed by rich contributors."[25]

The worry that the system might be corrupted, or even appear that way, did not provide sufficient impetus to move Congress to action in the 1960s. Just as Sam Rayburn had buried earlier legislation to reform campaigns, so too did Wayne Hays (D-Ohio), chair of the House Administration Committee and an unapologetic opponent of any change in the campaign finance system, now kill any bill that would endanger what he saw as a vested right—the ability of incumbents to secure more funds than their challengers. Moreover, he had allies on his committee, northern Democrats who did not want anything to get in the way of labor support for their party, and southern Democrats who wanted to keep the financing of party primaries as veiled as possible. But pressure built, and if a reform package could get past the obstructionists, like Hays, it stood a good chance of passage. Finally, Congress acted, not once but several times, in the 1970s.

* * * * *

A variety of reform proposals had been batted around during the 1960s, following the report of the presidential commission. Some emphasized full disclosure of contributions and expenses, and a broadening of the parties' financial bases (by limiting contributions of big donors) to provide a fairer and more stable finance system. Other groups, such as the Citizens' Research Foundation, recognized the need for greater campaign resources, to be kept in check by stringent reporting requirements and the spotlight of publicity. Such publicity, they believed, would keep the candidates, the parties, and the system honest. A third approach, championed by public interest lobbies such as Common Cause, a citizens' lobby headed by former cabinet secretary John Gardner, introduced a new idea—limit campaign resources by imposing ceilings on both campaign contributions and expenditures. The tight limits on individual contributions would be offset with public funds. The ideas of this third group, although quite different from the traditional reforms that had been pushed since the end of World War II, nonetheless caught the attention of key members of Congress. Aware of the escalating costs of campaigning and the ever more difficult and time-consuming task of fund-raising, they found the idea of limitations on both income and expenditures very attractive.

In 1970, both houses of Congress passed a relatively limited campaign finance reform bill. Among other things, the measure would have suspended §315 of the Communications Act (the equal-time provision) for presidential and vice-presidential candidates, and required stations to sell air time to all legally qualified candidates at a price not to exceed "the lowest unit charge of the station for the same amount of time in the same time period." Another feature limited the amount that candidates could spend for the use of broadcasting time to 7 cents for each vote cast for all candidates for that office in the previous election, or $20,000, whichever was greater. This part applied to president and vice president, senators and representatives at the national level, and governors and lieutenant governors at the state level. For primary campaigns, candidates (with the exception of those seeking the presidency) could spend no more than one-half of the limit for the general election. To enforce this provision, each candidate or a representative had to certify in writing to the station that buying the requested time would not exceed the legal limits. Stations could not sell time to candidates refusing to submit such affidavits.[26]

Despite the limited nature of the bill, President Richard M. Nixon vetoed it, on grounds that it did not go far enough. He described the measure as a "good aim, gone amiss." The problem with campaign spending, he declared, "is not radio and television; the problem is spending. This bill plugs only one hole in a sieve." Nixon also disapproved of the fact that, as he saw it, the bill discriminated against broadcasters. Since the expenditure ceilings applied only to radio and television, the broadcast media would be at a disadvantage. Candidates could spend their quotas, and then spend as much as they wanted in other venues, such as newspapers, billboards, and mailings. As a result, Nixon claimed, overall campaign spending would not be curtailed. The president had a number of other objections, and although critics might discount them as self-serving, since at the time his reelection committee had already begun amassing the biggest campaign finance war chest hitherto seen in U.S. politics, he made a number of valid points. The bill would favor incumbents, would discriminate against broadcasters, and the formula did not take into account differing costs in different markets.[27] Although defenders of the bill believed that one step in the right direction would be a good start, Nixon in essence said that if Congress really wanted to reform campaign finance, then it should do so.

Shortly after the Nixon veto, Common Cause filed a suit challenging the nonenforcement of the Federal Corrupt Practices Act, the 1925 act that still governed campaign expenses. The suit sought to enjoin the Republican and Democratic National Committees as well as the Conservative Party of New York from violating two sections of the FCPA. Common Cause alleged that the committees had encouraged the formation of multiple committees on behalf of individual candidates in order to get around the law's limit of $5,000 on an individual contribution to a committee and the expenditure by any one committee of more than $3 million in one year.

The courts eventually dismissed the suit, but it served a useful purpose in focusing attention on the shortcomings of the FCPA, and showing how easily the major parties circumvented its restrictions. Moreover, Common Cause may well have wanted to prod Congress to act quickly, aware that with the 1972 presidential campaign just around the corner, the potential for even greater abuse could not be ignored.

* * * * *

To everyone's surprise, Congress did in fact completely overhaul federal campaign law by passing two measures, the Revenue Act of 1971[28] and the Federal Election Campaign Act (FECA) of 1971.[29] The Revenue Act finally put into effect the Long Amendment of 1966 by creating a general fund for presidential and vice-presidential campaigns, and permitting taxpayers to check off a dollar of their taxes to underwrite the fund. In order to get Nixon's approval, Congress agreed to delay implementation until the 1976 presidential election. FECA had two main goals—tightening reporting requirements and limiting expenditures for media advertising. But it also looked at other aspects of modern campaign finance, and brought many of the provisions of the old 1925 law up-to-date.[30] The law broadened the definitions of both "contributions" and "expenditures" in order to include almost any donation and cost associated with a political campaign. In a clear effort to reduce the advantage of wealthy candidates, the law imposed a ceiling on what candidates for federal offices could spend out of their own pockets or those of their immediate families—$50,000 for president or vice president, $35,000 for senators, and $25,000 for representatives.

The FECA set up fairly specific rules for reporting contributions and expenditures, which made the law far more effective than its predecessor. On the contribution side, the names of all donors or lenders who gave $100 or more had to be reported, and the names of all committee officials had to be listed. The drafters of the measure had such great confidence in the reporting provisions that the bill repealed the largely unenforceable prior limits on contributions and expenditures. Only the old prohibition against direct contributions by corporations and labor unions remained intact.

The media provisions to some extent addressed some of the problems Nixon had pointed out in his veto of the earlier bill. Candidates now had limits on all media spending, both broadcast and print, with a maximum of $50,000 for the smallest district and up to $1.4 million for the senatorial candidates in California. Of this amount, no more than 60 percent could go to radio and television.

Recognizing that inflation could make these limits meaningless and therefore susceptible to evasion, the bill indexed the ceilings to adjust to changes in the cost-of-living index.

Only time would have told if the FECA regulations would do what its sponsors had hoped—shed the bright light of publicity on the abuses and excesses of campaign finance, restrict both large contributions as well as large expenditures, and provide a more level playing field for challengers and incumbents by having them both operate under the same rules. The bill, signed into law by President Nixon in January 1972, seemed to meet some of its goals in the 1972 election, and as Frank Sorauf noted, it "brought the fullest disclosure of campaign transactions in American history; and while it did not curb the growth of campaign spending generally, it did limit the use of media advertising."[31] Moreover, its provisions may have helped unravel one of the largest scandals in U.S. history—Watergate.

★ ★ ★ ★ ★

The break-in at the Democratic National Committee headquarters in the Watergate complex in Washington, D.C., by a group funded by the Committee to Re-elect the President (CREEP), proved to have been the first step in a chain of events that eventually led to the resignation of Richard Nixon in August 1974. But Watergate is far more than a botched burglary. The stories uncovered by investigative journalists and in House and Senate hearings detailed an unparalleled abuse of executive power.[32] For the purposes of our story, however, Watergate stands for the worst-case scenario of a badly flawed campaign finance system that failed to forestall corruption or prevent out-and-out criminal activity. That in the end constitutional safeguards worked to save the political system and forced Nixon from power provided little comfort to those seeking to reform the system of financing elections.

Nixon had decided to bypass the Republican National Committee as much as possible, in part because he and his top aides assumed that the committee would play by the rules, which would prevent them from raising and spending the massive amounts of money Nixon believed necessary to win in 1972. So his campaign created an independent body, the Committee to Re-elect the President, and the money flowed in. Financier Robert Vesco (who later fled the country after embezzling millions of dollars from his companies) delivered $200,000 in cash in an attaché case. Billionaire aviation manufacturer and movie producer Howard Hughes put $100,000 into a safe deposit box belonging to Nixon's friend Bebe Rebozo. Clement Stone reported giving $73,000, but later investigations showed that he had provided more than $2 million secretly. At least 13 corporations and their foreign subsidiaries made over $780,000 in clearly illegal contributions. All told, the committee received an estimated $5 million in large individual and corporate donations, most of them illegal under the law.[33] The committee, in order to hide these donations, kept a great deal of the money in cash on hand, allowing for payouts of $250,000 to Herb Kalmbach, the president's lawyer; $350,000 to Gordon Strachan, H. R. Haldeman's aide; and $83,000 to G. Gordon Liddy, this last money going to finance the Watergate break-in.[34]

How did sophisticated and wealthy men become dupes of the Nixon committee? After all, they had made donations, perhaps even large ones, before, but not since the days of the Tweed Ring in the late nineteenth century had there been stories of fat cats turning up at party headquarters with satchels stuffed with bills. In part Nixon turned the primary fear of the reformers on its head. They had worried that big corporations, eager to get government to act for their advantage, would offer money and essentially "buy" legislators and their votes. Nixon did the opposite. His lieutenants went to corporations and told them that if they hoped to be treated well, they had better pony up. One story illustrates this practice perfectly.

A Nixon fund-raiser, Herbert Kalmbach, approached George Spater, the president and CEO of American Airlines, at a dinner in New York on October 21, 1971. He asked Spater to make a contribution to the Nixon campaign of $100,000, a sum well beyond anything that Spater had ever given, and because of existing law, one unavailable from the American Airlines treasury. Spater said he might be able to come up with $75,000, but Kalmbach wanted more, and Spater knew that Kalmbach represented Nixon. At that time the company had at least 20 matters pending before various federal agencies, including a proposed merger with Western Airlines that would require the president's signature. Moreover, in his private law practice, Kalmbach represented United Airlines, American's major competitor and an opponent of the merger.

Figuring he had no choice, Spater first contributed $20,000 out of his own pocket. Then he transferred $100,000 of the airline's money to the Swiss account of a Lebanese agent, André Tabourian, who regularly handled legitimate overseas transactions for American Airlines. For accounting purposes, Spater had the amount entered on the books as a special commission to Tabourian for the sale of used aircraft in the Middle East. Tabourian then transferred the money back to a separate account in New York, and soon afterward he came to the United States himself. Tabourian withdrew the $100,000 in cash and handed it to an American Airlines official who put it into a safe. In March 1972, Spater took the laundered cash—now free of any traceable connection to the airline—put it into a large envelope and handed it over to the Nixon fund-raisers.[35] These and other tales not only illustrated the greed and criminality of the Nixon campaign, but also illuminated the shortcomings in existing laws, even in the major reforms enacted just as people delivered bags of money to the Nixon campaign committee.

The disclosures of Watergate fed the demand for reform. In the late 1960s there had been, as Seymour Martin Lipset and William Schneider noted from their study of public opinion polls, "a virtual explosion in antigovernment sentiment." Although the Vietnam War may have been the "catalytic event" creating this mistrust, Watergate heightened popular distrust of both government and its leaders.[36] The University of Michigan's Center for Political Studies runs a biennial poll in which it asks if the respondent thinks that "quite a few of .the people running the government are a little crooked," and if "the government is pretty much run by a few big interests." In 1968 only about a quarter of the people answered yes to the first question, a number that shot up to nearly 50 percent by 1974. Thirty percent of the people thought big business ran the government in 1964; almost 70 percent responded affirmatively to that question in 1974.[37] In the early 1960s, when serious discussion of public financing of campaigns began, Americans rejected the idea by a seven-to-one margin; by the fall of 1973, a poll showed 65 percent of the people favored tax support for both presidential and congressional campaigns, while only 24 percent opposed it.[38]

Common Cause attracted 100,000 members within six months of its founding; by the beginning of 1972 that number had increased to a quarter million. Common Cause and other groups dedicated to electoral and governmental reform played an important role in campaign finance reform over the next three decades. When the Federal Election Commission proved slow or unwilling to enforce the law, these groups stepped in and generated publicity as well as lawsuits. Common Cause filed its first lawsuit within months of its creation, challenging the efforts of both the Democratic and Republican National Committees to evade the 1971 FECA contribution and expenditure limits by setting up multiple committees. A key issue in the suit was whether or not the law gave nongovernmental groups standing to seek a right of private enforcement. Common Cause won a significant victory when the federal district court ruled that it had standing to bring class action suits on behalf of all voters.[39] The suit did more than just put the major political parties on notice that Common Cause intended to serve a watchdog function; it also gave the new group immediate legitimacy and a seat at the table in the discussion of future campaign reform measures. Common Cause next sued Richard Nixon's campaign committee to force it to disclose how much money it had raised before April 7, the date the law went into effect. When it became clear that the case would come to trial before Election Day, the committee reluctantly released the names of more than 1,500 people who had given more than $5 million.

As Robert Mutch notes, the Watergate hearings did for campaign finance reform in the 1970s what the Armstrong hearings had done for the 1907 and 1911 laws. Not only Common Cause but other groups signed on to the issue. To take but one example, Sears, Roebuck and Company heir Philip M. Stern, a liberal philanthropist and author, established the Center for Public Financing of Elections. The executive director, Susan B. King, had been the Washington, D.C., director of the National Committee for an Effective Congress, a liberal PAC, and she proved extremely adept at building a coalition of church, labor, and professional organizations, all committed to campaign finance reform. King, Gardner, and other reformers, all veterans of politics, knew how to lobby and they knew how to get their side of the story into the media. On some days, as Mutch dryly notes, "members of Congress might well have felt that the morning newspapers, nightly television news, constituent mail, and pro-reform lobbyists all over the Capitol had created pressure for new legislation that was too great to resist."[40]

★ ★ ★ ★ ★

Of course most of the crimes related to Watergate had little or nothing to do with campaign financing, such as the break-in at Democratic Party headquarters, obstruction of justice, or use of the Internal Revenue System to try to punish "enemies." Nixon had not been forced to resign because of violation of the 1971 FECA, nor did the trials and convictions of many of his associates deal with campaign finance. But as the facts of how Nixon had raised and used money became public, it fed a growing public outrage. Gardner noted that many of the illegal activities committed by the administration and its hirelings had been financed by money paid to the Committee to Re-elect the President, and that Watergate was "a particularly malodorous chapter in the annals of campaign financing."[41] The public outcry grew so powerful that it enabled reformers in Congress to push through substantial changes to FECA that in fact dwarfed the reforms of the 1971 act. Although known as amendments, the 1974 measures not only addressed the perceived shortcomings of the 1971 FECA, but tackled just about every item on the reformers' agenda.[42]

To begin with, Congress finally created a mechanism to police the candidates and the parties in their adherence to the campaign finance laws. The Federal Election Commission would be composed of six members, three Democrats and three Republicans, serving staggered six-year terms. The president, the speaker of the House, and the president pro tem of the Senate would each appoint two members, one from each party, and all six members would be subject to confirmation not just by the Senate but by the House of Representatives. In addition, the secretary of the Senate and the clerk of the House would serve as ex officio members.

The 1971 law set no limits on either contributions or expenditures, except for what wealthy candidates could give to their own campaigns. The amendments set a $1,000 contribution limit to any one candidate for each primary, runoff, or general election, with a maximum of $25,000 to all candidates for federal office in any election cycle. No contributor could give more than $5,000 to any political organization or committee, but there were no limits on the aggregate amount a person could give through multiple committee donations. A private person could not expend more than $1,000 on behalf of a single candidate. Contributions of over $100 had to be paid by check or money order, a clear response to people carrying envelopes stuffed with money into the Nixon campaign headquarters. Foreign contributions were barred completely.

On the expenditure side, candidates for president could not spend more than $10 million in the primaries. In any specific state primary, they could not spend more than twice what a senatorial candidate would be allowed to spend. For the general elections the law capped presidential expenditures at $20 million. Candidates for the House had a $70,000 limit in both the primary and general election, and people running for the Senate faced limits determined by the population of the state, but no more than $100,000 in the primary and $150,000 in the general election.

In an important step the new law finally implemented public funding of at least part of the presidential campaign, through a voluntary check-off on a taxpayer's return. A formula determined how much a candidate would get once he or she had raised a minimum of $100,000 in amounts of at least $5,000 in each of 20 states or more. In addition, the law tightened the reporting requirements and directed that periodic reports be delivered in a timely manner to the FEC. In other areas as well the law attempted to strengthen the rules set out in 1971.

To call these changes simply "amendments" to the 1971 FECA is clearly erroneous. This law went well beyond the 1971 regulations, attempted to avoid the problems revealed by the Watergate scandals, and in many ways fulfilled the agenda that many reformers had been advocating for more than two decades. In some of its goals the 1974 law was in fact a great advance over all previous measures. By extending public financing to all levels of the presidential campaign, it acknowledged the importance of both the primaries and the general election in choosing the nation's chief executive. But reformers could not get public funding for congressional campaigns, primarily because of the intransigence of Wayne Hays (D-Ohio), now the powerful chair of the Ways and Means Committee, and other representatives from essentially one-party districts who did not care to see their challengers paid for by tax dollars.

The question of whether spending limits would increase the advantage enjoyed by incumbents played a major role in the debates in both houses of Congress. In the House, William E. Frenzel (R-Minn.) had noted in the 1971 debate that "when you establish a spending limitation you literally insure that incumbents are not going to be defeated because the only weapon the non-incumbent has . . . is [money to] get his name known." By the time Congress debated the 1974 measures, it had figures from the 1972 elections showing that challengers to incumbents only did well if they spent a great deal of money, usually more than would be allowed under the new limits. Several representatives and senators said plainly that they would never have been elected if the proposed spending limits had been in place when they first ran for office.[43]

Part of the problem in setting a viable limit arose from the different experiences of those involved. Proposed limits for the expenditures for House races ranged from $30,000 to $190,000. Representative Frenzel thought that $150,000 made sense, because "that is what it cost me to get elected the first time." Wayne Hays and John Herman Dent (D-Pa.) thought that $35,000 to $40,000 would be enough, but both men ran in districts where they normally had weak opposition. In the end the House set a limit of $70,000 on the primary and an equal amount on the general election, with another 20 percent allowed to cover the costs of raising these funds. A single number, applying to all races, made sense for the House, since all districts are by law roughly equal in population.

Candidates for the Senate, however, faced a far different situation. Running in California or Texas meant covering more ground and persuading more voters than running in Rhode Island or New Hampshire. So the bill allowed senatorial candidates to spend the larger of two amounts—$100,000 or 8 cents per eligible voter, in a primary, and then $150,000 or 12 cents per voter in the general election.

Those who predicted that the 1974 limits would favor incumbents were proven right, and one need not be cynical to assert that the drafters of those limits recognized that such would in fact be the consequence. To begin with, the regulations embodied in the bill made it that much more difficult to raise money, and would-be donors tended to give to incumbents, who had not only the name recognition but also the power of an office they already occupied. Various studies showed that incumbents on the average raised twice as much as challengers, and that challengers had a difficult time (unless they had personal wealth) getting the start-up money to run a campaign.[44] The regulations for contributions also made it more difficult for both challengers as well as incumbents to raise money, with the result that much more time went into the effort to fund a campaign than went into the actual campaigning itself. Sixty-one percent of Senate candidates and more than half of the House candidates—both incumbents and challengers—responded in the affirmative to a survey taken after the 1976 election: that the new FECA rules made it more difficult to raise campaign funds.[45]

Perhaps some reformers considered this good news, but even before the bill had gone into effect some politicians began warning that no bill, no matter how comprehensive, could free campaign finance from the influence of money. Senator Edward Kennedy (D-Mass.) asked: "Who really owns America? Is it the people or is it a little group of big campaign contributors?" According to Kennedy, Congress had failed to solve the energy crisis because of the campaign gifts of the oil industry. National health insurance had been sabotaged by the American Medical Association and private insurers, while the National Rifle Association blocked meaningful gun control laws. Failing to provide for public financing of Senate and House elections, Kennedy warned, guaranteed that the influence of powerful interests would continue. As if in response, Senator Lowell Weicker (R-Conn.), one of the heroes of the Watergate investigation, urged the public not to place too great a faith in public financing, which, he declared, "is not a magical Clorox guaranteed to end forever the dirty laundry of Watergate. It does not cut the cost of campaigns; it just shifts the cost." Senator Howard Baker (R-Tenn.), another popular figure during Watergate, worried about the constitutionality of a law that used taxpayers' money to fund candidates they did not support. Public subsidies, he warned, could "abridge the individual's First Amendment right of freedom of political expression."[46]

As it turned out, the 1974 FECA amendments did abridge the First Amendment, but not in quite the way that Senator Baker had worried about.

★   ★   ★   ★   ★

The first challenge in the courts to FECA began in the spring of 1972, when three old-line liberal activists walked into the offices of the American Civil Liberties Union (ACLU) with an incredible story. On May 31, they and others had sponsored a two-page advertisement in the *New York Times* calling for the impeachment of Richard Nixon following the bombing of Cambodia, and praising those few members of Congress who had voted against the bombing. The ad included two coupons that readers could use to send in contributions to the National Committee for Impeachment. Almost immediately afterward, Nixon's Justice Department filed a lawsuit in federal court demanding to know how the group had been organized and who had paid for the ad. In addition, government lawyers threatened the dissidents with injunctions and ordered them not to engage in further political speech unless they filed reports and disclosures with the government, and otherwise obeyed a whole host of rules and regulations they had never heard about. All they had done, they told the ACLU, was sponsor an ad critical of the president. Wasn't this the very type of political speech protected by the First Amendment?

The irony, if one can call it that, is that the rules and regulations used by the Nixon Justice Department to threaten the committee had just been passed by Congress—the Federal Election Campaign Act of 1971. The government argued that, even though it spoke only about issues, the advertisement mentioned, criticized, or praised people who would be running for public office that year, and thus might affect the results of those elections. This comprised not political speech but political activity by a "committee" of the type Congress had intended to include within the limitations imposed by FECA. The Justice Department managed to get an injunction from a friendly district judge, only to be slapped down and reversed by a unanimous three-judge panel of the Second Circuit in October. The panel ruled that campaign finance laws could not be used against nonpartisan, issue-oriented committees engaged in commenting upon or even advocating policies related to important public issues.[47]

As Joel Gora points out, in one way the government had been right. Speech such as that in the ad might influence people's opinions about members of Congress and the president, and thus influence their vote at the next election. Even if that had not been the primary purpose of that ad, its sponsors must surely have hoped to influence those who read it. Moreover, the ad cost about $18,000, or $80,000 in current dollars, an amount, Gora notes, that makes it "serious money." So if one is to be consistent about campaign finance reform, then one would indeed have to include any type of paid speech that, directly or indirectly, might affect the electorate. Such controls, whether in FECA or in later legislation, all have one thing in common: they penalize people for exercising their First Amendment right to speak out on important issues.[48]

The ACLU not only won that case, it managed to get another provision of the 1971 bill nullified in court. The law placed a limit on media spending, and if every issue ad, or even an ad placed by a private citizen, came within the legal limits of $50,000 or 10 cents a voter, then that limit would soon be met, causing great harm to candidates seeking to place their own ads. The ACLU argued that just because a privately placed advertisement praised—or damned—a candidate, it did not make that ad part of campaign advertising. Once again the courts agreed, and held that FECA did not apply to groups like the ACLU, whose major purpose involved issue discussion, not the election of candidates.[49] Suddenly the warnings of those who had said campaign finance reform might run afoul of the First Amendment took on new life.

Whereas proponents of campaign finance reform saw FECA and its 1974 amendments as cleansing the political process of potentially corrupting influences, opponents saw it as restricting the free exchange of ideas and treading upon that most precious of American rights, free speech to criticize the government. The most telling of the criticisms might be summed up as follows:

- The law restricted the right of candidates to expend money, even if it all came from small contributors. The claim that big business or special interest groups could "buy" candidates through big contributions made no sense if the money all came from small donors.
- The amounts set by Congress were, even by the standards of the time, much too low. The $70,000 limit on House races came to less than House members on the average spent on the free mail privilege and other constituent services. These limits clearly favored incumbents, who already had the name recognition and could bypass limits by flooding their districts with materials sent out under the free postage privilege.
- The act limited what candidates could contribute to their own campaigns. If the idea had been to prevent corruption, then how could candidates corrupt themselves? Under this rule, the cam-

paign of John Heinz for the Senate in 1976, or the more recent presidential bids by Ross Perot and Steven Forbes, would have been illegal.

- The law silenced independent speakers by limiting how much any person could give in so-called political expenditures. The $1,000 limit at that time would have barely purchased a quarter-page ad in the *New York Times*. (This was, of course, the provision the Justice Department had attempted to use in *National Committee for Impeachment*, although the actual constitutionality of that provision would not be tested until later.)
- The law invaded one's privacy, because even the smallest contributor would have his or her name disclosed publicly and then put on file by the government
- Under the terms of the 1974 act, issue-oriented groups that reported on the voting records of members of Congress and then drew up "box scores" indicating how House members and senators had voted would have to file reports as "political committees."[50] What did political speech mean other than the right to evaluate and judge the performance of elected officials?

Given the fact that the 1974 act severely curtailed the amount of money that a candidate could raise and expend, it is not surprising that there would be a court challenge. But in order to make that challenge, there had to be a constitutional basis, and that is where the advocates of free speech came in. FECA would be challenged on the grounds that limiting how much money a person could donate to a political candidate, or how much a person could spend in running for public office, violated the First Amendment.

By 1975, moreover, even with the addition of more conservative justices appointed by Richard Nixon, the Supreme Court had adopted a highly speech-protective view of the First Amendment.[51] Although not going as far as Hugo Black and William O. Douglas, who had maintained, in their long careers on the bench, that First Amendment protections were absolute, the majority of the Court adopted the position that in order for the state to curb expression, it had to show a compelling governmental interest. If it could meet this heavy evidentiary burden, it then had to show that the means adopted were the least restrictive in manner.

Free expression can take many forms, and although the Court's record over the years has been erratic in some areas (such as obscenity and commercial speech), for the past half-century it has adhered to the notion that political speech is at the very core of First Amendment protection. While drawing upon theorists such as Zechariah Chafee, Jr., Alexander Meiklejohn, and Thomas Emerson to develop the notion of protected free expression, one can also point to one of the most influential opinions in the Court's history, the concurrence of Justice Louis D. Brandeis in *Whitney v. California* (1927).[52] In that opinion Brandeis provided what has become the root rationale for the protection of speech. The First Amendment, he explained, protects both the speaker's right to expound unpopular ideas and the listener's right to hear and evaluate such ideas. In a democracy each person, in order to be a good citizen, needs to be informed about public issues in order to make intelligent choices through the political system. The protection of political speech is thus crucial to each citizen's ability to perform civic obligations, and although the content of that speech may at times be offensive, in the final analysis the people in their collective wisdom will choose the better ideas and discard the less useful. Rather than stifle "bad" or unpopular speech, Brandeis declared, the remedy is more speech, and the result will be an informed citizenry and a vibrant democratic society.

In order to overturn the campaign finance laws, then, challengers would have to prove that the government had not shown any compelling interest in limiting the purest form of political speech, campaigning for office. Opponents of FECA believed they had a good chance at doing so, and on January 2, 1975, a coalition of both conservatives and liberals filed suit attacking key parts of FECA. The litigants included James Buckley (brother of conservative columnist and icon William F. Buckley, Jr.), then a Conservative Party senator from New York; former Senator and liberal presidential candidate Eugene McCarthy; financier and liberal activist Stewart Mott; the conservative journal *Human Events*; the ACLU; the New York Conservative Party; and the American Conservative Union. The coalition had been put together by David Keene, an assistant to Senator Buckley, who realized that opposition to the law ran across the political spectrum, and that it would be expedient if all these individuals and groups could pool their resources to cover the costs of the suit.[53]

The coalition attacked the law on several grounds. They opposed the public financing of presidential campaigns because, in accepting public money, candidates had to agree to abide by spending and contribution limits. They alleged that such limits, whether tied to the public financing provisions of the presidential campaign, or freestanding in regard to House and Senate races, violated the candidates' First Amendment rights. Similarly, contribution limits invaded private citizens' rights of political expression.[54] In essence, money, whether given by a willing contributor to a campaign, or expended by a candidate seeking office, constituted speech. Moreover, as political speech, it stood at the apex of the type of expression protected by the First Amendment.

The case, *Buckley et al. v. Valeo,* began in the U.S. District Court for the District of Columbia, which upheld the act, and from there was certified for appeal to the Court of Appeals for the District of Columbia, which, sitting *en banc,* upheld all but one provision of the act.[55] That provision, §437a, required issue advocacy groups, including those who rated members of Congress on their voting records, to file detailed reports with the government disclosing contributors and the amounts they had given. All of the circuit court judges, ranging from the liberal David Bazelon and J. Skelly Wright to the conservative Edward Tamm and Malcolm Wilkey, upheld the law.[56]

★ ★ ★ ★ ★

Buckley did not mark the first time that the High Court had heard cases involving political corruption (but these had usually involved corruption in office rather than questions of campaign finance),[57] and as recently as 1972 had decided a case in which a Senator had accepted a bribe and claimed legislative immunity from prosecution, a claim the Court rebuffed.[58] In three cases there had been First Amendment issues involved. First, the Court had dismissed an indictment under the Federal Corrupt Practices Act against the Congress of Industrial Organizations for publishing an internal newsletter that endorsed political candidates.[59] Second, in 1957 the Court had sustained the indictment and conviction of a union for illegally using union dues to sponsor television commercials supporting prolabor candidates.[60] Third, the Court had held that the 1971 FECA did not prevent unions from making political contributions if the money had been given voluntarily and through a segregated fund.[61]

In none of these cases, however, had the Court actually reached the First Amendment issue, and had always based its conclusions on other grounds. The Court had not hitherto directly addressed the question raised by the plaintiffs in *Buckley*—did limitations on campaign contributions and expenditures, without any evidence of wrongdoing, violate the First Amendment?

The Court heard oral arguments on November 10, 1975, and handed down its decision fairly quickly, on January 30, 1976, no doubt wanting to clear up any questions about the validity of portions of the act before campaigning for the 1976 elections began in earnest. The opinion is somewhat complicated and came down in per curiam form—that is, as the opinion of the Court with no justice listed as the author. Only three members of the Court, William Brennan, Potter Stewart, and Lewis Powell, joined in all parts of the opinion. In addition there were separate opinions by Chief Justice Warren Burger and Justices Byron White, Thurgood Marshall, Harry Blackmun, and William Rehnquist, all joining the opinion in part and dissenting in part. Justice John Paul Stevens, who had recently joined the Court, did not participate in the decision.

In essence, the Court in *Buckley* upheld the limits on individual contributions, the reporting provisions, and the public financing scheme for presidential elections. But it struck down on First Amendment grounds all limits on campaign expenditures by candidates or by political action committees. According to the Court, spending money in a campaign constitutes a form of expression, since it buys time or space in public forums to get across ideas; limiting expenditures, therefore, limits speech. The Court rejected a similar argument against contribution limits, even though they also imposed some restrictions on expression, because it accepted the government's argument of a compelling governmental interest in preventing corruption and maintaining the integrity of the political process.[62] In addition, the Court invalidated the means of appointing FEC members, and ruled that appointments could only be made by the president, by and with the concurrence of the Senate.

The Court ruled that FECA restricted "the voices of people and interest groups who have money to spend and reduce[d] the overall scope of federal election campaigns. . . [since] the alleged 'conduct' of giving or spending money 'arises in some measure because the communication allegedly integral to the conduct is itself thought to be harmful.'"[63] In other words, the only reason one would want to restrict contributions and expenditures would be to restrict the message being circulated, and this could not be done without violating the First Amendment. The Court also noted that, unlike earlier cases in which it had approved content-neutral time, place, and manner restrictions, this action, although technically content-neutral, in fact aimed at squelching the message completely.

Recognizing the realities of current campaigning, the Court noted that restrictions on money spent in political communication necessarily reduced the amount of that expression and the number and variety of issues discussed, "because virtually every means of communicating ideas in today's mass society requires the expenditure of money." In particular, the Court singled out the $1,000 ceiling on spending by interest groups, which "would appear to exclude all citizens and groups except candidates, political parties, and the institutional press from any significant use of the most effective means of [communication]."[64] In terms of preserving the right to expression, the Court held that so long as a political advertisement did not use certain words, later called "magic words"—such as "vote for," "elect," "defeat," or "reject"—the ads did not come within the definition of political advertising.[65] Although no one recognized it at the time, this was the first step in what would eventually become the avalanche of "issue advertising." The Court did, however, approve the reporting requirements, holding that by themselves such requirements did not limit free expression, and served the legitimate purpose of public scrutiny of campaign finance and expenditures.[66]

The opinion then drew a distinction between limits on expenses, which would restrict expression, and limits on contributions, which the Court said would not have that great an effect. "A limitation upon the amount that any one person or group may contribute [entails] only a marginal restriction upon the contributor's ability to engage in free communication. A contribution serves as a general expression of support for the candidate and his views, but does not communicate the underlying basis of the support. [At most], the size of the contribution provides a very rough index of the intensity of the contributor's support for the candidate. A limitation on [contributions] thus involves little direct restraint on political communication." Although admitting that greater contributions would allow the candidate greater expression, the Court noted that it was not the contributor's free expression, but that of the candidate, that reached the public.[67] Moreover, the Court found that no evidence showed that contribution limits would have any dramatic effect on the ability of political campaigns to raise the money they needed.

As for the First Amendment issues, the decision brushed them aside almost casually. "It is unnecessary to look beyond the Act's primary purpose—to limit the actuality and appearance of corruption resulting from large individual financial contributions—in order to find a constitutionally sufficient justification for the $1,000 contribution limitation. . . . The deeply disturbing examples surfacing after the 1972 election demonstrate that the problem is not an illusory one."[68] Clearly the Court, like the Congress that passed the 1974 FECA amendments, had Watergate on its mind, and used that example to undergird its constitutional argument that the necessity of avoiding corruption or its appearance provided the compelling interest to justify the act.

The Court's reasoning is confusing. If spending money is expression, then the amount of money one has in hand clearly enables or limits candidates or parties in sending out their message. The more money, the greater the capacity for expression; the less money, the less the ability to express. The Court seemed to assume that if candidates could no longer count on the big givers, they would still raise the money they needed by tapping larger numbers of small givers. If, however, a rich person strongly believed in an idea or program championed by a candidate, then it is plausible to assume that by financing that candidate, the donor is also making an expression. In our society there are many instances in which a person expresses his or her ideas through others. This contradiction becomes even more puzzling when we note that the Court struck down the limits on amounts that a candidate could give to his or her own campaign. A Nelson Rockefeller or a John Heinz could pour millions of their own money into their own campaigns. Rich candidates, in other words, had unlimited expression rights, but not rich donors. The Court ignored the claim that contributors were also expressing their views. And as we shall see in Chapter 3, this forced the political system to create alternative means by which those with deep pockets could give vent to their expressions, devices that within a short time would change the landscape of U.S. political campaigning.

In the third major part of the opinion, the Court upheld the provisions providing for public financing of presidential campaigns. "Subtitle H is a congressional effort, not to abridge, restrict, or censor speech, but rather to use public money to facilitate and enlarge public discussion and participation in the electoral process, goals vital to a self-governing people. Thus, Subtitle H furthers, not abridges, pertinent First Amendment values."[69]

Buckley has had its supporters and detractors ever since. The decision lifted the limits on expenditures by candidates and by groups operating independently of candidates, and the bar on how much candidates could give to their own campaigns. The limits on contributions remained in effect, restricting how much PACs, individuals, and political parties could give to specific campaigns; the public funding of presidential elections through a voluntary tax check-off remained untouched; and the Federal Election Commission would now be the official federal agency overseeing campaign finance. But although the Court apparently equated the expenditure of money by candidates with free expression, the lack of rigorous analysis in the opinion would cloud the issue of campaign finance reform for the next quarter-century.

⋆ ⋆ ⋆ ⋆ ⋆

Even after *Buckley*, the 1974 amendments still marked a significant improvement over the nearly useless scheme that had been in effect before 1971. As Anthony Corrado noted, "The new campaign finance system represented a major advancement over the patchwork of regulations it replaced. The disclosure and reporting requirements dramatically improved public access to financial information and regulators' ability to enforce the law."[70]

The new regulatory plan did include one very familiar element, a ban on corporate and union contributions and expenditures in federal elections, and the law now put a little bite into these prohibitions by making it unlawful for anyone—a candidate or a committee member—to accept such contributions. But the law did allow for a political action committee (PAC), whose administrative and fundraising expenses could be paid for by a parent corporation or union, so long as the actual funds expended politically came from voluntary contributions. One wonders if the drafters of this provision realized that, far from reining in campaign finance abuses, PACs would be the proverbial camel's nose in the tent.

The 1974 law also treated political party committees as a type of political entity that had to register with the Federal Election Commission, and it subjected them to fairly specific limits on donations they could receive and expenditures they could make. But party committees, as part of the official political party structure at national, state, or local levels, did in fact receive special treatment as well. Individuals could contribute up to $20,000 a year to national party committees and an additional $5,000 to a state party committee. These committees could then transfer unlimited sums to other party committees without the transfer being treated as a contribution. A national party committee could also transfer $17,500 during an election cycle to a senatorial candidate, and both national and state parties could make limited "coordinated" expenditures on behalf of their candidates for federal offices. These amounts varied by office (representative, senator, president) and by state population (more in New York and California than in Nevada and Mississippi), and were indexed to the rate of inflation.

In what would prove the greatest flaw in the new plan, the law made no distinctions between various types of party accounts, some subject to federal law and others not.[71] The statute makes no mention of "federal" or "nonfederal" accounts, and this created the first problem that arose after the law went into effect in 1976. The limits set on coordinated party spending clearly had a harmful effect on traditional grassroots party activity, and this led Congress to amend the law in 1979 to correct this problem. Neither did the 1974 law distinguish between what we now call "hard" and "soft" monies. The 1974 law and the 1979 revision created what would become the bane of reformers for the next two decades; the difficulty resulted, as we shall see, from the response of the Federal Election Commission to concerns related to the federal system—how best to facilitate the work of party organizations that have roles in both federal and nonfederal election campaigns. One might add that the internal inconsistencies in the Supreme Court's decision in *Buckley v. Valeo* boded poorly for the future.

3 / The Failure of Campaign Finance Reform after 1976

> I have been in a number of campaigns, and
> I enjoy the campaigns. . . . But the most
> demeaning, disenchanting part of politics is
> related to campaign finance. . . . Most of us,
> when we campaign, are on the telephone,
> calling our friends, calling up committees,
> meeting with people, often times begging for
> help. Searching for campaign money is a
> disgusting, degrading, demeaning experience.
> It's about time we cleaned it up.
> —Hubert H. Humphrey

SHORTLY after Richard M. Nixon resigned the presidency in the wake of Watergate, Senator Edward M. Kennedy (D-Mass.) noted that "abuses of campaign spending and private campaign financing do not stop at the other end of Pennsylvania Avenue. They dominate congressional elections as well." Kennedy's comment pointed to one of the major problems that would confront campaign finance reform over the next quarter-century. The quadrennial presidential election, the largest, the most expensive, and the most visible of all campaigns, captures the public's attention, and abuses in the Nixon years epitomized for many people the corruption inherent in the campaign financing system. But 100 senators and 435 members of the House of Representatives also have to stand before their constituents. In addition, there are gubernatorial, legislative, and local elections in all 50 states, the District of Columbia, and the territories.

That most astute political commentator, former Speaker of the House Tip O'Neill (D-Mass.), once famously declared that "all politics is local." It stands to reason, therefore, that people wishing to influence political decisionmaking have to target those elected officials whose actions will most directly affect their interests. Developers will be more interested in the decisions of local zoning boards and county supervisors than in the deliberations of members of Congress and will direct their political contributions toward local campaigns. Policies that affect many businesses are enacted by the states, and businesses with large stores in specific states will try to shape state laws on sales taxes, labor regulations, and the like. Although the president of the United States has enormous power to affect the implementation of regulations, those rules flow from statutes enacted by Congress, and large national and multinational corporations prefer to have Congress act in their favor. Of course, some groups like the National Rifle Association, the National Organization for Women, the Sierra Club, and the Christian Coalition operate at all political levels—local, state, and national—since policies affecting them may be implemented at all these levels.

To view campaign finance reform, therefore, just as a question of cleaning up presidential politics is to look at the tip of the iceberg and fail to realize that most campaigning goes on below that level. Reforming the system, therefore, requires that members of Congress place limits on themselves; yet the variety of districts and states represented in Congress precludes any simple one-size-fits-all solution. Although some of the limits imposed on presidential candidates would make sense in congressional and senatorial campaigns, others would not. In terms of state and local politics, Congress does not have the constitutional authority to impose regulations.

The reforms enacted in the 1974 Federal Election Campaign Act amendments would not have greatly affected the vast majority of campaigns in the country. Congress responded to the *Buckley* decision by amending the FECA in both 1976 and 1979, but these changes had little impact on campaign financing. In fact, in the opinion of many, the problems only grew worse in the next 25 years as party officials and professional fund-raisers found ways, some of them ingenious, to get around the FECA proscriptions. Reformers pointed to ever worsening scenarios, Congress held hearing after hearing, and nothing happened. The costs of running for office, however, kept rising, and candidates became ever more dependent upon campaign contributions.

★　★　★　★　★

Following *Buckley*, Congress moved to correct some of the FECA deficiencies struck down by the Court. It reconstituted the Federal Election Commission, this time providing that its members be nominated by the president and confirmed by the Senate. In order to maintain its influence over the FEC, Congress gave itself a veto power over any rules proposed by the commission.[1] The drafters also took the opportunity to fine-tune some of the regulations, such as raising the limit on individual contributions from $1,000 to $5,000. But although allowing larger donations to campaigns, Congress also tightened the reporting requirements and limited solicitations by political action committees (PACs) to members or defined constituent groups. The 1974 law, modified by the 1976 amendments[2] and indexed for inflation, remained the basic law governing campaign finance until the passage of the Bipartisan Campaign Reform Act (McCain-Feingold) in 2002.

In 1979 Congress passed a series of noncontroversial amendments that supposedly tightened federal election law but—with one significant exception—had little effect.[3] Although seeming to strengthen the wall that had been created to reduce the influence of money in federal elections, the 1979 amendments proved more cosmetic than substantive. Responding to complaints about the excessive detail required by FEC regulations, Congress eased the reporting requirements and made adherence to the spirit of the law—"a good faith effort" at compliance—rather than to the letter the criterion for enforcement. The amendments, because they worked to the benefit of party committees, faced practically no opposition, and passed both houses of Congress by wide margins. The main provisions made no significant changes in federal election law, but a seemingly innocent provision on party-building within a few years mushroomed into the bête noire of campaign finance reformers—soft money.

Two main trends emerged in campaign financing between 1974 and the early 1990s. First, there was growth in the total sums expended, much of it supplied through PACs, with the rate of increase greatest not at the presidential level but in congressional races. The second trend was that a large percentage of the money raised went to incumbents. Scholars who follow campaign spending trends note that the large growth in spending took place mostly in the late 1970s and 1980s, and then leveled off or even decreased slightly (in terms of constant dollars) in the early 1990s. For example, the average expenditure of victorious House candidates rose from $178,000 in 1980 to $410,000 in 1990, when it dropped back slightly.[4] Expenditures remained steady through most of the Clinton years, and then costs jumped again around the 2000 election.

Much of the jump in expenses can be traced to the ever-increasing role that media played in campaigns. As Larry Makinson of the Center for Responsive Politics noted, it takes a multimillion dollar campaign to run for the presidency. "But in the four decades since the first 'I Like Ike' TV commercials hit the air, the business of political advertising and consulting has penetrated to nearly every level of office-seekers."[5] In order to raise that money, candidates and parties have tapped into three main sources: soft money, political action committees, and personal wealth.[6]

★ ★ ★ ★ ★

Soft money is the result of a provision in the 1979 FECA amendments that eliminated any limits on donations to political committees providing that (a) they are not placed in the budget of any particular candidate's campaign, and (b) they are at least nominally directed toward so-called party-building activities, such as get-out-the-vote efforts, polling, and state campaign coordinating efforts. One may wonder whether the sponsors of this legislation ever intended or even imagined that it would create the greatest single device for evading both the letter and the intent of the FECA. As Mr. Dooley remarked of antitrust legislation in another era, lawyers could take what had been erected as a solid wall and turn it into a triumphal arch. By the mid-1990s, total soft money contributions rivaled the amount raised by the campaigns themselves, even in presidential elections where the federal government put in nearly $100 million in funding. According to some analysts, the soft money frenzy drove the costs of campaigning for the presidency from $325 million in 1984 to $500 million in 1988, and to more than $600 million four years later, of which less than one-sixth constituted the federal funding designed to place a cap on campaign costs.[7]

When the Court in *Buckley* upheld the FECA's limits on contributions, it assumed that "contributions" included any "funds provided to a candidate or *political party* or campaign committee either directly or indirectly through an intermediary," in addition to "dollars given to another person or organization that are earmarked for political purposes."[8] Congress in the FECA defined contributions and expenditures as the donation of and use of money or anything of value "for the purpose of influencing an election for federal office."[9] The statute did not go into any greater detail, leaving clarification of particulars to the FEC, which issued formal regulations in 1977. In those rules and in several advisory opinions, the FEC seemed to take a tough stance on how political committees could use money for party organization-building or voter registration drives. At the time, however, the FEC only addressed the issue of money raised under FECA provisions, and not "nonfederal funds," or what we now call "soft money." In subsequent rulings and advisory opinions, the FEC moved to the position that registration and get-out-the-vote drives could be financed by a combination of federal and nonfederal funds. Although for audit purposes they could maintain separate accounts of federal and nonfederal monies, it seemed that both would be subject to the same regulations. By 1979, however, the FEC ruled that both national and state parties could solicit and accept donations that would not be subject to FECA source and amount limits, so long as the parties maintained these funds in separate accounts, and that these funds could be used to influence elections for nonfederal offices. The only restriction the FEC imposed involved auditing practices, whereby the committees had to allocate administrative and certain other costs between federal and nonfederal funds.

Then in 1979, Congress amended the FECA to relieve state and local party organizations from many of the law's strictures, on the grounds that federal requirements interfered too greatly with traditional grassroots and volunteer activities. The new law exempted activities such as state party expenses for campaign materials (buttons, bumper stickers, lawn signs, and the like) used to support candidates, but the exemption rested on the use of "hard money"—that is, money raised under FECA guidelines for the support of a candidate. In other words, if Mr. Jones gave $1,000 to the Republican Party to elect Representative Smith, and the party allocated that money to Smith's local campaign committee specifically for the use of campaign materials, that money would not count against the expenditure limits imposed on Smith's campaign by FECA. Similarly, party expenses for voter registration and get-out-the-vote, if paid for by hard money, also would not count against the FECA expenditure limits. But, money given by Mr. Jones directly to a committee—either an established political committee or a special committee—specifically for these purposes would not count in any manner against FECA limits, and as a result, by the following year, had become an important part of national party campaign finance.[10]

Professor Thomas Mann of the Brookings Institution, a well-known student of campaign finance, noted that the 1979 amendments did not create soft money, and in fact Congress had no venal motives at the time. The amendments simply grew out of the recognition that political parties at the local, state, and national level had roles to play in both federal and nonfederal elections, and that the limits established by the 1974 FECA amendments hampered what most people considered valuable work of these committees in motivating voters, and getting them registered and to the polls. By 1979, the FEC had significantly relaxed its rules regarding what state and local committees could do with nonfederal funds, so long as the expenditures did not violate state laws. The Democratic and Republican National Committees then argued to the FEC that they, too, should have the flexibility that the FEC allowed to state and local committees. The 1979 amendments did not authorize national committees to accept unlimited donations from individuals or from corporate or union treasuries. Instead, they expanded the uses state and local parties could make of hard money.[11]

Once Congress permitted state and local committees to spend unlimited funds on grassroots activities that benefited federal as well as state and local candidates, the FEC permitted national party committees and the campaign committees of federal candidates to pay for a portion of these activities with funds outside the FECA limits. Beginning in the 1980 election cycle, soft money—that is, funds not subject to FECA limits and outside the scrutiny of the FEC—could be used by all political groups to finance certain activities. National parties could thus approach corporations and unions for direct contributions to these separate funds that ostensibly would be used solely for grassroots, voter registration, and get-out-the-vote drives. In addition, soft money could be used for so-called party-building activities, and the only limitation would be applicable state law, which in many states was either nonexistent or ineffective. Therefore reports of soft money were notoriously unreliable, since there were practically no required filings for the amounts raised or spent. The best estimate we have was done by Anthony Corrado, and from his fig-

Table 3.1. Hard- and Soft-Money Campaign Expenditures, 1976–2000

	Democrats			Republicans			Total		
Election	Hard	Soft	Total	Hard	Soft	Total	Hard	Soft	Total
1976		19.4 − 19.4			40.1 − 40.1			59.5 − 59.5	
1980	35.0	4.0	39.0	161.8	15.1	176.9	196.8	19.1	215.9
1984	97.4	6.0	103.4	300.8	15.6	316.4	398.2	21.6	419.8
1988	121.9	23.0	144.9	257.0	22.0	279.0	378.9	45.0	423.9
1992	171.9	32.9	204.8	256.1	47.5	303.6	428.0	80.4	508.4
1996	214.3	121.8	336.1	408.5	149.7	558.2	622.8	271.5	894.3
2000	265.8	244.9	510.7	427.0	252.8	679.8	692.8	497.7	1,190.5

ures, shown in Table 3.1, we can get an idea of how important soft money became in the two decades following 1980. (Figures are in millions of dollars.)[12]

In 1980, the first year that the national committees could raise and spend soft money, it accounted for only 8 percent of their total outlay; by the 2000 election, soft money accounted for 42 percent of the total expenditures of the national committees. Even in off-year cycles, the national committees raised and spent millions in soft money—$98.8 million in 1994 ($1 in $5 of the total), and $220.7 million in 1998 ($1 in $3). By 1988, parties raised much of their soft money through gifts from large contributors, with more than 400 persons, corporations, or unions each giving $100,000 or more. In that year the Republican National Committee set up "Team 100," a roster of contributors who donated at least $100,000 to the party, most of it in soft money. After the election the Republicans announced that they had received gifts of at least $100,000 from 267 donors; the Democrats that year received gifts of similar sizes from 130 donors. Four years later, the top category went to donors who gave $200,000 or more.[13]

A half billion dollars buys an awful lot of campaign buttons, bumper stickers, and yard signs, so clearly the party definitions of grassroots activities, voter registration, and get-out-the-vote expanded from what had been the relatively limited definition intended by Congress in 1979. The figures for 1980 and 1984 indicate that the parties appear to have been sticking to fairly narrow uses for soft money. The $21.6 million raised in 1984 represented only little more than a 10 percent increase from 1980, and in fact actually constituted a decline in the total amount spent, from 8 to 5 percent. Then the parties learned what they could do.

Throughout the 1980s and early 1990s, party organizations used soft money to finance a wide range of party expenses and activities. Both national party committees and their Senate and House campaign committees paid for administrative expenses, staff salaries, fund-raising costs, and general advertising (ads not expressly directed to favor a candidate). Of course, some of it actually went for buttons, bumper stickers, and yard signs.

Technically, soft money could not go to financing the campaigns of federal candidates, but in fact that is exactly where it went. Diana Dwyre, a political scientist at California State University–Chico, has detailed how soft money raised by political parties ended up in federal campaigns. The process began with the national party raising soft money, primarily through large donors, who made out their checks to nonfederal party accounts. The parties then transferred the money to state and local parties in districts and states where competitive elections were expected to occur. This transfer then allowed the state or local party to cover administrative costs or to make contributions to state or local candidates. This freed up hard money that had been raised to cover such purposes, which could then legally be given to federal campaigns. State and local committees simply could not transfer national-party soft money to federal candidates, but by exploiting the wording of the law—and with careful accounting procedures—soft money could be used to cover costs normally associated with hard money expenditures. The transfer allowed state parties to help federal candidates by essentially "washing" the soft money.[14]

Campaigns have open and hidden costs, both of which are necessary. The general public sees the television ads, billboards, bumper stickers, and yard signs, and may hear the voice of a staff member calling to urge support for the candidate. What are not seen are the overhead costs—rental of office space, purchases of computers and other office equipment, staffing for phone banks, telephone charges, costs of polling, transportation, the ad agencies that create the media spots, and the like—all of which are every bit as essential to a successful campaign as the appearances by the candidate and the constant mention of his or her name in the press, on billboards, bumper stickers, and so on. One may read about the amount of money raised at a $1,000-a-plate dinner for a candidate, but how much did it cost to rent the hall, pay for the catering, flowers, and liquor, solicit the contributors, and make sure that the committee sold all the seats?

If a candidate had $300,000 to pay for the overt costs, and did not have to worry about the hidden expenses, then in fact she had far more than $300,000 on which to campaign. Although the FECA had been amended in part to support the election of nonfederal candidates, the bulk of the money went to helping federal candidates. In the 1992 election, barely $2 million of the $80 million in nonfederal funds went to state and local candidates. The two national parties transferred $15 million to state party committees, nearly all of which they had to use in support of federal candidates. Approximately two-thirds of the soft money transfers of each party went to 10 states considered up for grabs in the presidential election. The bulk of the money, it is true, did go to financing voter identification and get-out-the-vote activities, the latter through large phone banks in which voters received not only the message to get out and vote, but also information on the candidates responsible for their getting that call; for example, "William Jackson, the Republican candidate for Congress in the 10th district, urges you to go out on election day and cast your vote." These campaigns also admittedly benefited state and local candidates, but only incidentally. The extra people hired, the phone banks created, the computerized voting lists—all of these had one aim to elect federal candidates. The people who raised the soft money—the national committees—wanted state and local candidates of their party to win, of course, but they raised and spent the money to benefit candidates for the Senate, the House, and of course, the White House.

The parties also used soft money for so-called generic advertising. Mostly television ads run in key states, they reinforced the message of the presidential candidates. Generated by the FEC rule that allowed for joint federal/nonfederal activities, the two parties spent about $14 million in this effort in 1992. The ads never mentioned the candidates' names, since both parties believed that only hard money could be used for candidate-specific ads. Rather, the ads urged the citizenry to "Vote Democratic" or "Vote Republican," and stressed the major themes of the presidential campaigns.[15]

For people with large amounts of money that they wanted to invest in candidates and campaigns, soft money opened a door that had supposedly been shut in 1974. An individual under the FECA could only give a candidate $1,000 per election (primary and general), $5,000 to a PAC, and a total of $20,000 in a year to political parties. But there were no limits at all on independent expenditures for or against a candidate, or on how much could be given to an interest group or a political party for issue advocacy or to a political party's soft money accounts. Before long the amounts solicited from, and given by, wealthy contributors easily rose above the old pre-Watergate levels.

Although the growth of soft money increased at an exponential pace, the FEC did essentially nothing to control it or even to have the amounts spent reported in a meaningful manner. Since much of the soft money supposedly went to state and local activities, the FEC reasoned, state and local governments ought to have the responsibility of policing their expenditures. This led Common Cause to request the FEC to issue new allocation laws on how the national parties could spend soft money, and to charge that the Democrats and the Republicans had improperly used nonfederal funds to influence federal elections by taking advantage of the FEC's loose guidelines. When the FEC refused to act, Common Cause took the agency to court, and the federal district court ordered the FEC to revise its regulations, give party committees more specific guidelines on how monies could be allocated and spent, and also to keep records of how much soft money the committees expended.[16] The case, decided in 1987, had little impact on the growth of soft money spending. In 1988, the soft money total for both parties reached $45 million; four years later it went to $80 million, then to $271 million in 1996, and nearly half a billion in 2000. From a little over 10 percent of the total expenditures by the national party committees, soft money had gone up to 42 percent by the time George Bush faced Al Gore in 2000.

By the end of the 1992 campaign, it had become clear that soft money and its use directly contravened the purposes of the FECA. The FEC, whose initial rulings had treated soft and hard money similarly, had essentially abandoned the field, and had to be dragged into court and forced to issue minimal regulations. State and local candidates, the object of congressional intent in permitting nonfederal funds, had been marginalized as national committees used soft money everywhere to help federal candidates. Soft money had become a means of financing federal elections, not funding grassroots state and local activities.

★　★　★　★　★

Prior to the 1996 election, most people assumed that one could not run candidate-specific ads except with hard money. Then President Bill Clinton and Dick Morris, his political consultant, devised a method to get around this limitation, through what they called "issue advocacy."[17] Starting in the fall of 1995, the Democrats spent some $34 million of soft money on television ads to promote Clinton's reelection. Although the spots featured Clinton, the party did not charge them against the Clinton campaign committee. Instead, the party paid for them with soft money and utilized a totally new legal argument—namely, that party communications that did not explicitly advocate the election or defeat of a federal candidate should be treated like generic party advertising, and, according to FEC rules, be financed by a mixture of hard and soft money (although in practice the greatest percentage came out of the soft money pocket). Such "communications," the Democrats claimed, constituted issue advocacy, a form of political speech subject neither to campaign spending limits nor to the source or size of contributions to political parties for this purpose.[18]

The argument could be traced directly back to *Buckley*, when the Court used an express advocacy test as a means of narrowing disclosure requirements and contribution limits. Political communications consisted of those messages that "in express terms advocate the election or defeat of a clearly identified candidate for federal office." The Court then elaborated in a footnote examples of such "express advocacy," which soon became known as the "magic words" test.[19] The Clinton ads, by carefully avoiding the magic words, sidestepped the intent of the FECA, the FEC regulations, and the *Buckley* test. Moreover, no limits existed on what donors could give to this issue advocacy campaign, a fact that Clinton, a champion fundraiser, put to good advantage. As he told a gathering of donors:

> My original strategy had been to raise all the money for my campaign this year [1995], so I could spend all my time next year being president, running for president, and raising money for the Senate and House Committee and for the Democratic Party.

And then we realized that we could run these [issue] ads through the Democratic Party, which meant that we could raise money in twenty and fifty and hundred thousand dollar lots, and we didn't have to do it all in thousand dollars. And run down. . . what I can spend, which is limited by law. So that's what we've done. But I have to tell you I'm very grateful to you. The contributions you have made in this have made a huge difference.[20]

Of the $34 million expended on such ads, the Democratic National Committee paid $12 million in hard money and $22 million in soft money. It accomplished this feat by transferring most of the soft money directly to state committees, which operated under more favorable FEC rules regarding the allocation ratios of hard and soft money, and the state committees purchased the air time.

The Republicans soon realized that the FEC would not oppose issue advocacy, and launched their own campaign. In May 1996 the Republican National Committee announced a $20 million issue advocacy campaign to show "the differences between Dole and Clinton and between Republicans and Democrats on the issues facing our country, so we can engage full-time in one of the most consequential elections in our history." Like the Democrats, the Republicans financed the campaign with a mixture of hard and soft moneys, funneled most of the soft money through the state committees, and targeted what they expected to be the key battleground states in the upcoming election.[21]

One might suggest that issue advocacy, at least in the abstract, ought to have been welcomed, if it in fact gave voters greater information on where candidates stood on issues and explained those issues to the people. If President Clinton, for example, had spent some time explaining why health insurance mattered to the nation, and then simply said, "And that's why I fought for it," the message would have been clear. If Robert Dole had tried to make clear why integrity constituted the one indispensable character trait of a president, and then said, "That's why I am in this race," many people would have preferred that to a three-second sound bite. Such ads would also have passed the "magic words" test of *Buckley.* But neither party wanted to operate on that plane, and before long issue advocacy ads appeared that barely, if at all, passed the *Buckley* test, and that in many cases proved virtually indistinguishable from regular campaign ads. Moreover, the practice soon spread into the congressional and Senate races, and provided a golden opportunity for individual interest groups to support candidates who passed the litmus test on their issue and oppose those who did not. None of the following ads, under the rules then in effect, were considered to be election advertisements:[22]

- "Working families are struggling, but Congressman [. . .] voted with Newt Gingrich to cut college loans, while giving tax breaks to the wealthy. . . . Tell him his priorities are all wrong." [AFL-CIO, for use in many districts]
- "Congresswoman Andrea Seastrand has voted to make it easier to dump pollutants and sewage into our water. . . . Fact is, it's time to dump Seastrand, before she dumps anything else on us." [Sierra Club]
- "Tell President Clinton: You can't afford higher taxes for more wasteful spending." [Republican National Committee]
- "Who is Bill Yellowtail? He preaches family values, but he took a swing at his wife. And Yellowtail's explanation? He 'only slapped her.' But her nose was broken." [Citizens for Reform]

According to the Annenberg Center, issue advocacy ads cost between $135 million and $150 million in the 1996 election cycle, about one-third as much as all federal candidates combined spent on direct candidate ads. Political parties spent about half this money, and interest groups spent the other half. The AFL-CIO by itself accounted for half the sum spent by interest groups.[23] Because these ads stood outside the contribution limits of FECA, corporations and labor unions could tap their own treasuries to run the spots, either under their own names or through an anonymous intermediary. Although some candidates began to complain that they could no longer set their own campaign agenda, by the late 1990s most candidates, especially challengers, realized that large issue-advocacy promotions had become critical to their chances of success.[24]

*   *   *   *   *

Reformers saw soft money and its abuses as one of the two great villains of the campaign finance system; they saw political action committees as the other culprit. Such committees had been in existence well before Congress enacted the Federal Election Campaign Act. But the act, and especially the 1974 amendments, completely transformed the role of PACs in the political process. As Steven Gillon noted, "That's not what we meant to do."[25]

Prior to 1974, PACs had, with few exceptions, been relatively minor players in campaign finance. The leading PAC, the AFL-CIO's Committee on Political Education (COPE), had by the early 1970s emerged as an effective and powerful body that not only raised and distributed funds but led highly regarded voter registration and get-out-the-vote drives. The AFL-CIO had been forced to create COPE because of the Taft-Hartley Act restrictions on the use of regular union funds for political action. Corporations, on the other hand, had eschewed PACs, even though the Corrupt Practices Act also forbade the use of corporate treasuries to fund political activity. Corporate officials, however, had not been restricted in how much they could personally give to campaigns, and although company money, after suitable laundering, may have made its way into the campaign chests of some candidates, business owners personally faced no barriers in giving large amounts of money to candidates.

During the 1960s no questions had been raised about the legality of PACs, but in 1970 a court ruled a union PAC in St. Louis illegal. Although no one mounted a challenge to COPE itself, labor leaders worried about the possibility and worked closely with the Democrat-controlled Congress to put language into FECA that explicitly allowed unions and corporations to establish "separate segregated funds" to create and operate PACs. The clause gave corporations a legal basis to establish PACs, and a few did. Then Common Cause filed a lawsuit against several companies that had set up PACs, on the basis that FECA prohibited campaign contributions by firms or other groups that had contracts with the government. The suit, although aimed at business, also worried labor leaders. A number of unions had secured contracts from the government to train workers under Lyndon Johnson's War on Poverty programs. Once again the AFL-CIO went to Congress, and in the 1974 FECA amendments it responded by protecting not only unions with government contracts but corporations as well, and permitted companies that had large defense and other government contracts to use corporate funds to establish and administer PACs and to fund-raise for them.[26]

Because business had never utilized PACs to any great extent, union officials assumed there would be no reason for them to do so now. Common Cause, which backed the PAC provision in the 1974 amendments, thought that PACs would be a way to keep an eye on special-interest giving. The disclosure requirements imposed on the committees supposedly would discourage unions, corporations, and wealthy individuals from trying to spend their way into positions of influence in Washington. Moreover, small groups that could not by themselves mount an effective campaign could now unite, and, with a lot of small donations from middle-class citizens, obtain a voice in the political process. Both assumptions proved wrong.

Prior to 1974, wealthy persons could make unlimited private donations to campaigns, and thus had little interest in supporting PACs. The new law, however, placed restrictions on the amount of money individuals could give directly to candidates, but allowed them to give thousands of dollars more to PACs that would support those candidates or specific issues. In the six months following the FEC ruling implementing the 1974 FECA amendments, more than 150 companies established PACs. Moreover, all sorts of interest groups suddenly recognized the value of the newly legitimized committees. Common Cause thought that only groups like environmentalists or advocates of reform would create PACs; instead, interest groups from all over the political, economic, and social spectrum rushed to enter the fray.

Between 1974 and 1982, the number of PACs organized by business and labor unions more than quadrupled from 608 to 2,601. By 1999, 3,835 PACs had registered with the FEC, most of them corporate.[27] In 2000, 43 percent of all PACs represented businesses, and 8 percent labor;[28] the rest spoke for a variety of interests that ranged from religious and social conservatives to the National Rifle Association and to environmental groups like the Sierra Club. PACs not only helped to fund presidential campaign committees, but over the years came to play an ever-increasing role in congressional campaigns. In 1978 PACs accounted for 13 percent of all contributions to senatorial candidates; 10 years later that amount had increased to 22 percent. In the same period of time the percentage of funds provided to House candidates by PACs went from 24 to 40 percent. Common Cause, which had championed the provision legitimizing PACs, noted that despite the economic stagnation of the early 1980s, "PACs have become a truly remarkable growth industry." The Center for Responsive Politics declared the 1974 legislation a partial failure. Although ending the era of "unregulated, free-wheeling, under-the-table campaign finance," and instituting a system of reporting that provided fairly accurate information, the reforms "only served to sanitize, rationalize, and legitimize the same old system of privately financed federal elections dominated by wealthy individual and corporate contributors."[29]

It is hardly surprising that corporate America seized the opportunity provided by the 1974 amendments. Critics of corporate PACs charge them with legalized corruption, undermining the democratic process, buying undue access to government decisionmakers, and using the PAC device to bypass federal laws prohibiting the use of company funds for political purposes. The PACs have their defenders as well, and each of these points carries with it at least some truth:

- Corporate and other PACs represent individuals who subscribe to a common set of beliefs, and can therefore find greater expression in the political arena through collective action. PACs thus provide legitimate interest representation for individuals.
- The money provided by PACs enables candidates without personal wealth to seek office and have a chance of winning. The admission of these new voices into politics enriches the democratic process and opens it to greater diversity of participation.
- The rules that govern corporate PACs, such as disclosure requirements, have brought corporate political involvement, which always existed, out of the shadows and into the sunlight where it can be scrutinized. Instead of back-door exchanges of money satchels, corporations now operate in the open, and must do so according to the rules.
- PACs foster debate and competition in politics by emphasizing issues that might otherwise be ignored.
- Corporate PACs have helped to balance what had hitherto been the overwhelming political influence of organized labor.[30]

It is possible to quibble with each of these points, but the fact remains that corporations have interests that are affected by political decisions, and since the Supreme Court ruled over a century ago that corporations enjoy some of the rights accorded "persons" under the Fourteenth Amendment, then they ought to be able to defend their interests just as natural persons do.[31] Moreover, although government policy has always had an impact on the business community (through tariffs, land grants to build the transcontinental railroads, and protective labor legislation in the nineteenth and early twentieth centuries), the increase in government regulations in recent decades has made business even more sensitive to protecting itself in the political arena.[32]

The *Federal Register*, which lists all federal laws and administrative regulations, increased in size from 20,036 pages in 1970 to 77,497 pages in 1979; in other words, it nearly quadrupled in just under a decade. In the 1970s Congress created a number of regulatory bodies including the Environmental Protection Agency (EPA), the Occupational Safety and Health Administration (OSHA), the Consumer Product Safety Commission (CPSC), and others. In addition, several agencies established new departments to oversee the enforcement of new federal laws. The Department of Housing, Education, and Welfare set up an Office of Civil Rights to enforce new fair housing legislation. The Department of Labor created the Office of Federal Contract Compliance to monitor the 1964 Civil Rights Act. These new agencies embraced a far more expansive view of regulation than had previously existed, and went far beyond the economic regulations of the New Deal. In the past federal regulatory bodies had been reactive, responding to specific claims of wrongdoing. Historian Hugh Davis Graham describes the new regulations as "provocative, emphasizing future compliance to reduce risk and eliminate hazards." During the 1970s, he argues, the federal government shifted from an "administrative state," in which agencies gave money to the states for programs, with few strings attached, to a "regulatory state," in which Congress and the executive agencies established rules governing private and especially corporate behavior.[33] If labor, environmental, and other groups have the right to advocate for regulatory policies that could adversely affect business, then surely corporations ought to be able to counter that influence with efforts of their own.

PACs derived at least part of their influence from the mushrooming rise in campaign costs. Congress in the FECA amendments had put limits on campaign contributions at the same time that television and the new computer technology needed to manage campaigns and voter databases drove up the cost of running for office. By 1996 the average campaign for the Senate cost $4 million, and a House seat required half a million. A typical senator, therefore, needed to raise $15,000 a week, every week, for six years, in order to finance a reelection bid. Even the indexing provisions of FECA, which adjusted campaign limits on the basis of inflation, did not help, because the costs associated with running for office grew at a far faster rate than the overall inflation index. Television costs in particular skyrocketed, as the medium played an ever more crucial role in office-seeking, and by 1990 the two parties spent nearly one billion dollars on media advertising. As Senator Ernest Hollings (D-S.C.) admitted, "The hard fact of life for a candidate is that if you are not on TV, you are not truly in the race."[34]

PACs provided candidates with the most accessible means of money to pay for advertising, polling, and the other accoutrements of a modern campaign. In 1980 PACs gave $55.2 million to congressional candidates, a figure that almost quadrupled to $206.8 million by 1998.[35] The reason PACs became such an important source in campaign financing could be found in the Federal Election Campaign Act and its amendments. PACs could give no more than $5,000 per election directly to a candidate, up to $15,000 per year to a national party committee, and no more than $5,000 in combined contributions to state and local committees.[36] But PACs had no aggregate annual limit, so they could give money to multiple candidates, to state and local committees that would support those candidates, and to various independent committees for activities such as issue advocacy. Moreover, individuals could give up to $5,000 to each of several PACs. The American Petroleum Institute, an organization of petroleum producers and refiners, could not give $100,000 to a single candidate; but it could create 10 different PACs, and then give $10,000 to each one for transfer to a candidate. It is little wonder that PACs became so important.

Another aspect of PAC activity that drew the attention of critics lay in the fact that PACs fostered the advantage that incumbents had over challengers. Common sense tells us that unless he or she has displeased a good part of the constituency, an incumbent enjoys an advantage in fund-raising. By 1998 House incumbents on the average outspent challengers by a ratio of four-to-one, and 9 out of 10 incumbents won reelection. PACs, as a result, saw an incumbent as a good investment, one that would increase over time as a member gained seniority and, with it, plum committee appointments and chairmanships. From the beginning, then, PACs not only supported incumbents, but did so in a lopsided manner. In 1974 PACs gave 72 percent of their donations to incumbents, and only 28 percent to challengers. By 1998, congressional challengers received only 8 percent of PAC donations; the rest went to incumbents. Only wealthier candidates could afford to ignore the PACs, and one advocate of reform, Senator Robert C. Byrd (D-W.Va.), warned that without changes in the law, Congress would soon become the "exclusive domain of the very wealthy," and people with the "common man's background" (such as himself) would be discouraged from seeking office.[37]

★　★　★　★　★

What did the Federal Election Commission do during these years? The answer is, "Not much." Ten years after the creation of the FEC, the *Congressional Quarterly* described it as an agency "with no constituency, little money, and few friends, . . . an agency whose administrative decisions are vilified by politicians, ridiculed by lawyers, and overturned by courts."[38] The commission, created by the 1974 amendments, began its work as the *Buckley* case wended its way through the judicial system, and it soon became clear that although Congress had created the new agency, it had little love for its child. Four of the first six commissioners had been members of Congress, a fifth had strong ties to the Republican Party, and the sixth had been a lawyer for the AFL-CIO—all of them were naturally sympathetic to the campaign financing needs of congressional and presidential candidates. Congress also made sure that the commissioners understood that they had a limited role to play. The FEC initially asked for $20 million for two years, a figure Congress reduced to $7.8 million for 18 months. Using its veto provision, Congress nullified the first two regulations promulgated by the commission. The first regulation would have required that members of Congress include, as part of their campaign finance disclosures, the amount of money they kept in their office slush funds, and the second would have changed the initial point of entry for financial reports from the clerk of the

House and the secretary of the Senate to the FEC. In both instances, Congress charged the FEC with interfering in long-established congressional practices.[39]

Then came *Buckley,* in which the Court declared the manner of appointing FEC members—two by the Speaker of the House, two by the president pro tempore of the Senate, and two by the president—to be unconstitutional, and gave Congress 30 days to revise the procedure, so that all members would be nominated by the president and confirmed by the Senate. For some unexplained reason, it took Congress more than three months to work out this simple detail and to make other responses to the decision, and not until May 1976 did President Gerald Ford sign legislation bringing FECA and the FEC into compliance. Ford reappointed five of the six original members (the FEC also has two nonvoting members, the clerk of the House and the secretary of the Senate), but the sixth, former congressmember Thomas Curtis (R-Neb.), resigned because he believed the FEC would never truly be independent of Congress. Curtis believed the commissioners should be part-time, deriving their income from sources other than congressional appropriations, and that funding authorization ought to be given for a multiyear period rather than annually.

Congress, however, intended to keep a tight rein on the FEC through funding. Many agencies get multiyear appropriations, with adjustments made in each budget cycle. Wayne Hays (D-Ohio), the powerful chair of the House Administration Committee, learned that he might be the subject of a random FEC audit, and told Curtis: "You're not going to set the ground rules. [My] committee is. As Chairman, I'll tell you. You're coming back every year for an authorization."[40] When Congress passed the 1979 amendments, it prohibited the FEC from conducting random audits, even though the commission, which had begun the audits in 1976, believed that random selection was "the most nonpartisan and even-handed approach" to verify and correct the public record. In 1981, conservative Senate Republicans unsuccessfully attempted to kill off the FEC by cutting its funds entirely.[41] Although reformers have often charged that regulatory agencies frequently become captives of the industries they are supposed to regulate, "the FEC was not so much captured as it was kidnapped and held hostage."[42]

Most likely the FEC behaved pretty much as Congress intended it to, and in fact the rules make it almost impossible to secure any truly effective action. Most agencies, such as the Securities and Exchange Commission (SEC), the Federal Trade Commission (FTC), and the Interstate Commerce Commission (ICC), have five voting members, but the FEC has six. The agency is supposed to be politically neutral, with three of its members Democrats and the other three Republicans. But for the agency to agree on anything requires four votes, which means that either the proposed measure is so innocuous that it will not offend anyone or so egregious that it cannot be ignored. Although ideally the FEC should be nonpartisan or at the most bipartisan, in fact Congress has demanded partisanship, and presidents have acquiesced by nominating people who will act in a partisan manner to protect the interests of the parties. As Robert Mutch notes, "Congress wants more than the statutory balance between Republicans and Democrats on the Commission—Congress wants the right kinds of Republicans and Democrats, preferably ones who are both partisan and closely tied to congressional party leaders."[43] FEC members are quite aware of this, and when President Carter nominated Frank Reiche of New Jersey to the FEC in 1979, Senate Republicans expressed concern that he would not pay enough attention to Republican interests. Reiche himself acknowledged that "Congress views the FEC as a partisan body. There is no question that [a commissioner's] votes will be scrutinized as the time for reappointment approaches." The presence of the two ex officio members, the clerk of the House and the secretary of the Senate, both beholden to congressional leadership, ensures that congressional influence—and partisanship—are always present at commission deliberations.[44]

Given the partisanship and the four-vote requirement, it is hardly surprising that the FEC proved ineffective. In 1986, for example, the Democratic Congressional Campaign Committee filed a complaint against its Republican counterpart, charging that the Republicans had violated the FECA by not counting, against their limit on coordinated expenditures, $10,000 spent for a mailing in Rhode Island. The FEC general counsel, after looking into the matter, reported that there was reason to believe that a violation had occurred, and that the commission should look into it. The year before, the FEC had issued an advisory opinion on this same issue, under which the Republican mailing in Rhode Island would have had to be reported and counted. Nonetheless, the commission split its vote, three to three, and then quietly closed the file without any explanation of its decision.[45] The next year the commissioners again split along party lines and rejected their counsel's advice that there was reason to find the National Republican Senatorial Committee in violation for failing to report $3 million in contributions designated to 12 senatorial campaign committees.

Most of the work of the FEC during the 1980s and 1990s was noncontroversial and involved questions of campaign housekeeping and reporting; and by some estimates, only 1 in 10 cases aroused the type of partisan controversy noted above. The reason for this may be that the parties and the candidates held the FEC—and the laws it supposedly enforced—in such low regard that in many instances they just ignored the agency. The candidates and their parties appeared willing to take potentially illegal or controversial actions without seeking an advisory opinion from the FEC. They operated on the assumption that even if there should be an investigation, it probably would not take place until after the election had been held, and then the FEC vote would split three to three along party lines, negating any action at all. Daniel Swerlinger claimed that most candidates and their advisors take the view that "the Commission is never going to get four votes, so they can do anything they want. . . . It is undercutting what was anyway a rather weak enforcement system and making it even more toothless."[46]

To give an idea of how little regard candidates and campaign committees had for the FEC, and how little they feared its enforcement powers, one might look at a *Harper's Magazine* simulation in 1987 regarding how the 1988 presidential campaign would run. Robert Beckel, who had been Walter Mondale's 1984 campaign manager, and Harrison Hickman, a Washington-based pollster, agreed that their candidates would ignore state spending limits if necessary in order to win primaries and delegates. At worst, the FEC would take months to get around to investigating, and then even if they managed to overcome their squabbling, all that would happen would be a slap on the wrist and a small fine.[47]

Even when the FEC agreed to investigate, the process could drag on indefinitely. Early in March 1984 the FEC finally closed a complaint that had been filed in April 1979, by the National Committee for an Effective Congress (NCEC), against two of Ronald Reagan's committees, one a presidential prenomination group and the other a PAC Reagan had founded in 1977. The complaint alleged that the PAC had conducted activities that directly benefited Reagan's campaign, and thus had exceeded the $5,000 legal limit the law imposed on PAC donations to a candidate. It took five years before both the committee and the PAC agreed to pay small civil penalties. As the NCEC said, "The investigation was entirely too long for this kind of [petty] result." The NCEC had considered taking the FEC to court, but decided not to do so because of the costs involved in what would have been a protracted court fight. All sides agreed upon one thing: the FEC could move slower than any other federal agency, both in its own work and in the courts.[48]

If Congress, as is likely, had wanted to create a toothless agency to enforce the election laws, then it succeeded brilliantly. Structurally, the FEC is designed to fail. The appointment process emphasizes partisan loyalty rather than an ethical willingness to enforce the law. The requirement that there be four affirmative votes to take action has led to a stalemate on most issues coming before the commission. The chair serves only a one-year term, is chosen by the other commissioners, and has little or no independent power over selecting staff or instituting procedures. Congress has not given the FEC anywhere near the money necessary for the commission to do a decent job. In fiscal 1989 it received an appropriation of $16 million, compared to $43 million for the ICC, $66 million for the FTC, $99.6 million for the Federal Communications Commission (FCC), and $143 million for the SEC. Even allowing that these other agencies have a larger range of activities, the FEC appropriation, as the *Washington Post* noted, amounted to "chicken feed." This money paid for basic expenses and for a staff far too small to handle complaints with any degree of speed. Allegations of violations could take months or even years to go through the FEC, a fact that disturbed only such reformers as John Gardner's Common Cause.

When the FEC acted, it did so on minor issues and in a manner that was, at the least, embarrassing. It failed to act on claims that millions of dollars had been wrongly unreported, but when the Central Long Island Tax Reform Immediately Committee raised $135 to print a pamphlet that outlined a congress member's voting record on tax reform, the FEC found "reason to believe" that the committee had violated the law by not filing the appropriate financial disclosure report.

The commission then spent thousands of dollars and four years in court in a battle against the committee, being slapped down by one judge after another. U.S. Court of Appeals Judge Irving Kaufman tongue-lashed the FEC, declaring that it had "failed abysmally" in carrying out "its obligation to exercise its powers in . . . harmony with a system of free expression." Brooks Jackson, who has written an unsparingly harsh review of the FEC, said the case reflected the commission's record of taking "an unrelenting strict line on minor violations and an astonishingly relaxed attitude about big ones."[49]

Yet this is exactly how the two parties and Congress wanted it. Mark Braden, the former general counsel for the Republican National Committee, admitted this in an amazingly candid comment: "If we had an efficient commission, then we might have them having an impact on elections, which I don't think, at least from my perspective . . . I would be real happy with. In some ways I sort of like the snail's pace that you have now, so that they never get anything done, so it does not affect any election."[50] The responsibility for enforcing campaign finance laws, as so many have noted, rested in an agency created by Congress, with closer ties to Congress than any other federal agency had, and that had the responsibility for overseeing campaign laws without offending members of Congress who had to campaign under those laws.

In fairness, the FEC did carry out its statutory obligations on rulemaking and other matters.[51] It also kept making recommendations to Congress on ways that it could become more effective, and it asked for more money so that even within its crippling structure it might handle more complaints in an expeditious manner. It also recommended changes in the election law from time to time. All came to nothing, as Congress consistently turned a deaf ear. As Mark Braden said, "No one is really sure that they want [a commission] that works. Because they are afraid of what would happen if it works."[52]

★   ★   ★   ★   ★

Just as Congress attempted to deal with what it saw as the problems of financing federal elections, states also tried to keep themselves free of the corrosive influence of money and other inducements that might affect the ballot. In one of the earliest state laws on campaign regulation, Maryland in 1811 made it a crime to keep open any establishment at which "any victual or intoxicating liquors shall be gratuitously given or dealt out to voters." Some states closed down all bars and taverns on Election Day until after the polls closed, and others prohibited wagering on the elections. By the 1950s the general pattern of state regulation—complicated, of course, by the fact that the 48 states addressed the problem in a variety of ways—roughly mirrored that of federal legislation discussed as in Chapter 1. Many of the states, in fact, enacted campaign reform legislation, as before Congress did. California and Missouri, for example, placed limits on candidate expenditures in 1893; Congress first tried that approach in 1911.[53]

In a survey of state legislation made in 1960, well before the Watergate scandals led to FECA and its amendments, Alexander Heard found that four states had limits on individual contributions that ranged from $1,000 to $5,000. Thirty-one states had limits on campaign expenditures, although most of these rules applied only to candidates and to moneys spent with their approval. In addition, 43 of 50 states had some requirements for reporting of contributions and expenses by candidates and/or party or other campaign committees.[54] These laws varied in comprehensiveness and means of enforcement. As early as 1930, in commenting on some of the earlier laws (which remained on the books until the 1970s), Louise Overacker, one of the first scholars to study campaign financing, noted that "some are so obviously sketchy on the enforcement side as to arouse the suspicion that the drafters must have hoped and expected that they would remain dead letters upon the statute books."[55]

Even when states collected reports, they did little to analyze them or even make them available for public scrutiny—a major purpose of requiring the reports. Overacker noted that when one asks for reports, "one is taken into a tiny wash room where a series of dusty, paper-covered bundles repose upon an upper shelf. By climbing upon a chair and digging about among the bundles one usually finds what one wants if one persists in this 'trial and error' method long enough, but there is no file and no system, and for some of the earlier campaigns no record of what is supposed to be there and what is not."[56] These conditions could be found in many state capitals, not to mention being found in the clerks' offices in the House and Senate in Washington. In addition, in some states there are also local election laws requiring reporting. But with the exception of the California

Commission on Campaign Financing, there have been few efforts to analyze local reports in any meaningful manner.[57]

Concern about campaign financial practices has grown in the states, because the cost of running for state and local elections has mirrored or even exceeded the increases in federal campaigns. Between 1958 and 1986, for example, the cost of running for a seat in the California legislature increased by a factor of 40, or 4,000 percent! In 1990 the median cost of a California Senate race had risen to $713,974; and an assembly seat, to $341,324. Many races cost more than $1 million, and some exceeded $2 million. Although California may be an extreme example, in the state of Washington the total costs for legislative races jumped over 300 percent between 1976 and 1988. Studies of various states may report different rates of increase, but on one thing, all agree—it has grown increasingly expensive to run for public office at the state and even at the local level.[58]

Following Watergate, about two-thirds of the states revised their campaign finance laws. By 1980, nearly all states required reports on contributions and expenditures in connection with the general elections, and quite a few required similar reports on the costs of primaries. Twenty-nine states required the listing of all contributors who gave more than a minimum amount, although this number varied from $25 to $100. Seventeen states required fairly detailed expenditure reports, with all expenditures itemized. Most barred anonymous contributions and money given by one person in the name of another. A few states prohibited contributions of over a certain amount, usually $100, in cash.[59]

Perhaps most importantly, 16 states had public funding programs of some sort in place for parties and/or candidates. Six—Delaware, Kentucky, Maryland, Nebraska, North Carolina, and Rhode Island— gave money just to gubernatorial candidates and people running for statewide constitutional offices. In addition, Minnesota, Wisconsin, and, to a far lesser degree, Hawaii provided funds for legislative candidates.[60]

State laws focused primarily on disclosure and limitations more than on public financing. Nearly every state required reports on contributions and expenditures, although the laws varied enormously in what candidates had to report and in how much detail, and how often. Often these laws constituted sections of larger statutes regulating lobbyists, the type and value of gifts that state officials could accept, or, in some instance, so-called sunshine laws designed to ensure that the activities of elected officials would not be hidden from the public.

In line with *Buckley*, of course, states could not regulate the amount of money expended—except in those instances where candidates voluntarily agreed to spending limits in connection with some form of public financing. Before that decision, 35 states had enacted campaign expenditure limits, and 31 had ceilings on independent spending; all of these fell by the wayside after *Buckley*. Twenty-three states restricted individual and group contributions, although the top amounts ranged from $600 in New Jersey to $10,000 in Missouri, to a $150,000 limit on the sum of contributions to all candidates and/or committees in an election cycle. Most states adopted the same limits imposed by federal law—$1,000 per election (primary or general), with a total contribution limit of $25,000 per year to all campaigns.[61] Naturally, the key to the effectiveness of any law is how well it is enforced. Just as the FEC disappointed reformers by its performance in carrying out the FECA, state agencies also proved less than enthusiastic in monitoring compliance with state laws. These results did not encourage reformers:

- In Maryland, Governor Marvin Mandel used his office to dry up funds for any potential Democratic challengers by raising $1 million at a kickoff dinner held more than 17 months before the election. Nearly all the money came from labor unions and business owners who had profited greatly from their contracts with the state.
- Even before Watergate, Texas had done a major overhaul of state government. Nonetheless campaigns in the next few elections cost more than $8 million, even though no major office was seriously contested. Governor Dolph Briscoe, elected in 1972 as a reform candidate, advanced $645,000 to his reelection campaign in gifts and loans.
- In Florida, as the governor went beyond the demands of state law to limit his contributors to $100, another state official, deeply mired in scandal, easily won reelection because he extracted large donations from companies his office regulated.
- Although California reformers managed to push through a tough campaign finance law by using the initiative, Governor Pat Brown, a principal backer of Proposition 9, raised over $1.5 mil-

lion for the primary in 1974, and $2 million for the general election, nearly all in large contributions from individuals, public sector unions, and companies all doing business with the state.

- In Massachusetts, where corruption and reform run in almost predictable cycles, 1973 saw the passage of a comprehensive campaign finance law that, among other things, closed a loophole regarding funds from testimonial dinners. Before signing the law, Governor Francis Sargent had scheduled a number of $100-a-plate dinners to benefit his campaign. He then offered to return all of the money if the legislature would pass a public financing bill. Despite wide support for it, the state assembly refused to enact such a measure.
- In Georgia the man responsible for the new campaign finance law also proved the most adept at evading its strictures and exploiting its loopholes. He criticized his opponent for relying on loans from banks until it came out that he had accepted them as well, since the banks wanted to ensure favorable regulatory legislation.[62]

One could go on with other stories, all pointing to situations in the states comparable to that in federal campaign financing—supposedly rigorous laws on the books violated or ignored by candidates, especially incumbents. As reformers in general despaired, *Washington Post* correspondent David S. Broder found a silver lining in the state situation. The very fact that so much could be reported, he declared, "is in itself a direct by-product of the legislative reforms that preceded the 1974 campaign." Before then there would have been no reports of how much money had been raised or where it had come from. If corruption had not been eliminated—and it had not—at least the reporting system made it easier for the press and the public to see what was going on.[63]

*   *   *   *   *

Herbert Alexander, a noted scholar of campaign finance, has commented that the effort to reconcile the concept of "one person, one vote" in a democracy and the inequities of financial resources is the core issue of money in politics. Critics of soft money and PACs believe that the two cannot be reconciled, and that since money translates into political power, those who have the resources to give to PACs and to candidates will have an undue voice in political decisionmaking. Judge J. Skelly Wright of the Court of Appeals for the District of Columbia eloquently summed up this view:

> As individuals are squeezed out, as the behemoths of concentrated wealth dwarf the individual and bid fair to dominate the political field, the very purpose of direct democracy is defeated, and voters are bound to become disillusioned and apathetic. This picture might not trouble a convinced pluralist who sees democratic government as nothing more than the results of the pull and tug of aggregated interests in a field of political vectors and partisan forces of greater or lesser intensity. But I believe in the role of equal individuals in the process of American self-government, and I am convinced that this role cannot be snuffed out without at the same time destroying the integrity of our electoral process and the essence of our political faith.[64]

This problem—how to resolve the inherent tension between democratic equality and economic disparity—would be at the core of congressional efforts to reform the campaign finance laws, an effort that eventually culminated in the McCain-Feingold bill. The second issue, how to resolve the potential conflict between the demands of the First Amendment and efforts to regulate the political process, would confront the Supreme Court as it moved from *Buckley* to the challenge to McCain-Feingold.

4 / The Road to McCain-Feingold

> I can call Karl [Rove], and I can call about half
> the Cabinet, and they will either take the call or
> call back.
> —Member of George W. Bush's "Ranger" club
> who had raised at least $200,000 toward George
> W. Bush's reelection campaign

> If you think I'm giving money to get access to
> [President Bush], you're crazy. I'm just trying to
> get the right guy elected. That's all I care about.
> —Member of George W. Bush's "Pioneer" club
> who had raised at least $100,000 toward George
> W. Bush's reelection campaign

THE NORMALLY staid Association of the Bar of the City of New York began its special report on campaign finance reform in early 2000 with the alarmist cry that "our federal campaign finance system is in a state of disarray."[1] This idea, however, had by then become common parlance among those writing or talking about the financing of the U.S. electoral system. Thomas Mann of the Brookings Institution, who would be an expert witness in the case testing McCain-Feingold, called it a "regulatory regime in disarray."[2] Regardless of where they put the blame—on the courts, on PACs, on soft money, on the Federal Election Commission, or on corrupt and greedy politicians—most people agreed that the 1974 Federal Election Campaign Act (FECA) had been a dismal failure. Although providing better reporting of the dollars raised and spent, FECA had imposed no real controls on campaign finance.

If everyone accepted the fact that we had a broken system, little agreement could be found on how to fix it. Moreover, even if the system were in fact broken, that did not mean that everybody wanted it repaired. Soft money and PACs, the bugaboos of the reformers, benefited incumbents greatly, although few members of the House or Senate would admit this openly. Special interest groups also had no real incentive to push for reform, since they could spend almost unlimited amounts of money advancing their cause or supporting friendly candidates. Presidential candidates had such little difficulty raising money that some turned down the federal match, since accepting those dollars would have limited what they could raise and spend.

The debate in the 1980s and 1990s sounded strikingly similar to the very first debate over campaign finance reform, the Progressive era effort to get the Tillman Act passed in 1907. Academics, citizen lobbies such as Common Cause, many of the media, and journalists such as Elizabeth Drew (who had written widely on campaign finance)—all of them accepted the notion that large campaign donations inevitably corrupt the political system. A core belief of those Berkeley political scientists Austin Ranney calls "neo-progressives" is that "the great enemies of society are the big political machines, the business 'trusts' and other special interests that try to advance their selfish goals at the public's expense by buying elections and corrupting public officials."[3] Elizabeth Drew wrote that all the questions and answers about campaign finance could not have been more obvious: "Why is all this money floating about? What do investors expect? At a minimum they expect access, but access is only the required entry ticket for getting something done."[4]

True, not everyone thought that way. Senator Mitch McConnell (R-Ky.) denied that any corruption existed, because when you looked at the big picture, not all that much money was involved. "Federal campaign spending," he explained following the 1996 election, "amounted to $3.89 per eligible voter, about the price of a McDonald's value meal." McConnell has a point, and although people differ about the actual sums involved, some scholars have suggested that for $10 per person per year, all levels of elections—federal, state, and local— could be publicly funded.[5]

Whether the public believed that money corrupted the political process, or that corruption did not exist, events beginning in the 1980s and continuing through the Clinton administration led many people to call for something—indeed anything—to fix the mess. As one scandal after another broke on the political scene and as the amount of money spent in successive elections skyrocketed, the pressure for reform increased, until it finally succeeded in the passage of the Bipartisan Campaign Reform Act (BCRA) of 2002, commonly known as the McCain-Feingold Act. But whether that law would pass constitutional muster, or if in fact it could actually fix the system, remained to be seen.

★ ★ ★ ★ ★

Although some figures for elections appeared in the previous chapter, it would be well to note again how campaigns became more expensive.[6] In 1980 Republican John Connally became the first major party presidential candidate to decline partial federal funding of his campaign. The idea behind federal funding had been to offer candidates a fairly substantial sum of money, to be paid for by a check-off on individual tax returns, if the candidates agreed to limit their spending. Connally, a wealthy Texas businessman, intended to use his wealth and that of his backers to far outspend the Democratic candidate that year, President Jimmy Carter. Connally, however, never got to test this plan because he lost to Ronald Reagan in the GOP primary. Twenty years later, however, another Texan, George W. Bush, revived that strategy, and announced that he would forego partial federal funding. Bush raised a record $100 million and became the first major-party candidate to win the nomination without following the Watergate-era limits.[7] His huge war chest played a key role in his victory, as one would-be challenger after another dropped out of the race. In announcing her withdrawal, former Secretary of Labor Elizabeth Dole put it quite bluntly: "The bottom line is money."[8]

In the 2000 campaign, total spending for the presidential race reached a record $607 million (covering primaries and the general election). The major political parties spent an additional $693 million, with soft money accounting for $498 million. Although these categories cannot be accurately divided between presidential and congressional races, it is fair to say that the Bush-Gore contest alone cost in excess of $1.3 billion.

At the congressional level, spending increased from $666.2 million in 1988 to $1.05 billion in 2000. The average cost of running for a seat in the House of Representatives rose in those 12 years from $697,757 to $1.31 million, and the average Senate race increased in cost from $8.88 million to $13.17 million. The range for any election would have been very broad, with representatives in safe seats spending far less, and candidates in highly contested elections expending a great deal more. Rick Lazio and Hillary Clinton, vying for the New York seat in the Senate that had been vacated by Daniel Patrick Moynihan, between them spent $70 million, and across the Hudson River in neighboring New Jersey, Jon Corzine spent $63 million, nearly all of it his own money, in a successful bid for the Senate.[9]

Critics of soft money found the figures for congressional races in the 1990s alarming. Democrats raised $44.6 million in nonfederal or soft money in 1992; in 2000 that figure had gone to $245.2 million, an increase of 549 percent. The Republican numbers were not far different—$61.1 million in 1992, and $249.9 million eight years later, an increase of 409 percent.[10] To give readers an idea of how important a role soft money played in these elections, the Democrats raised $200.4 million in hard money in 1992, and $275.2 million in 2000, up a mere 37 percent, while the comparable numbers for the GOP went up only 43 percent, from $325.1 million to $465.8 million.[11]

★ ★ ★ ★ ★

The increase in campaign costs would have been enough for most reformers to urge a change in the system, but the numbers by themselves would have been insufficient to arouse public ire to the point where Congress finally felt it had to do something. One scandal after another reinforced the charges of reformers that the current system of campaign finance corrupted the political process.

The savings and loan collapse in the 1980s remains the most expensive regulatory scandal in U.S. history, with the ultimate cost to American taxpayers running into the hundreds of billions of dollars. Among the various horror stories emerging from that debacle, one is of particular relevance to campaign finance reform. A California savings institution, Lincoln Savings and Loan, received special attention because its president, Charles H. Keating, Jr., his family, and his associates contributed $1.3 million to influential legislators, a group eventually tarred by the epithet "the Keating Five."

Lincoln's questionable financial practices, especially large loans made to favored customers with minimal collateral, had begun drawing the attention of state and federal regulators in 1988. Keating either made or arranged direct contributions from others to five U.S. senators—$34,000 to John Glenn (D-Ohio), $47,000 to Alan Cranston (D-Calif.), $112,000 to John McCain (R-Ariz.), $55,000 to Dennis DeConcini (D-Ariz.), and $76,000 to Donald Reigle (D-Mich.). In addition to the $324,000 in hard money that went to senatorial campaigns, Keating also arranged for $200,000 in soft money to go to a committee run by Senator Glenn, the National Council on Public Policy, and for an additional $850,000 in soft money to go to committees working on voter registration and turnout, one of them a tax-exempt group managed by Cranston's son.[12] Keating gave $85,000 to the California Democratic State Central Committee for voter activities, and the American Continental Corporation, a company that Keating also headed, gave $90,000 to the California Republican Party in 1988. Lincoln Savings and Loan, despite laws to the contrary, gave $5,000 to California Republicans in 1987.

Although defenders of the system claimed that large donations made little difference in voting records and purchased little more than access to an official, in this instance Keating's money secured far more than "face time" with the senators. All of the Keating Five summoned the chair and key officials of the Federal Home Loan Bank Board, the agency responsible for savings and loan oversight, to discuss what the board intended to do about Lincoln and the possibilities of taking milder measures.

When information about the donations to the Keating Five—and their subsequent efforts to help Keating—became public, all of the senators denied doing any favors because of political donations. McCain, DeConcini, and Cranston explained that they had done no more than provide simple constituent services, since Keating was an Arizona resident with his holdings primarily in Arizona and California. However, at a news conference Keating said: "One question, among many, has to do with whether my financial support in any way influenced several political figures to take up my cause. I want to say in the most forceful way I can: I certainly hope so."[13]

Subsequent investigation indicated that Keating was not alone; many other savings and loan officials had contributed heavily to the campaign funds of House members and senators. The Senate Ethics Committee appointed a special counsel to look into the matter, and in July 1990 Senator Reigle, chair of the Senate Committee on Banking, Housing, and Urban Affairs, announced that he would donate about $120,000 of his savings and loan contributions to the federal treasury. Another senator, Tim Wirth (D-Colo.), also a member of the Banking Committee with Reigle, turned over almost $100,000 to the Colorado Department of Revenue. Three other senators returned smaller amounts.

In September 1990 a grand jury indicted Keating and three associates for violating California securities laws by misleading investors about the nature of Lincoln's assets, many of which turned out to be worthless junk bonds. All told, the grand jury returned an indictment of 42 separate counts (of which Judge Lance Ito dismissed 25), and Keating went to jail until he could post bond, originally set at $5 million and later reduced to $300,000. At his trial a jury found Keating guilty, and while awaiting sentencing he learned that he would be indicted for other fraudulent actions by the Securities and Exchange Commission (SEC).[14]

During the 1996 election, the most serious campaign finance violations since Watergate took place. Anthony Corrado, one of the leading political scientists studying campaign finance, declared that the election "was nothing less than the breakdown of the campaign finance system. The system we created in the early 1970s essentially collapsed. . . . It's the Wild West out there. It's anything goes."[15] Bill Clinton had been attacked by Republicans early in his first term for his aggressive fund-raising, but in 1996 he and Al Gore showed not only how easily candidates could circumvent the laws on the books, but also that they could just plain ignore many of them. First came allegations that the Chinese government, in order to maintain the friendly trade regulations promulgated by the Clinton administration, had made major donations to the Democrats through figurehead Chinese business owners in the United States. If true, this would have constituted a clear violation of the ban against foreign governments and nationals contributing to U.S. campaigns.

In 1997 the Senate Governmental Affairs Committee, headed by Fred Dalton Thompson (R-Tenn.)—rumored to be a potential candidate in 2000, but now an actor on the television series *Law and Order*—called a number of witnesses to testify about this so-called Asian connection. The cast included John Huang (who visited the White House 94 times and met with the president 15 times in Clinton's first term) and Charlie Trie, both friends of the Clintons from their

Little Rock, Arkansas, days. Trie is remembered for turning in two manila envelopes containing $460,000 in cash allegedly collected from penniless Buddhists, and Huang's donors included those with untraceable addresses or with identical handwriting, and a few who, reminiscent of Tammany Hall and Chicago politics, were dead! Mochtar and James Riadys, heads of the family-owned Indonesian Lippo group, a $12 billion conglomerate with major holdings in China and Hong Kong, were also longtime friends of the Clintons and raised money for the president. Veteran Democratic fund-raiser Johnny Chung, who raised money for Clinton, charmingly explained that the "White House is like a subway: You have to put in coins to open the gates." A group of Buddhist nuns testified about Vice President Gore's alleged fund-raising activities in a Buddhist temple. Although the election was over, the hearings proved embarrassing to Clinton and Gore, and the Democratic National Committee returned $1.6 million of the $3.4 million Huang had raised as well as $645,000 raised by Trie.[16]

Clinton and Gore well understood the mystique of the White House, and, again in seeming violation of laws against soliciting campaign money on federal property, raised tens of millions of dollars from those attending "coffee" sessions in the White House, where the president and/or vice president would stop in and chat. Then there were the infamous sleepovers in the Lincoln bedroom. Michael McCurry, speaking for the administration, declared that "the question is whether the president directly solicited funds during these occasions, and he did not." Although this statement was perhaps technically true, 90 percent of the people who attended the sessions had either made donations before being invited, or sent them in within a month after sharing coffee and pastries with the chief executive.

In addition, both Clinton and Gore solicited funds by telephone from the White House, although the White House counsel in 1995, Abner J. Mikva, believed these calls to be clearly illegal and issued a directive that "no fund-raising phone calls or mail may emanate from the White House or any other federal building." Clinton and Gore ignored him, and his successor, Lanny Davis, in 1997 issued a new memorandum approving such calls. In public comments defending his fund-raising calls from the White House, Al Gore repeatedly asserted, "My counsel tells me there is no controlling legal authority that says there was any violation of the law." If Gore had stopped there he might not have received the ridicule and suspicion that arose when he tried to explain that the money had not been raised "directly." But he added, "I never asked for a campaign contribution from anyone who was in a government office."[17] No matter where he called from, the real transaction—the offer of a contribution—took place at the receiving end of the line.

Although Republicans continued to make political capital by publicly denouncing Clinton's and Gore's sins, privately no one familiar with the landscape of campaign finance thought that anything unusual had occurred. As one Republican lawyer noted, "I would be flabbergasted if there was any criminal action," and he confidently—and accurately—predicted that there would be no civil action by the Federal Election Commission. To begin with, it makes little sense to force either the president, who lives in the White House, or the vice president, who works there, to have to leave and go across town to the Democratic or Republican National Committee in order to make a phone call. As for the coffees and overnight stays, Clinton essentially did what many of his predecessors had done—that is, use the mystique of the Oval Office to influence potential donors or to reward those who had already written a check. He just took it to an extreme. What upset reformers more than the coffees was that, as they later learned, Clinton had divided the money between hard and soft money accounts in order to give the DNC more money to spend promoting his candidacy. Under the law, money is raised as either hard or soft and should go into the appropriate accounts.

Although later impeached but not convicted for lying about his relationship with White House intern Monica Lewinsky, Clinton faced no legal problems regarding his fund-raising practices, and neither did Al Gore. In October 1997, the Republican-controlled Congress voted down all efforts to reform campaign finance, and in December Attorney General Janet Reno announced that no grounds existed to warrant appointing a special prosecutor to investigate charges of impropriety. Republicans predictably responded with outrage, but had they been serious about correcting the defects of the system, they could have acted in the one way that would have made a difference, passing campaign finance legislation (because they controlled Congress they could control the agenda of committee hearings).[18]

Moreover, the Republicans did not exactly come into the debate with clean hands. The GOP had its Asian connections as well. Haley Barbour, the chair of the Republican National Committee, had solicited a $2.2 million loan guarantee from Ambrous Tung Young, a wealthy Hong Kong businessman, in the last weeks of the 1994 congressional campaign. Theoretically, the loan went to National Policy Forum, a Republican-sponsored think tank, but according to its former president, Michael Baroody, any separation between the forum and the RNC was little more than a "fiction." In his resignation letter, Baroody told Barbour, "I told you . . . that you were right about the possibility foreign money could be raised, but thought it would be wrong to do so." The forum used $1.6 million of the Young loan to pay back money it owed to the RNC, which in turn immediately funneled it into some 20 Republican committees in key states around the country. Two years later the forum defaulted on the loan, leaving Young with a $700,000 loss, but the Republican party went into the 1996 campaign free of that debt.

The Republicans had other campaign finance irregularities that needed explanation. The FBI investigated Dan Burton (R-Ind.)—who had at times vociferously called for campaign finance reform—for allegedly threatening to deny a lobbyist for the government of Pakistan access to key government officials if a $5,000 donation to his campaign did not materialize. A Department of Education official claimed that Burton pressured him to delay eligibility standards for foreign medical schools involved in a U.S.-government student loan program, and that the meeting took place only one week after Burton received the second of two campaign contributions from the president of a Caribbean medical school. In addition, Burton asked the school to admit his daughter and to help his son-in-law get a job.

Simon Fireman, a vice chair of Robert Dole's 1996 campaign finance committee, had to pay a $6 million fine (half of which was assessed against his company) for evading the $1,000 limit on individual contributions by persuading his employees to make gifts with the understanding that they would be reimbursed from an overseas fund. Fireman thus had managed to raise $120,000 for the 1992 Bush-Quayle ticket. As some commentators noted, this constituted the largest penalty ever imposed by the Federal Election Commission, and it might just as well have been for stupidity, since Fireman could have legally given that amount or more in soft money.[19]

If Clinton and the Democrats raised large amounts of money through utilization of the White House and the presidential mystique, at least they never explicitly detailed just what particular contributions would buy. Not so the Republicans, who at the same time they were publicly bemoaning the "selling" of the Lincoln bedroom, put out a price sheet on what certain contributions might purchase. For a quarter million dollars, a "season ticket holder" would receive "the best access to Congress," meet with "the party's inner circle," and have private meetings with GOP leaders and key support personnel. One could become a member of "Team 100" by giving $175,000 over four years; this would earn meetings with high-ranking Republican leaders as well as invitations for "international Team 100 business missions." A $10,000 check secured admission into the "Senatorial trust," where one would have "intimacy" and "one-on-one" interaction with Republican senators." If a person could not afford the higher levels, no need to despair. According to a fund-raising letter sent out by Senate Majority Leader Trent Lott (R-Miss.), $5,000 put the donor into the "presidential roundtable," with "plenty of opportunities to share your personal ideas and vision with some of our top Republican leaders."[20]

This ought not to be seen as a contest over who abused the system more, Democrats or Republicans, because they both acted in gross disregard of the law. Candidates from both parties engaged in sloppy bookkeeping, accepted questionable contributions, looked the other way when donors funneled money through third parties (such as children or grandchildren), and, in general, simply ignored the laws. After all, what did anyone have to worry about? A cynical public expected politicians to act this way. Wealthy donors, whether for ideological or simple business reasons, rushed to write checks. The Federal Election Commission did practically nothing, and blandly presided over the collapse of what had been intended, in the wake of Watergate, as a system to rein in campaign finance abuses.

Two scholars who studied the Federal Election Commission in the 1996 election titled their article "Spitting on the Umpire" to give readers a sense of the low regard—indeed, the contempt—in which candidates and political parties held the FEC. The article explained how both political parties, in the raising and spending of hard and soft money in the 1996 elections, flouted existing campaign finance laws. "The result is a system that is fundamentally dishonest, where limitations and restrictions remain on the books but are ignored with disdain by those who practice the art of politics."[21]

To take but one example, in the wake of widespread allegations that Clinton and the Democrats had raised massive amounts of money illegally, much of it from foreign sources, reporters gathered at the FEC on October 24, 1996, to examine the DNC's last preelection report due by law, which covered the campaign finance figures and expenditures for the first two weeks of October. The report did not appear, and late in the day a reporter called the DNC to find out when it would be filed. He received the rather astonishing answer that the DNC had conducted no candidate-related activities during the first two weeks of October, and that it decided that legally no report had to be filed. The DNC did not bother to check with the FEC for a ruling on this claim; it simply ignored the commission, aware that an accurate report might be embarrassing. Eventually the DNC did file the report, not because the FEC—as it should have done—demanded it, but because the media would not let go of the story and insisted on knowing what the Democrats had tried to hide. Moreover, the reporting requirements of the FECA were generally acknowledged by all parties to be the simplest data to collect and file and the least controversial aspect of the law. The DNC did not fear the FEC, and neither did the Republicans; they and others considered the commission, along with the entire campaign finance regulatory system, basically irrelevant.[22]

★   ★   ★   ★   ★

The pattern of campaign finance reform appears to be that of cause and effect—the cause being a major scandal highlighting either the weaknesses in the system or out-and-out corruption, and the response being legislation addressing the perceived evils. Just as Watergate led to the Federal Election Campaign Act of 1974 and its strengthening amendments, so the Keating Five aroused Congress to consider new campaign finance regulations, although one suspects that it did so while fully aware that no matter how strong the measure, it would not matter. And so it happened.

Every year some House members and senators proposed legislation to reform the system, but with Republicans in control of the White House and the Senate following the 1980 election, there seemed little hope that a new bill would secure approval. In 1986 Senators David L. Boren (D-Okla.) and Barry M. Goldwater (R-Ariz.) proposed limits on the total amount of PAC money that a candidate could receive in any election cycle. Although the measure gained favorable notice both in and out of Congress, it never made it out of committee. When the Democrats regained control of the Senate after the 1986 election, Boren (after Goldwater had retired in 1986) reintroduced a strengthened proposal as Senate Bill 2. This time it looked as if something might happen, as Boren secured cosponsorship from an enthusiastic majority leader, Robert Byrd (D-W.Va.), and all but 10 of the Democratic senators. A strengthened bill passed the Senate Committee on Rules and Administration with a vote, along strictly party lines, of 8 to 3, on April 29, 1987.

The Boren bill provided for, among other things, public financing of senatorial candidates, who, like presidential candidates receiving public funds, agreed to observe spending limits in both the primary and general elections. To receive the public funding, they had to raise a minimum amount from individual contributors, the level depending upon the voting-age population of the state. Candidates also had to agree to limit the money they received from PACs to no more than 20 percent of their total expenditure. Even if a candidate decided to forego public funding, the Byrd-Boren bill imposed a limit of 30 percent of the state's allowable expenditures that could be raised from PACs. Other provisions included aggregate limits on how much national party committees could receive from PACs, prohibition of PAC bundling of contributions through related organizations, and expanded reporting requirements to cover more soft money expenditures.

The Byrd-Boren bill aimed primarily at reducing the influence of PACs and candidate dependence on PAC money. Had the bill passed, however, it might have run once again into the law of unanticipated consequences. As Herbert Alexander pointed out, one result would have been that candidates and parties would have focused their attention on the wealthiest PACs, since the easiest way to raise PAC funds up to the prescribed limit would have been to concentrate on those able to give the largest amounts. Smaller PACs, representing a variety of less affluent interests, would have been noncompetitive and ignored by all except the most desperate candidates. Moreover, the aggregate-limit provision, a new concept, would have undoubtedly raised constitutional issues under the then-prevailing *Buckley* precedents.[23]

The bill elicited near-universal opposition from Senate Republicans, who derided it as still another Democratic raid on the federal treasury. Senator Robert Packwood (R-Ore.) called Senate Bill 2 a Democratic effort "to take three or four hundred million dollars from taxpayers . . . to perpetuate their majority in the U.S. Congress." Moreover, the facts of the 1986 election seemed to undercut any urgency for reform. A majority of the 15 biggest-spending senatorial candidates lost, and five challengers beat incumbents who had outspent them by 2–1 or more in the campaigns. In June the Republican caucus voted not to accept any public financing or spending limits, even though Senate Minority Leader Robert Dole (R-Kan.) had accepted public financing in his failed presidential bid a year earlier, and Senator Ted Stephens (R-Ak.), who would lead a filibuster against the bill, had cosponsored a constitutional amendment providing for mandatory limits on campaign expenditures. Despite efforts to modify the bill to win some Republican support, party lines held firm, with only two Republicans defecting to support the bill and only two Democrats lining up against it. Although more than 430 newspapers and 73 organizations, such as Common Cause, endorsed the bill, the Republicans would not budge. They believed that since the GOP had greater access to PACs and other forms of financing, the bill would only work against their interests.[24]

Then came disclosures that some contributors had given more than $100,000 during the 1988 presidential campaign—a figure reformers believed had been prohibited by the post-Watergate legislation and the revelations related to the Keating Five. The multibillion dollar bailout of the savings and loan industry also spilled over into the campaign finance debate. Although no other scandals proved as titillating as that of the Keating Five, apparently many other legislators had attempted to help out constituents and had accepted money from PACs associated with the thrift industry. In addition, a public uproar over an alleged "salary grab" by Congress (the House voted itself a 25 percent pay raise) led the new Bush administration to seize the moment and propose a campaign finance scheme of its own, one that so blatantly favored the GOP over the Democrats that it had little chance of passage.

Presented in June 1989, the Bush proposal called for the near elimination of PACs (which had given three out of every five of their dollars to the Democrats in the 1988 election cycle), and strengthening the role of party committees (since Republican committees had raised three times as much money as their Democratic counterparts). Although the Bush plan sought to curtail or even shut off some sources of campaign funding, it made no provisions for raising money from other sources. It seemed a strange plan, with supposedly less money to spend, yet no limits on expenditures. In addition, the Bush plan would have

- reduced allowable PAC contributions to a candidate from $5,000 to $1,000 per election, although the original limit had been set when the dollar had been worth three times its value in 1989;
- prohibited bundling campaign contributions by PACs, while allowing party and special interest committees to do so;
- forbade candidates to maintain their own PACs, a practice used successfully by leaders in both parties, who used the funds to help other candidates;
- required union members to approve in advance the withholding of any funds for political purposes (union money had gone to Democrats over Republicans by a 12-to-1 ratio);
- banned all soft money to national parties as well as to state parties if the money were to be used in federal elections (again, a practice that in the 1980s had benefited Democrats much more than Republicans);
- removed all limits on party committee contributions to candidates except in a contested primary (benefiting the GOP, since the RNC normally raised far more money than did the DNC).[25]

The Congress now found itself confronted with two very different campaign finance reform bills and a public clamor that it do *something*. Party leaders in both houses recognized this, and believed they had little choice but to put campaign finance reform at the top of the legislative agenda. The House, which during the past several years had done nothing as it waited to see how the Boren bill would fare, now appointed a Bipartisan Task Force for Campaign Reform, but within a few weeks the members had deadlocked on every single issue. Once again the Senate took the lead, when Minority Leader Bob Dole suggested to Majority Leader George Mitchell (D-Me.) that they try an end run to break the partisan impasse. On February 8, 1990, they appointed a Senate Campaign Finance Reform Panel consisting of academics and lawyers with expertise in this area. Mitchell and Dole directed the ad hoc group to focus only on rules to govern election to the U.S. Senate and to report back within one month.[26]

The panel tried to walk a fine line between the public interest and partisan demands. Thus it proposed reducing the influence of PACs, both by imposing a limit of 30 percent of a candidate's total budget as well as by restrictions (including a prohibition on bundling) on how PACs could provide funds. Recognizing that media costs, especially television, had become one of the most expensive items in a campaign, the panel recommended that every candidate receive a total of eight hours of free air time as well as guaranteed prime-time and election slots. Individual campaign contribution limits, then set at $1,000, would be raised slightly and afterward indexed for inflation. The group did not propose public funding, nor did it impose any restrictions on soft money. Finally, in one of its more innovative proposals, the panel suggested flexible spending limits that would be reasonably high and so would not lead to candidates favoring large-source contributions in lieu of those from party committees and small in-state donors. For those candidates who abided by these limits, there would be preferential broadcast advertising rates, reduced or free postal rates, and tax credits for small in-state contributions.[27]

Why should anyone have expected even a distinguished and bipartisan group to develop an acceptable reform plan in the light of the partisan bickering that had gone on over the past few years? Although the task force members tried to be sensitive to the concerns of each party—that is, reducing the influence of PACs to satisfy the Republicans but allowing them to still play an important role to satisfy the Democrats—the partisan factions that had developed in each house allowed little room for compromise. Despite the fact that Senate leaders warmly praised the committee report initially, within a short time one after another of its proposals fell victim to attacks. Every now and then it would appear as if a new version of the Boren bill—now dubbed the "Boren again bill"—would garner the necessary support, but each and every time, partisan sniping sent it down.

Over the next few years proposals would arise and be greeted by reform advocates as the long-awaited breakthrough, only to disappear from sight as soon as someone zeroed in on one or more of its features. As a disgusted Herbert Alexander wrote, members of both houses of Congress had little interest in actually reforming the system; they essentially postured for public relations purposes, so they could tell the folks back home that they had really tried to secure campaign finance reform. Both parties, he complained "sought to maximize their partisan advantages and minimize the resources of their adversaries, appealing to popular notions of reform whenever possible—even when such notions were plainly misconceived or impossible to attain. And the role of President Bush and the White House staff was prominent throughout but mainly because of a premature announcement in July that the president would veto any legislation containing public funding or spending limits."[28]

On August 1, 1990, the Senate, by a vote of 59 to 40, agreed on a revised Boren bill, labeled Senate Bill 137, and two days later the House passed a similar bill by a vote of 255 to 155. The margins in both houses—60 percent in the Senate and slightly more in the House—masked the fact that the leadership in both houses did not really care for the measure. They took their time setting up a conference committee to iron out the relatively minor differences, and in fact the committee never met; the 101st Congress adjourned without passage of a campaign finance reform law.

The next several months did little to improve the congressional image in the eyes of the public. Repercussions from the Keating Five, the large raises the House and Senate voted for themselves in 1989 and 1991, the bounced checks in the so-called House Bank, the impetus behind term-limit campaigns in several states, and the Clarence Thomas nomination hearings—all of these led many people to ask about the Congress, "Can't they do *anything* right?" Congressional leaders apparently decided that some form of a campaign finance bill would have to be passed, and in April 1991, the Senate Rules and Administration Committee reported favorably on David Boren's latest draft, now known as Senate Bill 3. When it came to the floor vote, Boren made one final appeal:

> What are we talking about when we talk about campaign finance reform? What is the real issue? We are talking about whether we ought to do something to stop unlimited spending of money on political campaigns. Those of us who are supporting S.3 say yes, this is what is wrong with the politi-

cal system. . . . How long are we going to wait to stop the money chase in American politics and return this government back to the people? . . . Do we want to limit spending, or do we not? That is the issue.[29]

On May 23, 1991, the Senate adopted the Boren proposal by a vote of 56 to 42. The House took much longer, with intra- and interparty wrangling lasting more than six months. The full House passed its version of the measure in November, and this time a conference committee did meet and iron out the differences between the two versions, but not until April 1992. The House of Representatives approved the committee's reconciliation by a vote of 259 to 165, and the Senate followed on April 30 by a vote of 58 to 42.

The main provisions of the Campaign Spending Limit and Election Reform Act included increased spending limits for Senate races, ranging from $950,000 to $5.5 million depending upon the size of the state, with up to an additional $2.75 million for primaries (again, depending upon the state's size). The limit on House races went to $600,000 for the entire two-year cycle, with another $250,000 permitted if there were a primary fight. Although these limits were voluntary, candidates who abided by them would reap additional benefits. Senate candidates who raised money primarily in donations of $250 or less would get vouchers for broadcast time, and would also be allowed to buy additional time at 50 percent of the regular rate. House candidates could get up to an additional $200,000 in public money matching contributions of $200 or less, but would have to agree not to take any more than $200,000 in contributions greater than $250.

The bill made no changes in the existing $1,000 limit on individual contributions, but did reduce the amount a PAC could give to any one candidate from $5,000 to $2,500 for Senate candidates; it would remain at $5,000 for House candidates. PAC money could account for no more than 20 percent of a Senate campaign, and for House candidates it could be no more than $200,000, a figure that few congressional candidates then exceeded. The bill prohibited the national committees from using soft money in federal elections, but otherwise put no limits on the amount of soft money that could be raised or spent by other entities.[30]

Since the White House the previous year had indicated that the president would not sign any measure that limited campaign expenses, it is little wonder that George Bush, who in his one term used the veto more than many presidents have in two, refused to approve the measure. In his veto message he declared:

> For three years I have called on the Congress to overhaul our campaign finance system in order to reduce the influence of special interests, to restore the influence of individuals and political parties, and to reduce the unfair advantages of incumbency. S.3 would not accomplish any of these objectives. In addition to perpetuating the corrupting influence of special interests and the imbalance between challengers and incumbents, S.3 would limit political speech protected by the First Amendment and inevitably lead to a raid on the Treasury to pay for the Act's elaborate scheme of public subsidies.[31]

One suspects, perhaps a bit cynically, that a good many of the votes for S.3 were cast in the full knowledge that the measure would not become law, thus allowing the lawmakers to have their cake and eat it too. They could tell their constituents that they had supported and voted for campaign finance reform, without having to worry about the proposed reforms actually affecting their own campaigns. Neither house, even on the initial vote, had the necessary votes to override the promised presidential veto. Although the Boren bill had gone further than any other reform proposal in more than a decade, it, too, died, and the truth be told, few members in Congress mourned the passing.

★ ★ ★ ★ ★

Bill Clinton, aware that campaign finance reform played well with the voters, tried to capitalize on the Bush veto, and in the 1992 campaign promised to end big-money domination of politics. In fact, in his first inaugural, he proclaimed: "Let us resolve to reform our politics so that power and privilege no longer shout down the voice of the people."[32] In his first address to Congress he challenged the legislators to reenact the Boren bill, promising to sign it if they were to do so.[33] Whether Clinton really wanted a campaign finance reform bill or not is open to question, but he certainly pushed for one in his first year in office, and even proposed a modification of the Boren bill, focusing in on limits that PACs could give to presidential ($1,000) and senatorial ($2,500) campaigns as well as shutting off soft money. He also proposed that the tax laws be changed so that companies could not deduct lobbying costs as a business expense, and that individual citizens could raise the amount of their voluntary check-offs for elections from $1 to $5[34] Whether Clinton really meant what he said or not, he soon got caught up in the fight to reform health care insurance, and campaign finance wound up on a back burner, moving to the front every now and then for the rest of his administration.

After the Republicans won control of both houses of Congress in the 1994 midterm election, Clinton and Speaker of the House Newt Gingrich (R-Ga.) found themselves at a joint appearance at a senior center in New Hampshire in June 1995. The president declared that he would love to have a bipartisan commission look at meaningful campaign finance reform. Gingrich immediately joined in and said: "Let's shake hands right here in front of everybody. How's that? Is that a pretty good deal?" In the year that followed, Clinton, Gingrich, and Dole failed to name a commission; in fact, they hardly ever mentioned it again. In that same period various representatives and senators introduced hundreds of proposals, not a single one of which ever made it out of committee.

In his 1997 State of the Union address, Clinton again challenged Congress to give him a campaign finance reform measure that he could sign by July 4.[35] In the meantime, whenever appointments opened on the Federal Election Commission, Clinton nominated the same types of Democrats and Republicans to the vacancies, partisan political types who would never rock the status quo by attempting to enforce the law seriously. In September, after Congress failed to send him a bill to sign, Clinton threatened to keep the legislature in session until it acted. Dozens of House members and senators introduced bills, knowing the proposals would never get out of committee, but the claim for sponsoring campaign reform would be very useful for reelection purposes. Then suddenly a fluke occurred—in late September reform legislation somehow came straight to the floor of the House without going to the committee. Despite this surprise, congressional leaders made it very clear that they intended to kill the measure, which they did. As for Clinton, once again his priorities had changed—he wanted Congress to pass the North American Free Trade Agreement (NAFTA), and, with the full cooperation of Republican congressional leaders, he once again buried campaign finance reform.[36]

★ ★ ★ ★ ★

The fund-raising scandals of the Clinton administration, and the massive amounts of money raised and spent by both sides in the 2000 presidential election, constitute the immediate backdrop to the Bipartisan Campaign Reform Act of 2002 (BCRA), commonly known as the McCain-Feingold bill.[37] In many ways, however, BCRA is just one more step in a century-long effort to divorce the influence of money from federal elections, and although its supporters hailed it as a major step forward, detractors claimed it would eventually fail, as had earlier efforts. Perhaps Thomas Mann got it best when he declared: "It's not over yet, and it never will be. Campaign finance reform will be with us as it is with every country for a long, long and unending process."[38]

Despite the veto of the 1992 law by President George H. W. Bush, reformers kept plugging away in the House and Senate throughout the 1990s, trying in vain to impose some limits on both soft money and PACs. Although President Clinton on several occasions indicated that he favored such legislation, with the Congress being controlled by the Republicans for six of his eight years in office, he could do little more than stop enactment of measures he did not like; he never had the votes to put through important legislative reforms of his own. Nor, one can assume, did campaign finance reform figure high on his agenda, despite the lip service he gave to it. Clinton's greatest contribution to reform may have been his highly successful efforts to raise money, efforts that displayed all the weaknesses in the moribund system in effect. In the 2000 election, national and congressional party committees broke all previous records in raising soft money. The Republican National Committee raised $249.5 million, and the Democrats lagged only slightly behind at $245.2 million. The national committees transferred more than half this money to state party committees, primarily to pay for television advertisements.

The original version of the BCRA had been introduced as Senate Bill 1219 in the 104th Congress in September 1995. The bill not only provided restrictions on soft money but also called for voluntary spending ceilings in congressional races and free air time and reduced-rate mailing privileges for candidates who abided by these ceilings (both provisions were taken from the 1992 measure). It also placed limits on what candidates could spend out of their own pockets, a response to several recent races in which wealthy candidates had spent millions of dollars of their own money. The bill never made it out of committee, but at each succeeding session of Congress, Senators John McCain (R-Ariz.) and Russell D. Feingold (D-Wis.) reintroduced a version of their bipartisan campaign proposal.

The McCain-Feingold bill died due to a filibuster in the 104th Congress. During the following session, the House of Representatives passed a companion measure, H.R. 2183, known as the Shays-Meehan bill, after its sponsors, Representatives Christopher H. Shays (R-Conn.) and Martin T. Meehan (D-Mass.). Senate sponsors of the bill tried and failed three times in the 105th Congress to break a filibuster, but the reformers would not give up. In the 106th Congress, the House again passed the Shays-Meehan bill (H.R. 417), only to see their work thwarted once again by a Senate filibuster. Even a scaled-down version of McCain-Feingold, consisting of nothing more than a ban on soft money (S. 1593), fell before another filibuster.

Finally in the 107th Congress, the sponsors of the latest version of McCain-Feingold (S. 27) not only gained majority approval, but beat back 38 amendments designed to cripple the measure. On April 2, 2001, the full Senate passed an amended but still potent McCain-Feingold bill by a vote of 59 to 41.

Now the spotlight shifted to the House, which in previous sessions had passed the Shays-Meehan bill. But now, with a Senate-passed version on their desks and no indication from the White House that President George W. Bush would veto the measure, representatives had to deal with the very real possibility that a campaign finance bill would actually clear Congress. The House Administration Committee held hearings that lasted from April 2001 until March 2002. The committee then reported favorably to the full

House on the Ney-Wynn bill (H.R. 2360), a much-watered-down version of the Senate measure, and reported unfavorably on the Shays-Meehan bill (H.R. 2356), which more closely tracked the provisions of McCain-Feingold. On July 12, showing how many of the members did not really want to deal with the issue, the House rejected by a vote of 203 to 228 a proposed rule that would have brought discussion of campaign finance reform to the floor.

One week later, a group of so-called Blue Dog Democrats began circulating a discharge petition to force the House leadership to resume debate on the bills. The petition needed 218 signatures (a bare majority of the 435 members) to force a floor vote, and on January 24, 2002, the last four members signed on. The House approved the stronger Shays-Meehan proposal on February 7, 2002, by a vote of 240 to 189. Normally at this point House and Senate leaders would appoint a conference committee to iron out the differences between the two versions. When it became clear that such a committee would probably be stacked with opponents of campaign finance reform, Senate proponents decided to vote directly on the House version. On March 20, 2002, the Senate voted 68 to 32 to end debate on the bill, proving that supporters had the necessary votes to cut off a filibuster. Later in the day the Senate approved the measure by a vote of 60 to 40 and sent it on to President Bush.[39]

The president reluctantly signed the bill into law one week later. During the 2000 presidential primary season, John McCain had run a strong race against the ultimately successful George W. Bush, and a key feature of the Arizona senator's platform had been campaign finance reform. After his election Bush put forth a counterproposal, which allowed individuals to give as much soft money as they wanted. Bush decided to sign the bill, but without the usual ceremony where sponsors received signing pens. A legislative aide—not the president—called McCain at his home in Arizona to inform him that the bill had become law. Bush issued a written statement in which he essentially gave the back of his hand to the legislation. This bill "is the culmination of more than six years of debate among a vast array of legislators, citizens, and groups. Accordingly, it does not represent the full ideals of any one point of view. But it does represent progress in this often contentious area of public policy debate. Taken as a whole, this bill improves the current system of financing for federal campaigns, and therefore I have signed it into law."[40] When asked why there had been no formal ceremony, White House spokesperson Claire Buchan said "the manner in which the president signed the campaign finance reform into law was consistent with his views on the legislation."[41]

Bush thereupon left on a two-day fund-raising trip, where he hoped to raise more than $3.5 million for Republican senatorial candidates. Asked if he saw any irony in signing the bill and then embarking on such a trip, Bush said he saw no reason to stop his money-raising efforts. "I'm not going to lay down my arms. The Senate races are very important to me."[42]

★ ★ ★ ★ ★

Although BCRA had numerous provisions (see Appendix E), some key objectives in the legislation are discernible—an effort to do away with soft money, a redefinition of what constitutes campaign advertising, limits on contribution amounts and sources, and tougher disclosure and reporting requirements.[43]

The act banned soft money contributions to the national political parties after November 6, 2002, and required the national party committees to dispose of all soft money in their accounts by December 31, 2002. Under a congressional compromise, individuals and groups could contribute up to $10,000 in soft money (known as Levin funds) to each state and local party committee, if permitted by state law, for voter registration and mobilization drives in federal elections (§101). At the same time, the act increased the amount of hard money that could be given, partly in order to offset the loss of soft money but also because hard money faced tighter reporting and accounting regulations. Individuals could now give $2,000 instead of $1,000 per candidate, per election, and $5,000 to a political action committee. The amount that individuals could give to the national party committees went from $20,000 to $25,000, and donation limits for state and local party committees went from $5,000 to $10,000. The limits on PAC contributions to candidates and parties remained unchanged ($5,000 per candidate, per election; $5,000 per outside PAC, per year; $15,000 per national committee, per year, and $5,000 per state or local committee, per year) and were not indexed for inflation; moreover, the law imposed no annual aggregate limits on PACs, so although they faced limits on individual contributions, the wealthier PACs could continue to give hundreds of thousands of dollars a year across the political spectrum from local races on up to presidential candidates (§§102, 308).

In a provision that was sure to be challenged on First Amendment grounds, BCRA prohibited corporations, trade associations, and labor organizations from paying for "electioneering communications" within 60 days of a general election and 30 days of a primary using "treasury money." The law defined an electioneering communication as any sort of advertisement that referred to a clearly defined federal candidate and was targeted to that candidate's district (i.e., a congressional district for a member of the House of Representatives, a state for a senatorial candidate, and the nation for a presidential candidate). Although no corporation, trade association, or union could pay for such ads out of its treasury, its political action committee could run and finance such ads because under the law's definitions, such funds would count as hard money and be subject to those regulations (§201). Moreover, individuals who paid for political ads could no longer hide behind either anonymity or some front committee, but would have to identify themselves, and candidates would have to indicate that they had approved ads run by committees they controlled. ("This is John Doe, and I have approved this ad.")

Much to the distress of some reformers, the law kept the Federal Election Commission as the primary regulatory agency to enforce the law. BCRA required the FEC to issue new regulations to put the law's provisions into effect (§§307, 501, 502). (Within a very short time the FEC did issue regulations that, in effect, undermined the BCRA's ban on soft money, causing one of the law's chief sponsors, Christopher Shays, to file suit against the FEC.) Soon critics began calling for the abolition of the FEC, although some regulatory mechanism would then have to be put in its place to enforce the law and serve as a clearinghouse for reports.

In direct response to the Clinton scandals, the bill prohibited fund-raising on federal property, including the White House (§302), and also banned contributions from persons who were not citizens or permanent legal residents of the United States (§303). In response to concerns about millionaires self-financing elections, BCRA allowed opponents of self-financing candidates to raise and expend sums beyond the normal limits (§§304, 318).

One of the provisions of the bill forbade donations made through children and grandchildren (§318), a device that had commonly been used to circumvent the FECA limit on individual contributions. Between 1980 and 2000 contributions of $1,000 from "students" increased fourfold. Senator Edward M. Kennedy (D-Mass.) apparently holds the record for so-called kiddie cash, collecting more than $65,000 from people 18 and under in his 1994 campaign for reelection. Senator Fred Dalton Thompson raised more than $25,000 from children, some as young as nine. Business owner Vinod Gupta, for example, managed to give $50,000 to the Democrats, utilizing his 17-year-old son's trust fund. According to the FEC's own reports, in the 1996 election between 25 and 50 of the top 400 political donors also had their children and grandchildren—ranging from preteens to graduate students—contributing to their favorite candidates.[44]

* * * * *

The ink had hardly dried on George Bush's signature before the Bipartisan Campaign Reform Act came under attack. Senator Mitch McConnell (R-Ky.), a leading opponent of campaign finance reform, announced within hours of the signing that he would challenge the law in the courts and that he welcomed other groups, who believed that the BCRA deprived them of their constitutional rights, to join with him.[45] Anticipating the passage of the bill, McConnell had begun lining up his legal team. It included Floyd Abrams, a well-known civil liberties attorney and defender of the First Amendment; former solicitor general, appeals court judge, and special prosecutor Kenneth Starr; First Amendment scholar and Stanford Law School Dean Kathleen Sullivan, who had for several years attacked efforts to restrict funding and speech in campaigns; prominent Washington attorney Jan Baran; and James Bopp, the general counsel of the Madison Center for Free Speech.[46] "Today, I filed suit to defend the First Amendment right of all Americans to be able to fully participate in the political process," McConnell declared. "I look forward to being joined by a strong group of co-plaintiffs in the very near future."[47]

McConnell did not have long to wait. The National Rifle Association, which had used campaign contributions to oppose gun control for years, claimed that it had been the first to file suit after Bush had signed BCRA into law. Wayne LaPierre, the NRA executive vice president, and James Jay Baker, executive director of the NRA's Institute for Legislative Action, in a joint statement, challenged Congress's efforts to quiet the gun lobby. "The First Amendment," they announced, "*protects* us from such directives from the government. The First Amendment does not *allow* Congress to make laws which deny us the right to speak out on issues, the right of our members to associate together on public policy issues and the right to petition our government for redress of grievances. This is what this lawsuit is about."[48] Before long other groups joined in, although not necessarily agreeing with the position taken by McConnell and the NRA. The AFL-CIO was upset primarily over the limits placed on PACs. The U.S. Chamber of Commerce and the National Association of Broadcasters worried about how much the new law would cost in lost revenues, and also filed suit. Soon afterward the Republican National Committee, the California Democratic Party, the California Republican Party, and other local committees and officials joined the suit.[49]

The American Civil Liberties Union (ACLU), declaring that it had long supported campaign finance reform through public financing, found the BCRA a threat to the First Amendment, and used a particularly telling example of how the law could stifle open discussion. "Just last week," the executive director of the ACLU said, it had run "a series of radio and newspaper issue ads that would be outlawed under the new campaign finance legislation." The radio ads went out to more than 50,000 people in the congressional district of Speaker of the House Dennis Hastert, urging him to allow a floor vote on the Employment Non-Discrimination Act, a bill that would prohibit employment discrimination against gays and lesbians. The ad ran within 30 days of a primary election in which Hastert was unopposed. According to the ACLU this ad would have been prohibited by BCRA, even though it did not urge voters to support or oppose Hastert's reelection.[50]

Defenders of the bill reacted promptly. Immediately after McConnell's statement, the four major sponsors—McCain and Feingold in the Senate, and Shays and Meehan in the House—held a press conference to announce that they would intervene in the suit. Although the Department of Justice has the primary responsibility of defending the constitutionality of laws enacted by Congress, the four acted under a section of the BCRA providing a statutory right for members of Congress to intervene as parties. It is possible they had doubts about the enthusiasm with which the Justice Department would defend the law, and so they too rounded up a legal team to defend the measure. Seth Waxman, a former solicitor general in the Clinton administration and then a partner in the powerhouse Washington law firm of Wilmer, Cutler, and Pickering, led the effort.

In addition, there would be lawyers from both the private and academic worlds, all acting pro bono, as were the lawyers for McConnell.[51] In their statement regarding intervention, the four sponsors, plus Senators Olympia Snowe (R-Me.) and James Jeffords (Ind-Vt.), declared that they would show that the basic provisions of BCRA were not only constitutional, but actually protected core First Amendment values. "As the legislative record reflects, the American electorate is losing confidence in the democratic process because of the specter of actual and apparent corruption created by 'soft money' and other campaign finance abuses. . . . By closing loopholes in current law and prohibiting clearly identifiable abuses, the Reform Act encourages renewed citizen confidence and participation in all aspects of our democracy, thereby strengthening First Amendment values."[52]

★　★　★　★　★

The bill included a "fast track" provision: that any challenges would take place in the federal district court of the District of Columbia, and that appeals would go from there directly to the Supreme Court. After more than two decades, Congress had finally acted. Now the action shifted from the legislature to the judiciary.

PART II
THE COURTS AND
THE FIRST AMENDMENT

5 / The Supreme Court and Elections: From Buckley to McConnell

The First Amendment simply cannot tolerate restriction upon the freedom of a candidate to speak without legislative limit on behalf of his own candidacy.
—*Buckley v. Valeo* (1976)

The quantum of empirical evidence needed to satisfy heightened judicial scrutiny of legislative judgments will vary. . . . *Buckley* demonstrates that the dangers of large, corrupt contributions and the suspicion that large contributions are corrupt are neither novel nor implausible.
—Justice Souter, *Nixon v. Shrink Missouri PAC* (2000)

THE DRAFTERS of the Bipartisan Campaign Reform Act (BCRA) of 2002 knew that their handiwork would be challenged in the courts, primarily on First Amendment grounds. Although the law would not go into effect until after the 2002 midterm election, they wanted it—assuming it withstood constitutional challenge—to be in place for the 2004 cycle.

In the quarter-century since it had decided *Buckley v. Valeo*, the Court had heard a number of cases relating to both the election process and campaign finance. But although the justices hinted in their various opinions that they might no longer feel constrained to follow the *Buckley* rule, they had not negated it. The district court judges, therefore, had several choices before them. They could follow *Buckley*, the easiest path, and leave it to the High Court to determine if it wanted to go down a different route. They could assume that the various cases heard in the intervening years either established a new rule or hinted at one enough so that they could ignore *Buckley*. Or, if the judges were feeling very brave, they could try to make some sense out of the differing opinions following *Buckley* and come up with a new rule. Whatever path the three-judge panel chose, it could be sure of only one thing: the Supreme Court would have the last word.

★ ★ ★ ★ ★

If one were to ask a layperson whether the Supreme Court ever got involved in elections, the answer would probably be, "Oh, yeah, they decided the 2000 election." Although it is true that *Bush v. Gore*, which barred a recount of the Florida vote and thus gave that state's electoral ballots and the election to George W. Bush, may be the best known of the Court's election-related cases, it is far from the only one.[1] It is also far from being the most important in terms of constitutional doctrine. In fact the majority justices went out of their way to claim that their decision had little or no precedential effect, but rather applied to a unique set of facts.[2] Nevertheless, the Supreme Court has played a historic role in shaping modern election law.

The Fourteenth Amendment gave full citizenship to former slaves, but voting at that time remained completely a privilege granted by the states. The Fifteenth Amendment to some extent nationalized the right to vote by forbidding states to condition the suffrage upon skin color. In fact, the southern states soon disenfranchised nearly all black voters through a variety of devices such as poll taxes and literacy tests. Moreover, even if a black man learned to read and had the money to pay the poll tax (poor whites were excused from paying it through either grandfather clauses or good-character vouchers), his vote had little effect. From the end of the nineteenth century until the 1970s, the Democratic primary remained the only election that mattered in a region that voted overwhelmingly Democratic. With political parties defined as private organizations in the 1920s, African Americans essentially lost the franchise.

In 1935 the Court apparently validated black disenfranchisement in primaries in *Grovey v. Townsend*, but six years later the justices held that Congress could regulate a primary where it constituted part of the overall machinery for choosing federal officials.[3] That case, however, did not involve black voters, but a claim by registered white members of the Democratic Party in Louisiana that their votes in the 1940 election had not been counted. The *Classic* case looked more like a matter of voting fraud than a voting rights issue, but Thurgood Marshall, head of the NAACP's Legal Defense Fund, gambled that he might be able to use the narrow ruling in the case to launch a frontal attack on the white primary itself, and his gamble paid off. In *Smith v. Allwright* (1944), the Court reversed its ruling in *Grovey* and held that the primary constituted an integral part of an election, and therefore that it could not be closed to black voters.[4] Nine years later, the Court went even further, striking down the subterfuge used by the Jaybird Democratic Association of Fort Bend County, Texas, whereby a private poll was taken before the official primary, and was open only to the all-white club members. The winner of this poll would then be the candidate in the primary. In *Terry v. Adams* (1953), Justice Hugo L. Black denounced the scheme as a device tolerated by the state to defeat the purpose of the Fifteenth Amendment, and the Court struck it down.[5]

Although the Fifteenth Amendment and the primary cases theoretically gave blacks the right to vote in southern primaries and elections, intimidation and the social strictures created by segregation ensured that few blacks registered, much less tried to vote. The total of registered blacks in Alabama, for example, rose from 6,000 in 1947 to 110,000 in 1964, but not a single black had registered in Lowndes and Wilcox counties, where blacks outnumbered whites four to one. The 1964 Civil Rights Act, although the greatest legislative expansion of civil rights in the nation's history, nonetheless did not address the problem of black disenfranchisement.[6] The following year Congress, in the Voting Rights Act, authorized the attorney general to take strong measures to correct patterns of racial discrimination in registration and voting.[7]

Southern states quickly challenged the law, and the Supreme Court heard *South Carolina v. Katzenbach* on original jurisdiction. A unanimous Court (with Justice Black dissenting on a minor provision) upheld the law, declaring that Congress "may use any rational means to effectuate the constitutional prohibitions of racial discrimination in voting."[8] The act proved remarkably successful, and between 1964 and 1969 black registration in the South doubled. Before long these numbers translated into elected black legislators, sheriffs, and mayors. Moreover, the Twenty-fourth Amendment, ratified in January 1964, abolished the poll tax in elections for federal offices; the Court took the rationale of the amendment one step further and in *Harper v. Virginia Board of Elections* (1966) struck down state poll taxes as well.[9]

The 1965 Voting Rights Act aimed not only to ensure access to the ballot box but also to make sure that minority votes would count. Section 5 provided that in states with a history of racial discrimination in voting, new district lines might be required to give minorities proportional representation in the total makeup of a state's congressional delegation. Thus a state with eight congressional districts and a 25 percent African-American population might be required to draw district lines to create two so-called majority-minority districts. In 1960 the Court had held in *Gomillion v. Lightfoot* that states could not gerrymander districts to dilute minority voting strength.[10] But proportional representation had never been a tenet of U.S. democracy or law, and although the Burger Court seemingly approved race-conscious districting as a means of redressing past discrimination, the Court in the 1990s had to wrestle with the issue in several cases. After seemingly striking down the notion of majority-minority districting on equal-protection grounds, the Court in the end allowed states to create black-majority districts provided that they could be justified on political rather than racial grounds, a solution that has not satisfied everyone.[11]

Redistricting has been the concern of the Court in nonracial matters as well, and one of the most enduring achievements of the Warren Court involved apportionment. Although most states had constitutional requirements that legislative districts be redrawn every 10 years, quite a few states had routinely ignored this mandate. The growth of cities in the early decades of the twentieth century, and the mushrooming of suburbs after World War II, resulted in many states with legislatures dominated by representatives from rural areas that no longer commanded a majority of the state population. The first challenge to this problem came in 1946, when Professor Kenneth W. Colegrove brought suit against Illinois, which, despite massive population shifts, had not revised its district lines since 1901. A seven-member Court turned down the challenge by a 4–3 vote, with Justice Felix Frankfurter arguing that redistricting was a political problem not amenable to judicial solutions and warning that courts should stay out of the "political thicket."[12]

With the rise of the civil rights movement, agitation began anew to find a federal constitutional reason to force states to reapportion and to stop denying their urban and suburban voters an equal vote. Just as no one believed the southern states would voluntarily end segregation, no one believed the rural minorities who still held power because of malapportionment would voluntarily correct things. Although 30 states had redrawn their legislative boundaries in the 1950s, 12 states had not redrawn lines for more than three decades; Tennessee and Alabama had not reapportioned since 1901; and Delaware, since 1897. Discrepancies existed within states as well. In California, for example, the Los Angeles state senatorial district included 6 million people; in a more sparsely populated area the senate district had only 14,000. Following *Gomillion*, which involved a gerrymandering scheme aimed at disenfranchising African Americans, reformers began to ask whether urban and suburban voters deserved the same judicial protection of their vote as did Alabama blacks.

The Warren Court, never afraid to face what it considered an injustice, first held, in *Baker v. Carr* (1962), that questions of malapportionment were, despite Frankfurter's decision in *Colegrove*, susceptible to judicial resolution.[13] The very fact that the Supreme Court had agreed to hear the complaints led several states to voluntarily redraw their legislative district lines to reflect recent population changes. Then, in six cases grouped with *Reynolds v. Sims* (1964), the Court held that all voters were entitled to have their ballots count the same as those of other voters. In words that could have been taken from a civil rights opinion, Chief Justice Earl Warren ruled that "to the extent that a citizen's right to vote is debased, he is that much less a citizen. The weight of a citizen's vote cannot be made to depend on where he lives. . . . A citizen, a qualified voter, is no more nor no less so because he lives in the city or on the farm. This is the clear and strong command of our Constitution's Equal Protection Clause."[14]

★ ★ ★ ★ ★

Although racial discrimination and apportionment cases grabbed the headlines, the Supreme Court over the years has also heard a number of lower-profile cases involving political corruption, allegations of bribery, and the regulation of money in politics, both before and after *Buckley*. Although that case is pivotal in our discussion because it touches directly on the matter of campaign financing, one must keep in mind that the range of cases heard by our nation's highest court reflects all the concerns and problems that affect the democratic process. As Jack Rakove points out, corruption in the political system under the Articles of Confederation played a major role in the thinking of the framers of the Constitution, especially that of James Madison. Madison's ideas on federalism and separation of powers, for example, mirrored "his disillusionment with the failings of state legislators and citizens alike."[15] Whereas structural features such as checks and balances and separation of powers worked to ensure that no one part of government could gain ascendancy over the others, they also were intended to serve as a check on corruption.[16]

Alexis de Tocqueville asserted many years ago that in the United States all political issues eventually wind up as judicial matters. So it is not surprising that political corruption should come before the courts for resolution. Questions of corruption in government—whether through bribery or conflict of interest—have not been strangers to the Court, and when other branches of the government are involved, interesting constitutional points may arise.[17]

To take one example, the Court in *United States v. Brewster* (1972) had to decide whether the Speech and Debate Clause (Art. I, Sec. 6) provided immunity to a senator, Daniel B. Brewster (D-Md.), for allegedly accepting a bribe and then using his influence to obtain favorable postal rate legislation.[18] In his opinion for the Court, Chief Justice Warren Burger ruled that no immunity existed; the clause only prevents the executive or judicial branches from examining conduct relating to the legislative process as well as from attempting to search out the motivation behind related conduct. As for Brewster, the government had prosecuted him under a narrowly drawn bribery statute; it had shown that he had accepted a bribe, and it had not attempted to determine whether that bribe had led to specific conduct. For Burger, this meant the government could prosecute a senator for wrongdoing and at the same time preserve a basic element of separation of powers. The courts, therefore, would not be asked to adjudicate issues relating specifically to legislative actions.

Three members of the Court disagreed, and in his dissent Justice

William Brennan argued that "principles of legislative freedom" embodied in the Speech and Debate Clause immunized senators and representatives from any prosecution relating to their legislative activities, even if they involved criminal wrongdoing. The Constitution, in giving each house the power to discipline and even expel members, had intended to keep the other branches of government completely away from the legislative branch. Brennan pointed to a decision handed down just six years earlier, *United States v. Johnson* (1966), in which the Court had barred any noncongressional inquiry into why a senator gave a speech favorable to loan companies involved at the time in a conspiracy to defraud the government prosecution.[19] The *Brewster* decision, allowing prosecution of criminal activity by members of Congress, has since been the law.

Until *Buckley*, however, the Court had relatively little to do with campaign finance regulation. It did look at both the Tillman and Taft-Hartley Acts in a 1957 case involving political expenditures by a labor union.[20] In a thorough history of both measures, the Court concluded that Congress had had legitimate concerns about the effects on the political system of large contributions from both labor unions and corporations.[21] But prior to the Federal Elections Campaign Act of 1974 and its amendments, Congress had not tried to limit the amounts that individual contributors could give or that individual candidates and political committees could spend. When it heard *Buckley*, the Court had decided only a handful of political corruption cases implicating First Amendment values.

★ ★ ★ ★ ★

The Taft-Hartley Act, as noted earlier, attempted to regulate the use of money by labor unions for political purposes, and in §304 prohibited unions from using their internal newsletters to endorse a candidate. The majority of the Court evaded the First Amendment issue by holding that the legislative history of Taft-Hartley indicated that it had not been meant to apply to internal communications. But three justices joined an opinion by Wiley Rutledge that considered that provision a violation of the First Amendment's Freedom of Speech Clause.[22]

In 1957, a majority of the Court sustained an indictment against the United Auto Workers for using union dues to sponsor television advertisements supporting the election of certain candidates for Congress. The majority opinion by Justice Frankfurter held that is the Federal Corrupt Practices Act a valid exercise of congressional power, and he cited the act's legislative history to show that Congress had recognized that "money is the chief source of corruption." Frankfurter avoided dealing with the First Amendment issue by declaring it unnecessary to reach a decision; all the Court had to do was decide whether an indictment could be filed for the actions taken. William O. Douglas, joined by Chief Justice Warren and Hugo Black, dissented on the ground that the statute violated the First Amendment's guarantees of speech and assembly.[23] In a case involving a pipe fitters local union, the Court ruled that unions could make political contributions under the FECA if the money had been given voluntarily by the members and kept in a segregated fund. Although the union had challenged the statute on several grounds, including the First Amendment, the Court again avoided the constitutional issues in the case.[24]

Although two of these cases involved strong dissents on First Amendment grounds, the majority of the Court did not seem to equate campaign finance regulation with speech. Rather, the majority opinions emphasized the concern of Congress with maintaining the integrity of the political system by preventing corruption through large donations. In other cases the Court seemed very ready to respect congressional policy choices when they dealt directly with corruption or the possibility of corruption. For example, in *Barry v. United States* (1929), the Court had held that Congress had the power, under Article I, Sections 1 and 5 (judging elections, returns, and qualifications), to compel attendance of witnesses in an investigation of a Senate election in which excessive contributions had been made in the primary.[25] A few years later, the Court ruled that Congress had the power under the Federal Corrupt Practices Act of 1925 to require disclosure of political contributions by a committee that had attempted to influence the selection of presidential electors. In upholding the constitutionality of the law, Justice George Sutherland confirmed the power of Congress under Article I, Section 2, to preserve the purity of federal elections. "To say that Congress is without power to pass appropriate legislation to safeguard such an election from the improper use of money to influence the result," he declared, "is to deny to the nation in a vital particular the power of self protection."[26] A republican government, Sutherland explained, had to have sufficient power to thwart not only lawless violence, but also the corruption associated with the use of money in elections. Significantly, Sutherland implied that Congress, and not the judiciary, had the discretion to choose the means to address that danger.[27]

Looking at all the cases decided by the Court, in the half-century before *Buckley*, that dealt with elections, corruption, and redress of ills, it appears that the justices accepted the rationale of Congress that it had the power to deal with both the actuality and the threat of corruption in the political process. For the most part, the Court took congressional power as a given, and questions of First Amendment rights of speech and assembly, if they arose at all, appeared in dissents or minority concurrences. The Court did not by itself try to define corruption, but rather deferred to the policy choices made by Congress. All that changed with *Buckley v. Valeo* in 1976.

* * * * *

Although we briefly looked at *Buckley* earlier, we now need to examine the case in more detail. Just as the Federal Election Campaign Act and its amendments constituted the first serious effort by Congress to control the finances of campaigns, so *Buckley v. Valeo* was the first effort by the Court to reconcile the competing claim by Congress that corruption—both real and potential—in the campaign finance system required a new regulatory system, given the guarantees of speech and association protected by the First Amendment. The case involved eight distinct rulings, each of which would play a role in the law of campaign finance over the next quarter-century.[28]

First, five justices voted to sustain the FECA ceilings on individual contributions of $1,000 to any single candidate per election, and an overall limit of $25,000 on all donations by any one contributor. The Court held that these limits did not violate the speech and associational rights of the First Amendment, nor did they discriminate invidiously against nonincumbent or minority party candidates. The justices conceded that "a restriction on the amount of money a person or group can spend on political communication during a campaign necessarily reduces the quantity of expression by restricting the number of issues discussed, the depth of their exploration, and the size of the audience reached."[29] In using the strict scrutiny test, the Court held that the government's desire to limit actual corruption as well as the appearance of corruption constituted the compelling interest needed to limit speech. Indicating its awareness of the Watergate revelations only a few years earlier, the Court noted that the "deeply disturbing examples surfacing after the 1972 election demonstrate that the problem [of corruption] is not an illusory one. Of almost equal concern . . . is the impact of the appearance of corruption stemming from public awareness of the opportunities for abuse inherent in a regime of large individual financial contributions."[30]

In contrast to limits on contributions, the Court found, as we have seen, ceilings on expenditures, by individuals or by groups, to be unconstitutional. Although neutral on its face, (i.e., the law did not target any specific content), the law's spending limits nonetheless imposed substantial restraints on the quantity of political speech, the very type of expression that is "at the core of our electoral process and of the First Amendment."[31] Here the majority found that the governmental interest sufficient to limit contributions—the need to prevent corruption or its appearance—did not meet the requisite standard when applied to campaign expenditures.

The government had argued that limits created a more level playing field, so that those candidates and parties with greater funds would not be able to drown out the message of smaller, poorly funded campaigns. But the Court replied that "the concept that government may restrict the speech of some elements of our society in order to enhance the relative voice of others is wholly foreign to the First Amendment, which was designed to secure 'the widest possible dissemination of information from diverse and antagonistic sources' and 'to assure unfettered interchange of ideas.'"[32]

The Court also discussed the implications of §608(e)(1)—the limitations on private parties spending money for political purposes. The primary effect of this section, the Court noted, restricted the quantity of political speech by individuals, groups, or candidates. Even if facially neutral with regard to ideas, the law limited the very type of political expression protected by the First Amendment. Here the Court inserted the famous footnote 52, which held that such expression, provided it did not constitute actual campaigning, could not be regulated, and the Court provided a list of words that, by their very appearance, would make it a campaign ad—"vote for," "elect," "support," "cast your ballot for," "Smith for Congress," "vote against," "defeat," or "reject." Provided these words did not appear, the ads would be construed as issue advocacy rather than campaigning, and be exempt from regulation.[33]

The third holding flowed logically from the second—namely, that limits on what a candidate could spend out of his or her own pocket clearly interfered with constitutionally protected freedom. The provision, although trying to level the playing field, nonetheless cast its net too widely. A rich candidate might outspend an opponent because of greater success in fund-raising or, conversely, the public's perception that a rich candidate had great wealth might stop others from contributing. It made no difference, however, because "the First Amendment simply cannot tolerate [the] restriction upon the freedom of a candidate to speak without legislative limit on behalf of his own candidacy."[34] (Only Justice Marshall dissented from this part of the ruling, noting that in the seven largest states in the 1970 election, 11 of the 15 senatorial candidates were millionaires; the 4 who were not millionaires lost their contests. Congress had sufficient reason to believe that this disparity in personal wealth threatened the integrity of the political process.)[35]

Fourth, six members of the Court upheld the disclosure provisions of FECA, which required that every candidate and committee maintain records that included the name and address of every donor who gave more than $10 in a calendar year, and the name, address, occupation, and principal place of business for those who contributed more than $100 in a year. This information had to be submitted in quarterly reports to the FEC. The attack on the provision relied on the Court's decisions in *NAACP v. Alabama* (1958) and in *Gibson v. Florida Legislative Investigation Committee* (1963), in which the Court had turned back efforts by the states to compel branches of the National Association for the Advancement of Colored People to turn over their membership lists to state officials.[36] In both instances the Court had seen the demand as a means of intimidating the civil rights agency, and had held that the First Amendment protected individuals in their associational rights, and that the state had failed to provide a compelling explanation of why it needed these lists. There had to be a "substantial relationship" between a "compelling governmental interest" and the information required; in the Alabama and Florida cases neither state had been able to show either the substantial relationship or the compelling interest.

Although the "invasion of privacy of belief may be as great when the information sought concerns the giving and spending of money as when it concerns the joining of organizations," Congress had here provided both the substantial relationship and the compelling interest.[37] Disclosure provides the electorate with information as to where candidates received their campaign funds; second, disclosure deters actual corruption as well as the appearance of corruption; and third, the reporting requirements are an essential means of gathering the information needed. Only Chief Justice Burger dissented from this part of the decision, charging that the Court had failed to give traditional standing to an important First Amendment right, that of association, and that even if there were legitimate reasons, the means employed were too broad. There is no "relation whatever between the means used and the legitimate goal of ventilating possible undue influence. Congress has used a shotgun to kill wrens as well as hawks."[38]

(The majority conceded that the reporting requirements might work a hardship on minor parties espousing views different from those of the mainstream, but since that question did not figure in this case, the Court reserved judgment until a later time. That came within a few years, when the Socialist Workers Party claimed that the requirement would serve to chill donations because people would fear having their names associated with a fringe party. In an opinion by Justice Marshall, the Court agreed that the party had made a sufficient showing of a "reasonable probability of threats, harassment, or reprisals," and it could not be constitutionally compelled to disclose donor information.[39])

The Court dealt with the FECA-authorized public financing of the presidential election in two separate rulings. Although the act did not actually implement the process, Senator Buckley and others attacked public financing of presidential primaries and campaigns as contrary to several constitutional provisions—the General Welfare Clause, the First Amendment, and the Due Process Clause of the Fifth Amendment—on grounds that it invidiously discriminated against minority parties and their candidates. The Court dismissed all of these challenges, and in a footnote observed that "Congress may engage in public financing of election campaigns and may condition acceptance of public funds on an agreement by the candidate to abide by specified expenditure limitations. Just as a candidate may voluntarily limit the size of the contributions he chooses to accept, he may decide to forego private fundraising and accept public funding."[40] (Both Chief Justice Burger and Justice Rehnquist dissented from the public finance provisions, with Rehnquist arguing that public funding "enshrined the Republican and Democratic parties in a permanently preferred position."[41])

The last two parts of the ruling dealt with the mode of choosing members of the Federal Election Commission. Nearly all of the justices agreed that the principle of separation of powers implicit in the Appointments Clause, by which the president nominated and the Senate confirmed FEC members, had been breached, because the FEC would engage in rulemaking and adjudicatory and enforcement powers. However, the Court then granted de facto legitimacy to past rulings by the FEC, and stayed the Court's judgment on this matter for 30 days to give Congress the opportunity to take appropriate action and revise the means of appointing and confirming commissioners.

Chief Justice Burger, in addition to dissenting from the reporting requirements, also objected to the Court's ruling on contributions. He agreed that the FECA's limits on expenditures violated the First Amendment, and so could not understand why the limits on contributions did not also restrict speech. "For me contributions and expenditures are two sides of the same First Amendment coin. . . . Limiting contributions, as a practical matter, will limit expenditures and will put an effective ceiling on the amount of political activity [that] Government will permit to take place." The effort to distinguish contributions from expenditures, in terms of the First Amendment, he argued, "simply will not wash."[42]

Justice White took a similar position in chastising the Court for distinguishing between contributions and expenditures, but whereas Chief Justice Burger would have held both types of limits unconstitutional, White would have upheld them both. He did not understand how the Court could accept Congress's rationale in limiting contributions and then deny it in regard to expenditures. "I would take the word of those who know," he wrote, "that limiting independent expenditures is essential to prevent transparent and widespread evasion of the contribution limits." White went on to say that "the argument that money is speech and that limiting the flow of money to the speaker violates the First Amendment proves entirely too much."[43]

★ ★ ★ ★ ★

Buckley has been one of the most criticized cases in the Court's recent history. Frank Sorauf has written that "the majority opinion in *Buckley* is one of the Court's less impressive monuments. . . . It is long and rambling, an obvious pastiche of differing agendas and prose styles. Very likely it is also the longest per curiam opinion in the Court's history."[44] Those who denigrate the decision do so primarily for what they see as the logical inconsistency between legitimizing caps on individual contributions and voiding expenditure limits as conflicting with the core values of the First Amendment protections of speech and assembly.

Critics also charge the Court with failing to provide a consistent rationale to justify the various holdings. Disparate sections of an opinion are permissible, provided that some unifying jurisprudential thesis holds them together. Commentators have been unable to discern what such a rationale might be in *Buckley*. The Court's emphasis on corruption or the appearance of corruption has convinced few people. Brown University political scientist Darrell West claims that in the debate over campaign financing, many people forgot about Watergate and how fund-raising abuses lay at the core of the Nixon scandals. The Court's reasoning in *Buckley*, according to West, "in favor of disclosure rules, contributor limits, and voluntary spending caps in the presidential elections was based in large measure on the importance of avoiding either the reality or the perception of corruption in government." The problem, West believes, lies not in *Buckley*, but in the "sad irony" that subsequent decisions have rushed to elevate one good—freedom of expression—over every other virtue, allowing those who can provide large amounts of money, the very undue influence that the Court decried in *Buckley*.[45]

In contrast, Professor Vincent Blasi of the Columbia and Virginia law schools and a noted First Amendment scholar, charges that nowhere in the opinion does the Court give serious attention to the broader issues of republican democracy. Americans, he claims, ought not be obsessed with a simple quid pro quo type of corruption, but should be concerned about the entire perversion of the campaign finance system that one saw in Watergate.[46] On the contrary, Bradley Smith, a critic of efforts to reform the campaign finance system, and later chair of the FEC, believes the corruption argument not only overblown, but wrong. "The constitutional Achilles heel" of *Buckley*, he argues, "is its holding that the alleged anticorruption interest of the government justifies the burdens that certain campaign finance regulation places on First Amendment rights. Political speech is not free when it is burdened by regulation."[47]

Even if one believed that the Court had paid appropriate attention to congressional fears of corruption, it appeared to have defined corruption quite narrowly. "To the extent that large contributions are given to secure a political quid pro quo from current and potential officeholders, the integrity of our system of representative democracy is undermined."[48] Although this might be an intellectually defensible position, it does not necessarily reflect political reality. Whereas elected officials are clearly sensitive to sources of campaign funds, it is not at all clear just how directly a campaign contribution translates into a specific vote for or against a measure. According to Bradley Smith, the Court should have requested a much more encompassing definition of corruption before it could be the "compelling interest" needed to abridge First Amendment rights.[49]

Others believe that corruption is not really the rationale underlying the opinion, but rather the desire to impose equality on the playing field, the same way the Court imposed equality through the apportionment decisions. The "true targets of campaign reform," writes David H. Strauss, "are inequality and certain potential problems of interest group politics that are endemic to representative government."[50] He and others believe that because democracy is not a neat and ordered form of government, neither can its politics be entirely clear and well defined. Professor Lillian BeVier of Virginia Law School argues that "neither political equality nor enhancement of democratic dialogue is a permissible legislative goal under the First Amendment."[51] The problem is that the Court (like academic reformers) refused to recognize the realities of the messy but workable system in place; and in *Buckley* and its progeny the Court made the mistake of treating the system as an ideal, what *it should be*, rather than a reality, *what it is*.[52] Along this line, Cass Sunstein likens the *Buckley* decision to the infamous opinion in *Lochner v. New York* (1905).[53] The Court, he charged, assumed that the political marketplace was ideal and just, and therefore should not be tampered with, and then it invalidated a truly democratic reform.[54] BeVier, Daniel Ortiz, and others argue that the Court failed to understand that the political system has many of the characteristics of the marketplace, and as in most markets, simple rules of supply and demand will keep the system running well.[55]

★ ★ ★ ★ ★

Buckley v. Valeo did not put an end to litigation over campaign finance regulation. Some states tried to devise reform measures that would pass the Court's tests. At the same time the Federal Election Commission, confronted with that part of the FECA and its amendments that had either passed judicial scrutiny or had not yet been tested, found itself in court repeatedly as it tried to fashion workable rules. In the more than a quarter-century between *Buckley* and the time it heard the challenge to BCRA in *McConnell v. FEC*, the Supreme Court had several opportunities to revisit the issue of campaign finance regulation and to clarify some of the questions left by *Buckley*. Most commentators believe that, if anything, the situation on the eve of *McConnell* was more confusing rather than less in terms of what the First Amendment and the Court required.

As late as 2000 a majority of the Court seemed to maintain the *Buckley* methodology and to draw a distinction between contributions and expenditures, although the growing scandals associated with campaign financing in the 1990s led some of the justices to advocate dropping *Buckley* and adopting a new standard. In *Nixon v. Shrink Missouri Government PAC* (2000), the Court heard a challenge to a 1994 Missouri law imposing limits on contributions to candidates for state office ranging from $250 to $1,000, with the amount to be adjusted in even-numbered years to take into account inflation.[56] In 1998 the amount was adjusted to $1,075 for contributions to candidates for statewide offices. The PAC gave a contribution of $1,025 in 1997 and another $50 in 1998 to Zev David Fredman, a candidate for state auditor, and then announced that it would have given more but for the state law. The PAC and Fredman then brought suit in federal court alleging that the law violated both the First and Fourteenth Amendments.

The Supreme Court rejected the argument. Writing for a 6–3 majority that relied on *Buckley*, Justice Souter held that state limits may, if consistent with the First Amendment, be placed on political contributions. Although expenditures are protected by the First Amendment, contribution caps will survive if they are closely drawn and reflect a "sufficiently important interest" such as prevention of corruption or its appearance. States are not bound to impose the same dollar limits as the federal government did in FECA, and so long as the limits did not restrict a candidate's ability to run for office, they would be upheld.[57] The challengers had claimed that the state had not produced the type of evidence necessary—that corruption existed or might appear to exist—to warrant imposing limits. To this Souter replied that the statute did not fail for want of such evidence. "The quantum of empirical evidence needed to satisfy heightened judicial scrutiny of legislative judgments will vary up or down with the novelty and plausibility of the justification raised. *Buckley* demonstrates that the dangers of large, corrupt contributions and the suspicion that large contributions are corrupt are neither novel nor implausible." Although the Missouri legislature did not rely on the same sort of evidence referred to in *Buckley*, the record showed that it had taken into account local facts sufficient to warrant concerns over corruption or the appearance of corruption in the state.[58] In effect, *Buckley* remained good law, both for the states and for the federal government, and the contribution/expenditure distinction continued in effect.

What is perhaps most interesting about the Missouri case is that the Court's majority seemed to be lowering the bar for state and federal laws limiting contributions. The Court (1) ratcheted down the level of scrutiny it would apply to contribution limits; (2) expanded the definitions of "corruption" and the "appearance of corruption" to make it easier to sustain contribution caps; (3) lowered the evidentiary burden on the government in terms of what it had to prove to justify fear of corruption; and (4) created a very difficult test for those who would challenge campaign limits as too low. As one scholar noted, the majority "show[ed] dramatic new deference toward contribution limits."[59] In doing so the justices heartened reformers, since if the Court would pay greater deference on the contributions side, then perhaps it might also come around to the same position on limiting expenditures. "The Supreme Court is aware of realities now," wrote Anthony Lewis. "It is not in a First Amendment ivory tower, indifferent to the consequences of absolutism."[60]

Three justices dissented, primarily on First Amendment grounds. Justice Kennedy called the *Buckley* contribution/expenditure distinction a "wooden" one that over the years had "adverse, unintended consequences." In particular, Kennedy claimed, *Buckley*

> forced a substantial amount of political speech underground, as contributors and candidates devise ever more elaborate methods of avoiding contribution limits, limits which take no account of rising campaign costs. The preferred method has been to conceal the real purpose of the speech. Soft money may be contributed to political parties in unlimited amounts, and is used often to fund so-called issue advocacy, advertisements that promote or attack a candidate's positions without specifically urging his or her election or defeat. Issue advocacy, like soft money, is unrestricted, while straightforward speech in the form of financial contributions paid to a candidate, speech subject to full disclosure and prompt evaluation by the public, is not. Thus has the Court's decision given us covert speech. This mocks the First Amendment.[61]

Had the legislature imposed such a system, it would be suspect under the First Amendment, but Congress had nothing to do with it; the fault lay with the Court and its decision, one that had "created a misshapen system, one which distorts the meaning of speech."[62] If it were up to him, Kennedy concluded, he would overrule *Buckley*.

Justice Thomas, joined by Justice Scalia, also dissented, and in his opinion attacked *Buckley* and its contribution/expenditure distinction as well. He believed "the Constitution leaves it entirely up to citizens and candidates to determine who shall speak, the means they will use, and the amounts of speech sufficient to inform and persuade." The majority, he charged, had used "vague and unenumerated harms" and fears of corruption to lower the exacting standards required by the First Amendment.[63]

Of special interest is Justice Kennedy's observation that all *Buckley* had done was to force contributors to give their money in different and unaccounted ways. Since *Buckley* had upheld the reporting scheme of FECA, it would have been better to have all money coming into a campaign accounted for and open to public scrutiny. Instead, donors could not only evade the limits, but avoid publicity by giving through soft money channels.[64]

Although political action committees (PACs) were neither widespread nor a matter of reformers' concerns at the time of *Buckley*, they soon became so, and the Court heard several cases involving PACs. The FECA recognized the existence of PACS, defined as multicandidate committees, "which received contributions from more than 50 persons and made contributions to five or more candidates for federal office." In these cases the Court also followed the reasoning attached to the contribution/expenditure dichotomy. In *California Medical Association v. FEC* (1981), a nonprofit, unincorporated medical association formed a PAC that registered with the FEC, and thus became subject to FECA rules regarding PACs.[65] One of these rules prohibited individuals and unincorporated associations from contributing more than $5,000 per calendar year to any multicandidate committee; a related rule prohibited political committees from knowingly accepting contributions exceeding this limit. The PAC did accept contributions in excess of this limit, and when the FEC announced it would institute a civil suit, the medical association, its PAC, and two individual members filed suit in federal district court seeking to have the relevant portions of the FECA declared unconstitutional, on the grounds that here the money went not to a candidate but to a political committee.[66]

Although the Court could not devise a rationale that won the support of five members, Justice Marshall's plurality opinion (joined by Brennan, White, and Stevens) found *Buckley* to be controlling. Nothing in the law limited the amount the PAC or any of its members could spend to advocate their political views; rather, the law imposed a cap on contributions, and money given to the PAC, for either direct expenditure or passing on to a candidate's own committee, constituted a contribution. Marshall rejected the claim that, because the contribution went to a political committee, rather than to a candidate, the provision did not "further the governmental interest in preventing the actual or apparent corruption of the political process."[67] The provision was necessary to prevent circumvention of the contributions limits upheld in *Buckley*.

A second decision involving a PAC also followed the contribution/expenditure rationale of *Buckley*. A provision of the Presidential Election Campaign Fund Act prohibited PACs from spending more than $1,000 to further the campaign of a presidential candidate who accepted public financing. In *FEC v. National Conservative PAC* (1985), the Court struck down this provision on the grounds that efforts to regulate expenditures violated the First Amendment.[68] Justice White, joined by Brennan and Marshall, dissented on grounds that when PACs spent money they did so as proxies for the contributors, and by treating PACs differently than candidates (a distinction the Court had refused to draw in the California case), the Court was essentially allowing donors to exceed campaign contributions to candidates by routing them through a PAC. Perhaps of even greater interest was Justice Marshall's separate dissent, in which he said:

> Although I joined that portion of the *Buckley* per curiam that distinguished contributions from independent expenditures for First Amendment purposes, I now believe the distinction has no constitutional significance. . . . In both cases the regulation is of the same form: It concerns the amount of money that can be spent for political activity. . . . I have come to believe that the limitations on independent expenditures challenged in *Buckley* and here are justified by the congressional interest in promoting "the reality and appearance of equal access to the political arena," and in eliminating political corruption and the appearance of such corruption.[69]

The Court found that political parties, like individuals, candidates, and PACs, have a right under the First Amendment to make unlimited expenditures on behalf of a candidate. In *Colorado Republican Federal Campaign Committee v. FEC* (1996) (*Colorado I*), the Court considered an FECA provision imposing dollar limits on political party expenditures in connection with the general election campaign for a congressional candidate.[70] Even before a Republican candidate had been selected for the 1986 senatorial election, the Colorado federal Republican committee bought radio time to air advertisements attacking the presumptive Democratic candidate. The Democrats and the FEC charged the Colorado Republicans with violating the FECA by exceeding the allowable party limit.

Once again the Court relied on *Buckley*, but, once again, could not muster a rationale on which five justices could agree. Justice Breyer, joined by O'Connor and Souter, invalidated §441a(d)(3) of the FECA on grounds that "the First Amendment prohibits the application of this provision to the kind of expenditure at issue here—an expenditure that the political party has made independently, without coordination with any candidate." Declaring that the issue of unregulated expenditures had long been settled, "we do not see how a Constitution that grants to individuals, candidates, and ordinary political committees the right to make unlimited independent expenditures could deny that same right to political parties."[71] The plurality rejected the government's contention that party expenditures on behalf of a candidate ought to be presumed to have been coordinated with the candidate's campaign, and therefore treated as contributions, which, of course could be regulated.

Justice Kennedy, joined by Chief Justice Rehnquist and Justice Scalia, concurred in part and dissented in part. In essence, these three would have gone further and invalidated the party expenditure limits on their face, whether applied to independent or coordinated party expenditures. Justice Thomas, also joined by Rehnquist and Scalia, would have voided party spending limits in their entirety because the anticorruption rationale at the heart of *Buckley* just did not apply here. "What could it mean," Thomas asked, "for a party to 'corrupt' its candidate or to exercise 'coercive' influence over him? The very aim of a political party is to influence its candidate's stance on issues and, if the candidate takes office or is reelected, his votes. When political parties achieve that aim, it is not corruption; that is successful advocacy of ideas in the political marketplace and representative government in a party system."[72] Only Justices Stevens and Ginsburg dissented, claiming that party expenditure limits met the constitutional test because they served important governmental interests both in avoiding corruption and in "leveling the electoral playing field by constraining the cost of federal campaigns."[73]

Justice Breyer's plurality opinion in *Colorado I* declined to deal with the hypothetical question of what rule would apply if in fact there had been coordination; that issue came back to the Court a few years later in a case labeled *Colorado II*.[74] Breyer, O'Connor, and Souter, the plurality in the first case, were now joined by the two dissenters, Stevens and Ginsburg, to provide a 5–4 majority ruling that limits on a party's coordinated expenditures were constitutional. To reach this conclusion, the five justices rejected a series of assumptions from both sides. They denied the party's contentions that its coordinated spending should be as free from regulation as its independent spending, and that the point of organizing a party is to run candidates, so the coordination is integral to a party structure. The majority also rejected the government's claim that coordinated spending is the same as contributions and should be treated as such, and that if coordinated spending were unlimited it would only aggravate the use of a party as a money funnel to bypass the contribution limits upheld in *Buckley.*

Conceding that each of these arguments appeared "plausible at first blush," the Court rejected them and announced that the limit applied to a party's coordinated expenditures would be subject to "the same scrutiny we have applied to the other political actors, that is, scrutiny appropriate for a contribution limit, enquiring whether the restriction is 'closely drawn' to match what we have recognized as the 'sufficiently important' government interest in combating political corruption."[75]

Although admitting that no recent evidence existed to evaluate unlimited coordinated spending, the Court contended that "the question is whether experience under the present law confirms a serious threat of abuse from the unlimited coordinated spending as the Government contends. It clearly does. Despite years of enforcement of the challenged limits, substantial evidence demonstrates how candidates, donors, and parties test the limits of the current law, and it shows beyond serious doubt how contribution limits would be eroded" if the Court were to strike down the limits on coordinated spending. Moreover, unlike *Buckley* and even *Colorado I,* where the choice was between limiting pure contributions and pure expenditures, here "the choice is between limiting contributions and limiting expenditures whose special value as expenditures is also the source of their power to corrupt. Congress is entitled to its choice."[76]

The majority opinion, even though it claimed to follow *Buckley,* in fact became the first instance in which a majority of the Court strayed from a strict distinction between contributions and expenditures, and despite Souter's effort to differentiate between the *Buckley* test and the problem of coordinated money, critics had for a long time been arguing that the *Buckley* distinction made no sense in the real world of politics. Moreover, all four of the dissenting justices— Rehnquist, Scalia, Kennedy, and Thomas—agreed that they would overrule *Buckley* in part and apply to contribution limits the full strict scrutiny test hitherto applied only to expenditures. Justice Thomas also argued that even if the *Buckley* restrictions made sense in some way when applied to individuals and political committees, they did not make sense when applied to parties, which are inextricably intertwined with candidates.

A third area of campaign finance in which the Court attempted to make sense after *Buckley* concerned the activities of corporations. Federal law had long prohibited contributions from corporate treasuries to federal campaigns. But what about campaigns that did not involve candidates but instead involved referenda? Could a state prohibit a company from advocacy in a referendum where the results might seriously affect its welfare?

Massachusetts had enacted a prohibition against corporations making donations or expenditures in an effort to influence the vote in any referendum, "other than one materially affecting any of the property, business, or assets of the corporation." Moreover, the law specifically excluded any referendum concerning taxation of income, property, or business transactions from being considered as "materially affecting" a corporation. In 1976 the state's ballot included a proposal to authorize a graduated individual income tax. Banks and other financial corporations opposed the measure, and went into state court to challenge the validity of the restrictive corporate statute. The Supreme Judicial Court of Massachusetts upheld the measure, ruling that the First Amendment rights of a corporation were limited to issues that materially affected its business, property, or assets, and that the state had it within its power to define certain matters, including taxation, as not materially affecting corporate interests.[77]

The Supreme Court, by a 5–4 vote, reversed this decision in *First National Bank of Boston v. Bellotti* (1978).[78] Justice Powell wrote that the state court had asked the wrong question. The issue was not whether corporations had First Amendment rights similar to those of natural persons; rather, "the question must be whether [the state law] abridges expression that the First Amendment was meant to protect. We hold that it does." The issue that the banks wanted to talk about—a proposed constitutional amendment—lay at the very heart of First Amendment protection. "It is the type of speech indispensable to decision-making in a democracy. . . . The inherent worth of the speech in terms of its capacity for informing the public does not depend upon the identity of its source, whether corporation, association, union, or individual." [79] Once Powell had found that the type of speech warranted First Amendment protection, then the appropriate test would be strict scrutiny, and by this standard the state law failed. If the legislature could tell a bank to mind its own business, then it could say that to any other type of corporation, be it religious, charitable, or civic.

Justice White, in a lengthy dissent joined by Brennan and Marshall, asserted that the majority had committed a fundamental error in failing "to realize that the state regulatory interests [are] themselves derived from the First Amendment," namely, promoting the free marketplace of ideas by preventing domination by wealthy corporations. Although White agreed that corporate speech lay within First Amendment protection, corporate speech was "subject to restrictions which individual expression is not."[80]

Bellotti seemed to open another gap in the wall that Congress and some states had attempted to erect to keep corporate funds out of election campaigns. Even if corporate treasuries could not send money to a candidate, it now appeared that corporations could speak out on political issues of interest to them. So if, for example, two candidates differed over raising or lowering tariffs, a company that would benefit from lower rates could pay for an "issue ad," and voters would not have to go far to guess which candidate agreed with the company's position.

Although the Court had implied in *Bellotti* that restrictions on corporate entities would fail whether applied to businesses or civic associations, in *FEC v. National Right to Work Committee* (1982) the Court drew a distinction between the Massachusetts statute and a federal restriction on nonprofit corporations raising funds to contribute to candidate campaigns.[81]

The National Right to Work Committee, a nonprofit corporation without capital stock, established a separate segregated fund in order to receive and make contributions on behalf of federal candidates. This fund then sent letters to individuals who had previously contributed to the committee, soliciting contributions to the fund. Another lobbying group then filed a complaint with the Federal

Election Commission, asserting that the corporation had solicited contributions from persons who were not stockholders, executive or administrative personnel of the corporation, or their families, in violation of the solicitation restrictions of the FECA. The committee responded that, within the meaning of the FECA, those who received the solicitation letters were "members" of the corporation. The FEC disagreed and the committee filed suit; it lost in district court but then won in the court of appeals, which held that the term "member" had to be given an elastic definition in order to avoid infringement of First Amendment associational rights.

The Supreme Court reversed this decision in a unanimous opinion by Justice Rehnquist. The Court refused to accept the idea that anyone who had ever made a donation to the committee, or had even been solicited by them, constituted a "member" under the provisions of the FECA. The solicitation letter made no reference to members, and those solicited played no part in the operation or administration of the fund, nor did they have any control over the expenditure of their contributions. In addition, the fund's own articles of incorporation explicitly disclaimed the existence of members. As a result, the FECA prohibition against nonprofits engaging in this type of political activity met all constitutional tests, and the associational rights of the committee were overborne by the governmental interest in "ensuring that substantial aggregations of wealth amassed by the special advantages which go with the corporate form of organization should not be converted into political 'war chests' which could be used to incur political debts from legislators who are aided by the contributions."[82]

A few years later, however, the Court gave nonprofit groups greater leeway in the political arena, holding in a 5–4 opinion that nonprofits could issue pamphlets indicating their position on certain key issues and listing the voting records of candidates, provided they did not actually endorse any specific person.[83] The nonprofit Massachusetts Citizens for Life had prepared a "special election edition" of its newsletter urging citizens to vote "prolife" in an upcoming primary, and reporting the positions of various candidates on prolife legislation. Although the newsletter carried the pictures of candidates who supported such legislation, the committee explicitly denied endorsing any particular candidates.

Justice Brennan's majority opinion distinguished the prolife committee's actions from those of the right-to-work group. The latter had attempted to provide money for the use of candidates and thus violated the FECA. But the antiabortion group had simply broadcast its views, and since people joined that group because they shared that viewpoint, it did not have to set up a segregated fund in order to make known its views. Chief Justice Rehnquist, joined by White, Blackmun, and Stevens, dissented, and said the Court should defer to the judgment of Congress that corporations of any sort are a distinct category with respect to what type of speech regulation is constitutionally permissible.

Four years later, however, the Court reversed itself, and upheld a Michigan statute restricting independent corporate campaign expenditures substantially identical to the federal restriction that had been struck down in *Massachusetts Citizens*. Although the Michigan state law barred corporations from using their treasuries for political purposes, it did allow them to set up segregated funds. The statute exempted expenditures by any television or radio station, or any print media, in regard to either covering a race or even airing an editorial, a clear attempt to avoid First Amendment problems with the press. Justice Marshall's 6–3 opinion in *Austin v. Michigan Chamber of Commerce* (1990) repeated much of the language that the Court had used in *National Right to Work Committee* about the potential abuses of large corporate wealth in the political process.[84] The Michigan act "aims at the corrosive and distorting effects of immense aggregations of wealth that are accumulated with the help of the corporate form and that have little or no correlation to the public's support for the corporation's political ideas."[85] Given this fear of corruption, the state had articulated a sufficiently compelling rationale for restricting corporate involvement in politics.[86] Moreover, because the Michigan Chamber of Commerce was involved in a very wide range of activities, it had a large number of members, many of whom might not share the chamber leadership's political agenda.

Justice Scalia wrote a scathing dissent that began:

> Attention all citizens. To assure the fairness of elections by preventing disproportionate expression of the views of any single powerful group, your Government has decided that the following associations of persons shall be prohibited

from speaking or writing in support of any candidate. . . . In permitting Michigan to make private corporations the first object of this Orwellian announcement, the Court today endorses the principle that too much speech is an evil that the democratic majority can proscribe. I dissent because that principle is contrary to our case law and incompatible with the absolutely central truth of the First Amendment: that government cannot be trusted to assure, through censorship, the "fairness" of political debate.[87]

Scalia accused the majority of attempting to overrule or undercut *Buckley's* rejection of limits on expenditures solely on the basis of resources available to the speaker. Rich corporate bodies, because they had wealth to spend, could be restricted in their speech. He ridiculed the reasoning that the mere potential of harm justifies restrictions on speech. Yet a key element of *Buckley* had been just that. In sustaining the limits on contributions, the Court had relied on Congress's determination that large donations to candidates and political groups indicated either outright corruption or the perception of corruption. In what was certainly the most forceful rejection of this assumption since *Buckley*, Scalia argued that the same strict scrutiny should be applied to contribution caps as well as expenditure caps, and that all speakers, individual as well as corporate, should be treated identically in terms of First Amendment rights.

In another dissent, Justice Kennedy, joined by O'Connor and Scalia, also went back to *Buckley* and charged that the majority had upheld "a direct restriction on the independent expenditure of funds for political speech for the first time in history." The Michigan statute, he believed, failed the strict scrutiny test required by the First Amendment. In *Buckley* and *Bellotti*, he claimed, the Court had rejected the argument that expending money to increase the quantity of political speech somehow fosters corruption. "The key to the majority's reasoning appears to be that because some corporate speakers are well supported and can buy press space or broadcast time to express their ideas, government may ban all corporate speech to ensure that it will not dominate political debate," Kennedy asserted. "The argument is flawed in at least two respects. First, the statute is overinclusive because it covers all groups which use the corporate form, including all nonprofit corporations. Second, it assumes that the government has a legitimate interest in equalizing the relative influence of speakers."[88]

By this point one might well wonder how much of the expenditure/contribution rule in *Buckley* had survived. The Court had both negated and upheld limits on expenditures, and although several of the justices had urged doing away with the distinction altogether and applying strict scrutiny to both sides of the equation, that view never commanded a majority of the Court in any given case. The logical inconsistencies of these cases could not be masked. How could a corporation be allowed to engage in political speech on referenda (*Bellotti*) but not support candidates (*Austin*)? Or could they support candidates, if they disclaimed doing so (*Massachusetts Citizens for Life*)? Academics attempting to make sense of this pattern threw their hands up in bewilderment.[89]

Other decisions of the Court in the post-*Buckley* era did little to clarify this confusion. In *Citizens against Rent Control v. Berkeley* (1981), the Court struck down a local ordinance establishing a $250 limit on personal contributions to committees established to support or oppose referenda.[90] Chief Justice Burger's majority opinion found this limit an unconstitutional interference with freedom of association as well as individual and collective rights of expression. *Buckley*, he claimed, did not support contribution limits to committees favoring or opposing ballot measures, although in *Bellotti* the Court had relied on the *Buckley* rationale to strike down state limits on advocacy related to ballot measures. Only Justice White dissented, and, repeating his views from *Buckley* and *Bellotti*, argued that the ordinance represented such a negligible intrusion on expression that it ought to be upheld.

* * * * *

In all of these cases the Court had to wrestle with just what *Buckley v. Valeo* meant as applied not only to candidates and their committees, but to PACs, referenda, corporations, and nonprofits as well.[91] Although a few cases—mostly minor—managed to win over a full Court, in nearly all of them slim majorities tried to make sense out of *Buckley* but confronted strong dissents that called for greater

First Amendment analysis that would apply strict scrutiny to both expenditures and contributions.

By the time McCain-Feingold gained congressional approval, constitutional experts could not be sure just how the courts would respond. *Buckley*, according to at least one critic, stood "for the proposition that if [a campaign finance law] is effective, it must be unconstitutional." E. Joshua Rosenkranz charged that scores of promising reforms that have been enacted into law have fallen to a *Buckley* challenge. Lampooning the Court's distinction between contributions and expenditures, Rosenkranz said that the case stood for the proposition that "a [Ross] Perot or a [Michael] Huffington has an absolute right to buy his way into office. It means that a fat cat has an absolute right to saturate the airwaves with a message advocating for or against a candidate."[92]

One could go on citing one view after another, each one taking a different slant on *Buckley* and its progeny. Martin Redish probably put it best when, on the eve of the passage of McCain-Feingold, he wrote: "To this point, it would be difficult to declare a clear winner. Indeed, the Supreme Court's decisions on the subject not only have failed to provide a coherent resolution of the competing and complex arguments, they have instead given rise to their own doctrinal and theoretical confusion."[93]

Into this constitutional morass the three-judge panel of the district court would now venture.

6 / Getting the Ducks in a Row: Briefing the District Court

> The average Republican is a small
> businessperson who doesn't have time to get
> involved for a candidate. He doesn't have time
> like a labor union worker to go door to door for
> a Democrat. He runs a business and wants to
> participate by writing a check to the candidate
> who is going to protect the way he does
> business.
> —Senator Mitch McConnell (R-Ky.)

ALTHOUGH everyone knew that the final decision regarding the constitutionality of McCain-Feingold would rest in the hands of the nine justices of the Supreme Court, the time spent in preparing for trial in the district court served several useful purposes. First, it allowed both sides to line up their allies, those who would be coplaintiffs or interveners, and decide who would file briefs. Second, both sides would have to lay out their arguments in as cogent and persuasive a manner as possible. Once the district court had decided, there would be an appeal, but neither side would be allowed to make new constitutional arguments when filing in the High Court. Unless the justices wanted new issues brought in, the appeal would be limited to the problems argued below. Both sides would be able to present expert testimony to back up their views, and these papers by many of the leading scholars in the fields of the First Amendment and campaign finance, would be part of the record on appeal.[1]

Moreover, the Supreme Court often utilizes the grounds put forth by lower courts in explaining how it has reached a decision. Although the justices are not bound to the lower courts' conclusions or logic, the district court opinion would, at least initially, frame how the appeals were filed, and what sort of arguments would be at the basis of those appeals.

★   ★   ★   ★   ★

Even before George Bush signed the Bipartisan Campaign Reform Act (BCRA), opponents had lined up to attack it in the courts. The American Civil Liberties Union (ACLU) declared that, although it had long supported campaign finance reform through public funding of races for federal offices, the BCRA, in its view, impinged upon traditional First Amendment rights. The act, according to Stephen Shapiro, ACLU legal director, would severely restrict nonprofit, nonpartisan organizations (such as the ACLU itself) "from expressing their views on important public issues in the period immediately preceding an election, a time when those issues are most urgently debated."[2] Within Congress there had been an informal understanding that Senator Mitch McConnell (R-Ky.) would be the lead plaintiff, and as soon as George Bush signed the bill, McConnell announced that he would challenge the law in the courts. He welcomed others to join him if they believed that the BCRA deprived them of their constitutional rights.[3] "I look forward to being joined by a strong group of coplaintiffs in the very near future."[4]

McConnell did not have long to wait. Within a few days more than 80 interest groups or individuals announced that they intended to challenge BCRA in the courts. In the end, these 84 coalesced into 11 separate law suits against the Federal Election Commission, and all suits were heard and decided as one case, although the emphasis in each suit differed somewhat from others. For example, both the AFL-CIO and the National Rifle Association (NRA) opposed the bill on First Amendment grounds, but differed in both large principles and particulars. Wayne LaPierre, the NRA executive vice president, and James Jay Baker, executive director of the NRA's Institute for Legislative Action, in a joint statement, challenged Congress's efforts to quiet the gun lobby. "The First Amendment," they announced, does not *allow* Congress to make laws which deny us the right to speak out on issues."[5] The AFL-CIO was primarily upset over the limits placed on PACs. The National Association of Broadcasters worried about how much the new law would cost in lost revenues.

Soon afterward the Republican National Committee, the California Democratic Party, the California Republican Party, and a variety of local committees and officials joined the suit.[6] The most comprehensive and the lead grouping (27 litigants) was that associated with Senator McConnell's, and included Representatives Bob Barr (R-Ga.) and Mike Pence (R-Ind.).[7]

A formidable army of lawyers represented the various plaintiffs. Altogether, some 55 lawyers signed the plaintiff briefs. Although some of them were staff members (usually the general counsel) of specific organizations, others worked for private law firms, and all of them apparently gave their services on a pro bono basis. In the list one could find some of the most important civil liberties attorneys in the country, such as Floyd Abrams of New York and Joel M. Gora of the Brooklyn Law School, who had represented the ACLU in the *Buckley* case. Kathleen M. Sullivan, dean of the Stanford Law School and coauthor of a leading case book on the First Amendment, had been one of the first to volunteer her services to Senator McConnell. In addition, former Solicitor General Kenneth W. Starr, a member of the Washington law firm of Kirkland and Ellis, acted not only for McConnell but for several of the coplaintiffs.

The Federal Election Commission argued in favor of the new law, joined by several members of Congress. Although the solicitor general's office would be nominally responsible for defending a federal law in court, in this case it would have the help of some high-powered attorneys and law firms who, like those assisting Senator McConnell, donated their services on a pro bono basis.[8] Because the Justice Department had the responsibility of prosecuting violations under the criminal provisions of the law, it represented the United States. Robert D. McCallum, Jr., assistant attorney general, headed a team of 10 lawyers from the Department of Justice. Seventeen lawyers, nearly the entire legal department of the FEC, signed the brief, led by general counsel Lawrence H. Norton. In addition, the powerful and politically well-connected Washington law firm of Wilmer, Cutler and Pickering represented the members of Congress who had intervener status.[9] Although numerous lawyers from the firm worked on the case, only three signed the brief: Roger Witten, Randolph Moss, and former Solicitor General Seth P. Waxman.

On April 16, 2002, less than three weeks after the president signed BCRA, the case was assigned to a three-judge panel consisting of district judge Richard J. Leon, appointed just that year by President George W. Bush; district judge Colleen Kollar-Kotelly, appointed by President Bill Clinton in 1997; and court of appeals judge Karen LeCraft Henderson, named by President George H. W. Bush in 1990. One week later the judges met with lawyers representing both sides in a status conference, in which they heard the parties' proposals on matters of consolidation of suits, intervention, discovery, and the filing of motions. The very next day the court issued a unanimous order outlining a discovery and briefing schedule. Because of the complexity of the issue and the many sections of the law that would be challenged, the court allowed five months for discovery (far longer than normal) and one month for cross-examination of key witnesses and experts. The three judges set November 25 as the deadline for briefs and supporting documents, and informed the parties that they would begin hearing oral arguments on December 4, 2002.[10]

★ ★ ★ ★ ★

Given the nature of the trial, both sides would not only try to build up the constitutional arguments on their side but also make it appear that unless their views prevailed, dire consequences would be in store for the country's political system. The briefs are full of worst-case scenarios; overblown rhetoric; warnings of slippery slopes, should the other side win; and quite often, reasoning according to horrid possibilities, that is, "If this provision is allowed to stand (or is struck down), then we can expect to see horrible event #1, then horrible development #2, etc." Nonetheless, picking one's way between the essential constitutional arguments and the surrounding hyperbole, one finds one of the most important public policy debates of the last decade—to what extent should Congress attempt to control campaign financing related to federal offices, including the political speech that makes up those campaigns, in order to prevent corruption or its appearance?

The bulk of the attack would be led by the McConnell group, in which 9 of the 11 suits would be consolidated.[11] Although the plaintiffs did not agree on all points (the ACLU, for example, did not join in attacking Title I on federalism grounds), they all argued that the major titles of the Bipartisan Campaign Reform Act of 2002 violated the Constitution, especially the First Amendment. As they put it in their introduction, "At stake in this litigation is nothing less than the future of political speech in our Nation. [BCRA] constitutes . . . the most threatening frontal assault on core First Amendment values in a generation."[12] BCRA, they charged, "exhibits a total absence of proportionality—such little narrow tailoring engaged in, such slight attention paid to First Amendment interests, such utter contempt shown for governing Supreme Court precedent." Title I, for example, would bar the California Democratic Party from using funds lawfully raised in California to pay for a radio ad urging California voters to reject an initiative relating to affirmative action. Title II would criminalize advertisements by the ACLU criticizing the Speaker of the House for not permitting a vote on an employment nondiscrimination act or the National Right to Life Committee from encouraging viewers to urge their senators to vote for a ban on partial-birth abortions. Title III would ban a child from contributing $20 of personal money to a congressional campaign waged by a favorite Sunday school teacher but would irrationally allow the same minor to give $5,000 to a political action committee (PAC).[13]

Although conceding that Congress may have had power to act in some of these areas, the plaintiffs insisted that it could not "simply ignore competing constitutional interests, disparage governing Supreme Court case law, and disregard well-established and deeply rooted constitutional limitations." Never before, they charged, had the First Amendment been "treated as some sort of impediment to progress, with speech about issues and candidates viewed as some sort of threat to public health requiring quarantine lest too much of it be permitted." Not since the Alien and Sedition Acts had Congress ever mounted such an attack on freedom of expression, and it had done so in a law that, at its heart, attempted to protect incumbents.[14]

The statute had a severability clause; that is, if courts struck down one provision of the law, this would not automatically invalidate the rest. As a result, the plaintiffs had to attack, and the government and the interveners had to defend, each provision of BCRA. It also meant that, at least to some extent, they had to, if not coordinate their arguments, at least be aware of what the others were doing so as not to create problems down the line. For example, Edward Warren of Kirkland and Ellis, who represented several parties on the McConnell side, wanted to use some of the work on disclosure by Professor Elizabeth Garrett of the University of Southern California, and they discussed the possibility of her writing a brief on full disclosure as a sufficient remedy to potential corruption. Warren believed that the courts would be more willing to strike down the other aspects of the law if they could believe that permissible and effective regulation through more comprehensive reporting of contributions and expenditures would be constitutional. This idea stalled, however, when other lawyers in the coalition objected, not wanting to concede that any aspect of campaign finance regulation would meet constitutional tests.[15]

Title I of BCRA outlawed soft money, banning national parties from either receiving or spending money legitimately raised under state laws. This prevented national party committees from using state-regulated funds for any purpose, including contributions to state and local candidates, issue advocacy, voter registration, administrative expenses, or other functions. Such a sledgehammer approach, the McConnell group claimed, violated Article I, Section 4, of the Tenth Amendment to the Constitution by usurping the rights of states to regulate their own elections. But the ban on soft money also applied to federal elections, in which Congress clearly could impose some regulations on the states; the real issue to the plaintiffs lay in the fact that BCRA violated the First Amendment rights of free speech and association and the Fifth Amendment right of equal protection.

The most comprehensive attack on Title I came from the Republican National Committee, which denounced the ban on soft money on three grounds. First, it violated the federal structure of the U.S. government by exceeding the powers delegated to Congress. Second, it impinged on political parties' First Amendment right of association and restricted the pure speech protected by the First Amendment. Finally, Title I singled out political parties and subjected them to unique discrimination, thus violating the equal protection components of both the Fifth and Fourteenth Amendments.[16]

The RNC claimed that soft money, in essence nonfederal funds, had been raised under state regulations, and hard money had been subject to the FEC, or federal rules. The FEC itself, the RNC claimed, had always seen soft money as a state issue, recognizing that committees that supported both federal and nonfederal candidates had to abide by two sets of rules, and soft money ought to be seen as no more than a "by-product" of the federal system. Admittedly, sometimes activities for the benefit of both federal and nonfederal candidates could blur the lines, but the FEC had developed rules that allowed parties to fund up to one-third of their mixed activities with nonfederal funds; BCRA, on the other hand, required that 100 percent of such activities be funded by hard money.

Such a requirement ignored the historical origins of the important role that political parties had played in U.S. democracy. Political parties have coordinated activity among state, federal, and local entities, have encouraged a "democratic nationalism, have been critical agents in developing consensus, and have helped cultivate a sense of community—all critical features in maintaining a stable constitutional order." The RNC then went into an extended exposition of its many activities: how it raised money from a variety of sources, and how it spent money at the national, state, and local levels. If it were restricted to using only hard money, much of its activity would be limited, as would that of the Democrats. The Constitution recognized and encouraged government at different levels; therefore it made sense that political parties would operate at different levels, and under the rules appropriate to those levels. In Title I, Congress attempted to impose a one-size-fits-all regime that it did not have the power to enact because that violated the ideas of federalism that lay at the heart of the constitutional scheme.[17]

The brief filed jointly by the Democratic and Republican Parties of California claimed that BCRA so amended the Federal Election Campaign Act as to make it impossible for them to run traditional local fund-raising activities. They charged that the definitions of federal election activity contained in BCRA included "virtually any political party activity that takes place in an election cycle in which a federal office is on the ballot, without regard to the purpose of the expenditure."[18]

Interestingly, the California parties took part of Senator Feingold's deposition and turned it back on him. He had claimed that Title I would establish a "firewall" between state and national parties, and that the restrictions would be good for state parties. With BCRA, he said, "maybe we could get back to knocking on doors and putting up yard signs and having barbeques and bean feeds." As it turned out, the Yolo County Democratic Central Committee, one of the plaintiffs, actually had an annual Bean Feed whose proceeds went to voter registration and get-out-the-vote activities. Contributions from unions and corporations—of money and the raffle prizes, the printing of invitations, and the food itself—were all legal under California law. But under BCRA the Bean Feeds, which promoted local Democratic officeholders and candidates, including the local House member, were now considered "federal election activity" and the proceeds "soft money." Because of BCRA, the county committee had to cancel the past year's Bean Feed. "Surely," the committees claimed, "the framers of the Constitution never intended for Congress to reach so far into state and local politics."[19]

The equal protection argument was more fully developed in the Thompson brief, which claimed that the attack on the ideal of "one person, one vote" had reared its "Medusa-like head" once again in BCRA. Any interference with the right to cast one's vote interfered with the free association provision of the First Amendment, and this meant not only diluting the equity of one's vote, but also limiting the choice of candidates who could vie for the vote. Unequal treatment of candidates, according to the Supreme Court, violated a voter's right to cast an effective ballot.[20] By attempting to limit corruption or even the appearance of corruption, BCRA unduly limited the participation of all citizens in the political process. The inability to contribute to a candidate of one's choice or for a candidate to raise funds "is every bit as exclusionary to poorer candidates and voters as the regime of high filing fees and the poll tax."[21] The fact of the matter is that no one can be a serious candidate for any office without sufficient money to fund a viable campaign. Money by itself cannot guarantee victory, but its absence almost always assures defeat. Raising the half-million dollars or so needed to run a race for Congress is especially difficult in poorer districts and in those areas where large groups of people were discriminated against prior to the passage of the 1965 Voting Rights Act. The restriction of money, according to the brief, would have little impact on corruption—real or perceived. Its practical effect would be to discriminate "against grassroots activity, economically challenged candidates in economically challenged districts, and the citizens therein."[22] The Thompson group asked the court to either strike down Title I, "or, in the alternative, by the revision of the Act to include a 'Pauper's Provision' to allow hard and soft monies to be obtained and spent in the campaigns of economically challenged candidates."[23] The brief did not suggest to the court how to define such candidates, where to draw the line, or how to deal with the inevitable equal protection challenge to such a provision.

All told, the briefs in regard to Title I downplayed or ignored the corrupting influence that reformers had considered in their decision to do away with soft money. The RNC went back to the original FEC provision and concentrated on traditional party activities to justify its need for soft money, and Thompson tried to make it appear that without soft money, poor constituencies would be deprived of their right to free association because they would not have an equitable choice in candidates. Although the plaintiffs cited some Supreme Court cases, it seemed dubious that either the federalism claim or the associational-rights claim provided a sufficient rationale for the court to nullify BCRA. As for the demise of the Bean Feed, although perhaps a good example of the law of unintended consequences, by itself it did not seem to rise to the level of a constitutional impairment. Congress had, with the approval of the judiciary, reached much further down into local activities. In the 1965 Voting Rights Act, for example, it had authorized the Justice Department to take over the work of local registrars and to abandon literacy tests.[24]

Title II of BCRA imposed limits on certain types of electioneering ads in the period before primaries and general elections, a restriction that the plaintiffs charged flatly contradicted the constitutional command that speech be "uninhibited, robust, and wide-open."[25] Although perhaps less pressing matters to reformers than the abolition of soft money, these reforms raised very serious First Amendment issues. Such a ban on "electioneering communications" could not be reconciled with *Buckley*. The BCRA ban used much too broad a definition of such communications, and applied it to too many types of groups, including charitable corporations and nonprofit ideological groups as well as political committees. The type of speech outlawed comprised the very heart of the First Amendment—political speech. All sorts of groups could potentially face civil or political penalties for "broadcasts that inform the public that elected officials and candidates support or oppose pending legislation, address public policy issues, or otherwise comment on their official conduct."[26]

This may have been the plaintiffs' strongest point, since a number of Supreme Court decisions, especially *Buckley*, had stressed the near sanctity of "discussion of public issues and debate on the qualifications of candidates."[27] The First Amendment, according to the Court, affords political speech the "broadest protection" from government regulation, and is "at the core of [our] electoral process and our First Amendment freedoms."[28] Because any effort to regulate any part of the discussion in a campaign could only create more First Amendment problems, the Court in *Buckley* had created a bright-line test, the often-ridiculed "magic words" that made it clear that an advertisement was in fact an effort to elect or defeat a particular candidate. McConnell and his allies could live with that, so long as they could still discuss issues. They claimed that the *Buckley* Court had attempted to set up a rule that government must err on the side of the First Amendment in leaving protected political speech unregulated.[29] "Expenditures for issue advocacy," they argued, "may neither be limited in amount nor subjected to disclosure requirements."[30]

The *Buckley* mandate, according to McConnell, had withstood the test of time. Lower courts had followed it faithfully, and even the Supreme Court's 1990 decision in *Austin v. Michigan Chamber of Commerce* did not seriously alter the *Buckley* rule.[31] The chamber had sought to use its corporate treasury to fund newspaper advertisements supporting a specific candidate; thus the bright line between discussion of issues and advocacy of candidates had not been compromised. As the defendants admitted, all groups had unlimited First Amendment rights to discuss issues, and BCRA should not be allowed to change that.

Perhaps the strongest attack resting on traditional First Amendment grounds came from the ACLU, which, for more than three-quarters of a century, had been a protector of the Bill of Rights in general and the First Amendment in particular.[32] The ACLU had been a party or an amicus (friend of the court) in nearly every campaign finance case since *Buckley*, and, in that case and afterward, had opposed limits on both contributions and expenditures as restrictions on speech. The ACLU's remedy for campaign finance abuse had been public financing, which it believed was the only way to do away with corruption and its appearances and still preserve freedom of expression.

In the past 30 years, the ACLU claimed, the courts had established "several fundamental principles" of First Amendment law. The government could not regulate "political speech that does not expressly advocate the election or defeat of particular candidates," nor could it prohibit "issue advocacy corporations [like the ACLU itself] that are primarily supported by individual contributions from engaging in issue advocacy." Although the government could treat coordinated campaign expenditures as contributions, it could not "treat every conversation with a legislator as a sign of coordination." Finally the government could not impose overbroad disclosure rules "that threaten the right of anonymous political speech." Each of these principles, according to the ACLU, "is violated by Title II in ways that work to the direct detriment of the ACLU."[33] Although talking primarily about the ACLU's own activities, the ACLU brief made it clear that the restrictions BCRA imposed on it would affect every public advocacy group in the country. Preventing the ACLU— or any other issue advocacy group—from making statements at any time eliminates important voices from the political process. The fact that issue advocacy may affect an election is irrelevant; its suppression, in fact, would be quite hostile to the democratic process.

The blackout periods imposed by BCRA, 60 days before a general election and 30 days before a primary, may often be periods of intense legislative activity. During an election year candidates stake out positions on a variety of issues, and elected officials, especially presidents, may use the preelection period to put forth legislative initiatives. For example, during the 2002 election cycle (when the case was submitted), legislation creating a new Department of Homeland Security was under consideration during the blackout period. The legislation to create that agency had significant civil liberties ramifications, and the ACLU had taken out full-page advertisements urging legislators and others to be aware of the impact of the legislation and to incorporate safeguards for civil liberties. Under BCRA all such advertisements would have been banned. Opponents of the BCRA argued that it threatened not only the activities of issue advocacy groups, but the rights of all Americans.

Although they differed on many matters, the ACLU and the National Rifle Association agreed that BCRA violated their First Amendment right of advocacy. NRA activities did not encompass the gamut of civil rights and liberties that concerned the ACLU; rather, they focused on the Second Amendment, which the NRA claimed protected every American's right to own firearms. Well funded and very active, the NRA has long been considered one of the most powerful interest groups in the country, able to block almost every proposal at the state and federal level to control guns. In 2000 alone, the NRA purchased more speech on television—300,000 minutes—than all other issue advocacy groups and unions combined.[34]

Although the ACLU denied that its advocacy of issues was intended to affect elections, the NRA explicitly said that its activities "educated and informed its members and the public on specific legislative threats to Second Amendment rights . . . [and] defended itself against attacks on its positions made by the media and anti-NRA politicians. . . . In almost all of this speech, the NRA refers to federal officeholders and candidates." After having said that, the NRA claimed that "none of the speech that furthered these purposes in 2000 was intended to influence a federal election."[35]

In the very next sentence, however, the NRA conceded, "To be sure, the NRA also aired approximately 30,000 minutes of speech documenting Vice President Gore's hostility to the Second Amendment. In airing this political speech the NRA sought, among other purposes, to inform the public of the grave threat that Mr. Gore's presidential candidacy posed to Americans' Second Amendment rights."[36] The differences and the similarities between the ACLU and NRA positions are clear. The ACLU concerns itself with a broad range of issues, and it is quite possible that it will criticize a senator's position on one matter and praise him or her on another. The NRA is a single-issue organization. The NRA and its political action arm have but one purpose: to elect candidates supportive of their Second Amendment views and to defeat those who disagree. Yet both claim—legitimately—that their speech is political and therefore protected. One would be naïve to think that issue advocacy is candidate-neutral, but that is neither here nor there. Speech addressing public policy issues lies at the very core of political speech and is therefore the most protected type of speech. At no time is that speech more crucial than in the run-up to the elections, when voters need to hear different viewpoints as they make up their minds on how to cast their votes.

The NRA addressed head-on the claims by supporters of BCRA that negative-issue ads "poisoned" political discourse. Senator McCain claimed that issue ads, many of which lacked approval by the candidate, were "almost always negative attack ads and do little to further beneficial debate and a healthy political dialogue. To be honest, they simply drive up an individual candidate's negative polling numbers and increase public cynicism for public service in general." According to Senator Paul Wellstone (D-Minn.), "These issue advocacy ads are a nightmare. I think all of us should hate them. . . . We could get some of this poison politics off television."[37]

The NRA compared this effort to get issue ads off radio and television to a long and sordid history of undemocratic societies attempting to control information. According to the noted First Amendment scholar Harry Kalven, Jr., the idea of seditious libel has always been "the hallmark of closed societies throughout the world. Under it criticism of government is viewed as defamation and punished as crime. The treatment of such speech as criminal is based on an accurate perception of the dangers in it; it is likely to undermine confidence in government policies and in the official incumbents. But political freedom ends when government can use its powers and its courts to silence its critics."[38] Even in an open society such as the United States, BCRA's ban on electoral speech had antecedents, notably the Sedition Act of 1798.

The NRA's comparison of Title II to seditious libel may have been something of a stretch, but its logic made perfect sense in looking at the history of criticism of government. Not until the twentieth century had the Supreme Court finally ruled that the First Amendment forbade seditious libel as a crime; government could not use its powers to silence its critics. In *New York Times v. Sullivan* (1964), the Court had unanimously noted that the 1798 Sedition Act had been condemned "in the court of history," and then in 1969 it had driven the final nails into the coffin of seditious libel.[39] The Court's reasoning, with which the NRA fully agreed, recognized that political speech constituted the lifeblood of representative democracy, and that "debate on public issues should be uninhibited, robust, and wide-open."[40] It mattered not whether this political speech appeared in paid advertisements, since the First Amendment protects persons who may not themselves have direct access to publishing facilities. Moreover, it mattered not even if some of this political speech proved erroneous as to the facts, since as the *Sullivan* Court had recognized, "Erroneous statement is inevitable in free debate, and . . . it must be protected if the freedoms of expression are to have the 'breathing space' that they need to survive."[41]

Just as the NRA opposed Title II because it would have interfered with the group's efforts to advocate a particular reading of the Second Amendment, so too did the American Federation of Labor and the Congress of Industrial Organizations (AFL-CIO) oppose it because it would have impaired the union's efforts to influence legislation and to involve the public in the debate over issues affecting workers. Historically, the AFL-CIO had pushed for its legislative agenda by supporting or opposing candidates through its PAC. But in recent years it augmented that effort by running issue advocacy ads directed toward matters of importance for union members and other workers, for example, in favor of raising the minimum wage, against the outsourcing of jobs to foreign countries, and in support of providing greater health care and pension benefits. These and other matters "are perpetually the subjects of popular debate, prospective legislation and regulation, and federal government enforcement policies." No single body other than organized labor could advocate as effectively on these issues, according to the AFL-CIO, and BCRA would, in essence, silence that voice.[42]

The plaintiffs' arguments on Title II ranged across a broad gamut, from the more abstract and classic defenses of free speech embodied in the ACLU brief, to specifics on how BCRA would adversely impact the work of issue-oriented groups such as the NRA or the political campaigning of candidates, such as McConnell. All of them, however, reiterated the notions that political speech lay at the core of a democratic society, that such speech had to be robust and uninhibited, and that limiting it not only deprived the speakers of a constitutionally guaranteed voice but also robbed the public of its opportunity to learn about the different arguments involved in important issues. Of all the attacks on BCRA, those aimed at Title II seemed the strongest, especially in light of prior Supreme Court decisions.

Title III of BCRA included several provisions that plaintiffs attacked, including rules on what broadcast media could charge candidates, prohibitions on contributions by minors, and the so-called millionaire provisions. Section 305 of BCRA amended the provision of the Communications Act that had let candidates purchase broadcast time at the lowest unit charge available to other advertisers within 45 days of a primary or 60 days of a general election.[43] Under the new law, candidates could not get this cheaper rate unless they certified, in writing, that they would not make any direct reference to another candidate for the same office—even in a different advertisement. Candidates also had to include a four-second identification or visual statement in a television ad and an identification in an audio statement for radio, in both instances saying that they approved the ad.

McConnell attacked this provision as a discriminatory viewpoint and therefore unconstitutional. The courts had consistently held that speech could only be regulated under certain conditions, and that these rules had to be totally content neutral. For example, a township could establish time, place, and method limits (i.e., campaign rallies could only take place in the town square between 12 and 2 P.M., with only two amplifying units), but there could be absolutely no regulations determined by content (i.e., only those in favor of NAFTA could speak).

Although one could argue that these particular BCRA restrictions were in fact content-neutral—they did not control the message but merely required the speaker to identify himself or herself— McConnell claimed that, combined with the provision on lower rates, this indeed constituted content discrimination. It did not appear to be a winning argument, and McConnell's claim that "the very title of section 305—'Limitation on Availability of Lowest Unit Charge for Federal Candidates Attacking Opposition'—indicates that the section is intended, and *only* intended, to suppress direct criticism of officeholders and candidates" did not really make much sense.[44]

Another provision of Title III barred minors (defined as those 17 years old or younger) from making contributions to candidates. McConnell and others claimed that this violated minors' First Amendment right of free speech as well as the Fifth Amendment right of equal protection. Plaintiffs claimed that although Congress supposedly enacted this provision to prevent parents from circumventing contribution limits, federal law already prohibited one person from making a political contribution in the name of another.[45] Moreover, this provision reached so broadly as to ban *any* contribution by *any* minor. "This bald restriction on the constitutional rights of minors cannot survive even the slightest scrutiny."[46] Similarly, the Thompson brief acknowledged that although it might be the case that some adults funneled money through their children to evade contribution limits, "to prohibit all American minors under the age of 18 from giving their money to the candidate or committee of their choice violates and silences their First Amendment Right of free speech."[47] The electoral process, according to Congressman Thompson, benefits from the involvement of minors, who thus learn about the mechanics of politics. Why should their rights be limited because of the illegal activities of a few? If in fact, as some reports indicated, a number of those who made contributions were only infants or toddlers, then the proper solution was to enforce an already existing and sufficient law against such behavior, rather than wield a bludgeon that takes away the legitimate rights of minors old enough to make intelligent choices as to what to do with their money.[48]

According to the McConnell brief, the so-called millionaire provision served only to protect incumbents. Sections 304(a) and 319 of BCRA came into effect when a candidate faced an opponent who used personal funds in Senate and House races. Under the normal contribution limits, candidates for federal office could only receive $2,000 per election from an individual (indexed for inflation). However, when a wealthy individual used his or her own funds exceeding a certain "threshold amount" that varied according to state population, then a candidate could receive up to $6,000 per election from an individual, or, if the wealthy individual spends more than a second threshold amount, up to $12,000. In reasoning that was, to put it charitably, quite muddy, the McConnell brief claimed that this provision "put in bold relief the poverty of the asserted governmental interest in preventing actual or apparent corruption." BCRA, according to McConnell, "is fundamentally seeking a different goal—to protect incumbent officeholders from competition in the marketplace of ideas, including (in this particular) wealthy challengers."[49] But what if the incumbent were the wealthy one? McConnell did not address this situation, but the brief of the Republican National Committee did.

The RNC brief pointed out that there was a logical inconsistency between imposing limits on contributions and coordinated expenditures, and then raising limits to $6,000 or even $12,000, in case one candidate used personal wealth. "If such limits are *necessary* to prevent corruption or the appearance of corruption, why are they any *less* necessary when a wealthy candidate enters the fray? And why is Jon Corzine, a multimillionaire with over $60 million to spend on his own campaign, *more* likely to be corrupted by a $12,000 contribution or by unlimited party coordinated expenditures than his opponent, a person with *no* personal wealth?"[50] The expert witness for the defendants, Thomas Mann, had conceded that the millionaire provision "simply demonstrated the fear, irrational as it may be, incumbents have of wealthy challengers." As for Senator McCain's claim that the provision would level the playing field, decisions since *Buckley* rejected that as a legitimate basis for campaign finance regulation. As Mann noted, it was doubtful that such a provision would pass constitutional muster.[51]

Finally, the plaintiffs challenged Title V of BCRA, which they claimed imposed onerous recordkeeping requirements on broadcasters.[52] Section 504 required them to collect and disclose records of all "requests" to purchase time for communications that "relate to any political matter of national importance," including but not limited to any "election to federal office" or any "national legislative issue of public importance." The plaintiffs relied on a deposition by Jack N. Goodman, president and general counsel of the National Association of Broadcasters, who testified that §504 was so "vague and ambiguous" that radio and television stations would have "serious difficulty deciding what information to collect and disclose." What if matters related to "national importance" were included in a regionally aired spot about a regional issue? The vagueness particularly worried broadcasters because violation of the provision could trigger substantial fines and burdensome inquiries from the Federal Communications Commission. In addition, the McConnell group alleged that the reporting requirements bore no "rational relationship" to any legitimate governmental objective.[53]

Three other groups also challenged Title V: the AFL-CIO and, in a joint brief, the Chamber of Commerce and the National Association of Manufacturers. The AFL-CIO also believed §504 vague and overbroad, two characteristics that, if sustained, would be enough to sink the provision on a First Amendment challenge, but added that the burden fell not just on the broadcasters but also on unions, corporations, and other groups that routinely purchase broadcast time. The union claimed that the key concept—"any political matter of national importance"—and one of its three illustrative examples, "a national legislative issue of public importance," simply defied definition "and failed to give notice as to what they cover. No person that seeks to broadcast any message, even on a matter that appears only local in scope, can know for certain whether or not its 'request' to purchase time triggers a disclosure."[54]

The U.S. Chamber of Commerce and the National Association of Manufacturers noted that they routinely ran radio and television spots dealing with matters of national interest, sometimes in their own name and sometimes in partnership with other groups. The issues ranged from problems dealing with computers in 2000 (the Y2K matter) to support of specific legislation, such as the president's tax cut proposals. Because §504 would cause confusion on the part of broadcasters and others as to how to categorize particular ads, it would interfere with corporations' rights to speak, associate, and petition the government, rights guaranteed by the First Amendment and confirmed in the *Bellotti* case.[55] Even regulated monopolies such as public utilities retained these rights.[56]

The two trade associations conceded that ever since the Tillman Act of 1907, corporations had been forbidden from using "express advocacy" of candidates. However, as Justice William Brennan had noted, "a State cannot prohibit corporations from making many other types of political expenditures."[57] In that same case the majority stressed that any regulation of corporate advocacy, even express advocacy, would be subject to strict scrutiny, since "the mere fact that the Chamber is a corporation does not remove its speech from the ambit of the First Amendment."[58]

The most interesting argument made by the two associations is that it would be impossible to distinguish between a true issue advocacy ad and one that fell under BCRA's vague definition of pertaining to a national legislative issue. It gave as an example an ad run during the 2000 campaign by the Health Benefits Coalition (to which the Chamber belonged) and Citizens for Better Medicare. Jim Matheson, a Democratic candidate for Congress in Utah, had not indicated what plan he preferred to improve Medicare coverage of drugs for seniors. He apparently supported neither a plan passed by the Republican-controlled House of Representatives nor an alternative proposed by President Clinton. The ad rejected the Clinton plan and urged voters to get Matheson to make up his mind as to what plan he would support. Senator Feingold testified that this was an electioneering ad that fell under the provisions of §504. However, Craig Holman, an expert on political advertising, testified that even though the ad included a candidate's name, it still constituted a legitimate issue ad, the type protected by *Bellotti* and *Buckley*.[59] If a regulation did not make it crystal clear just what sort of speech had to be reported, then it was vague and should be struck down as unconstitutional.

All told, the various plaintiffs contesting the BCRA presented some telling arguments, most of which followed the lines of legal reasoning laid out for the First Amendment in general and for political campaign speech in *Buckley*. The new law marked a radical departure from the bifurcated *Buckley* test, and beyond that placed some of the most restrictive regulations on political speech seen in this country since the Sedition Law of 1917. If the district court accepted their argument, it would not have to make new law; sufficient precedent existed in *Buckley* and its progeny as well as in a long line of First Amendment cases.

★ ★ ★ ★ ★

When a federal law's constitutionality is challenged in the courts, its usual defenders are the agency responsible for the law's implementation—in this case the Federal Election Commission—and the Department of Justice, the chief legal representative of the federal government in the courts. This time, several "defendant-interveners" —parties who claimed an interest in the case that gave them standing in the eyes of the court—joined the FEC as defendants, and Senators McCain and Feingold, and the other sponsors had the pro bono legal services of one of the top law firms in Washington: Wilmer, Cutler and Pickering.

The three legal teams appear to have worked fairly well together. For the merits briefing before both the district court and the Supreme Court, the two government agencies wrote one brief and the law firm another. These were then integrated at the order of the three-judge panel, although the divisions were fairly obvious. First would come a section written by the Department of Justice and the FEC, followed by a section on the same provision by the interveners. On matters of deposition and witnesses, the teams worked together, and according to Randolph Moss of Wilmer, Cutler, "we had a superb working relationship with the government lawyers."[60]

The defendants had the harder task, since defending BCRA ran counter to a lengthy trail of Supreme Court precedent, and the new law's limitations on political speech could not be blinked away. For the defense to win, it first had to convince the court that *Buckley* was not as restrictive as people had believed for more than two decades. Second, it had to make a convincing case that the need to do away with corruption and the appearance of corruption in the political process constituted the compelling governmental interest that the First Amendment required in order for the government to restrict speech; and that the methods chosen were not overbroad and vague, but narrowly tailored to meet the needs in the least restrictive manner. It was a formidable challenge.

The defendant-interveners, however, had three assets on their side. One lay in an unwritten rule of construction—namely, that courts will give the benefit of the doubt to Congress and assume that it has passed a constitutional law until proven otherwise. This presumption, however, would collapse if the challengers could convince the court that BCRA did, indeed, violate the First Amendment. The second asset could be found in the fact that plaintiffs had launched a full-scale attack on the law before it could be implemented. This so-called facial challenge implied that the law could never be applied in a valid manner, a difficult task since no factual record existed on which to base this claim. The court would have to be persuaded that under any and all circumstances the law, as written, was substantially overbroad.

The third asset consisted of millions of dollars of research funded by the Pew Charitable Trusts. Under the direction of program officer Sean Traglia, the trust underwrote a number of scholarly studies to reinforce the argument that the integrity of the system stood in such great danger that only restrictions on soft money, attack ads, and other provisions in BCRA could prevent its imminent collapse from the corrupting influence of money.[61] Political scientists at the University of Wisconsin, for example, researched campaign television advertising and how McCain-Feingold would purportedly correct its abuses. Pew had Norman Ornstein, one of the drafters of BCRA, write a column for its "PewWire" explaining the merits of the bill. It funded a number of "Buying Time" studies to pinpoint the relationship between soft money and issue ads. Pew funded other studies in cooperation with the Center for Public Integrity, the Center for Responsive Politics, Brigham Young University, the Alliance for Better Campaigns, and Colby College. It also established a new entity,

the Campaign Finance Institute, which, according to its announcement, is "a nonpartisan institute that conducts objective research
and education, convenes leading practitioners and experts in the field,
and provides resources to the media."[62] According to one scholar,
"Pew spent literally tens of millions of dollars to create scholarship
and publicity designed to influence the litigation's outcome. Virtually
every election law scholar and political scientist studying campaign
reform [was] on the payroll as [an] expert for one or the other side or
had been funded by Pew. NYU's Brennan Center led much of the
campaign—the entire effort was orchestrated much like the NAACP
orchestrated litigation but using very different tactics."[63] In addition
to the Brennan Center, Pew funded studies and activities by other
groups such as the American Enterprise Institute, the Brookings
Institution, and the League of Women Voters Education Fund.

The law's supporters recognized that they could never win on
First Amendment grounds unless they could create a factual record
so overwhelming that the courts would have to recognize and accept
the claim that the situation had become so bad that only radical sur-
gery—BCRA—could fix things, and that in order to do so, the courts
would have to expand the limitations on the freedom of speech, as
they had been limned in *Buckley*. Although some might argue that
Pew and the scholars it hired engaged in an activity at odds with the
objectivity supposedly associated with academic research, in fact
there had long been a split in the academic community over the
desirability of campaign finance reform and its potential effective-
ness. Pew did not have to bribe scholars to change their minds; it
merely went to scholars whose views were already known, and
offered them a chance to apply their theories and knowledge in a
practical way. Similarly, McConnell and his supporters also had a
long list of academics upon which they could draw. The factual
record submitted to the court ran into thousands of pages, and
included literally dozens of studies by academics on both sides. No
one, however, put more resources and effort into building a case than
did the Pew Charitable Trusts in defense of McCain-Feingold.

The brief by the government and defendant-interveners tracked
that of the plaintiffs, maintaining, of course, that Titles I, II, III, and
V met the test of constitutionality. Whereas the plaintiffs claimed
that *Buckley v. Valeo* prevented Congress from imposing the regulations it enacted in BCRA, the defenders of the act argued that

Buckley had never been intended to be read so narrowly, and that the new law's provisions easily meshed with the rules enunciated in that case. They began their defense of BCRA by limning the factual situation that led to its passage. The brief detailed the rise of soft money and how the two parties took advantage of the FECA's loopholes to raise millions of dollars they could spend outside FECA limits. The biggest of these loopholes, they maintained, "involves so-called issue advocacy, in which communications, paid for in whole or part with soft money, attack a candidate by name while claiming to be an issue discussion outside the reach of federal law."[64] In a section entitled "Repairing the System," the brief detailed how Congress had responded to specific campaign finance abuses found in numerous investigations, including most recently that of the Thompson committee.[65] Contrary to plaintiff allegations that Congress had used a meat cleaver rather than a scalpel to deal with the problems, the defendants showed how Congress fine-tuned different sections. For example, in sections dealing with political communications (Title II), Senators Olympia Snowe (R-Me.) and James Jeffords (Ind-Vt.) had proposed an amendment to the original bill to draw a bright line between genuine issue advocacy and a clearly defined category of radio and television advertisements. According to Senator Snowe, they had consulted with constitutional experts to develop a "clear and narrow wording," thus tailoring the bill to meet First Amendment requirements.[66] In all parts of the brief, the defendants not only submitted the usual legal arguments but also tried to make the court understand the real-world context they claimed lay behind BCRA—the rampant corruption or its appearance that bedeviled U.S. politics.

The soft money ban in Title I, they argued, met the test of constitutionality because Congress had broad authority to ensure that federal restrictions on the sources and amounts of campaign contributions would not be evaded. Conceding that much soft money was raised under the aegis of state law, they argued that this really made no difference, since a long line of Supreme Court cases had held that Congress, in regulating areas clearly under its control, could impinge on areas of state sovereignty in order for federal policy to be carried out.[67] BCRA, the government maintained, had been closely drawn for a single and specific purpose: to prevent the appearance and the reality of corruption in federal elections.[68] Beyond that, Title I regulated contributions, which under *Buckley* fell within the powers of Congress and did not violate the Freedom of Speech Clause of the First Amendment. If Congress could ban hard money donations, as the Court held it could in *Buckley* and *Shrink Missouri,* "it follows that Congress has the power to restrict or ban contributions of soft money to national political parties. The rationale is similar in both cases: the restriction or prohibition would serve to prevent FECA's limits on individual contributions to candidates from being circumvented, without at the same time unduly impairing the ability of donors to speak or associate freely, or the ability of parties to accumulate funds through permissible contributions."[69]

The importance of the soft money issue both to the government and to the intervening members of Congress cannot be overstated. In the debates over McCain-Feingold and in the legal maneuverings leading up to the court case, both sides indicated how critical this issue would be. For Senator McCain and others, soft money had been the great villain of the campaign finance scandals of the 1990s, and unless Congress could ban soft money, there could in fact be no real reform of the system. The government attorneys wanted the court to understand that soft money constituted a real evil in the political system, and they spent 15 pages of their brief detailing the origins of and problems associated with soft money.[70]

The interveners presented evidence of how corrupting soft money could be and how constituents believed that it had disenfranchised all but the big givers. The brief quoted Congressman Martin Meehan (D-Mass.), who said that his constituents "think the system in which I work is a system tainted by unlimited amounts of money contributed by special interests in the political process. They believe that the whole system is tainted." Former Senator David Boren, now the president of the University of Oklahoma, noted in his deposition that he told all of his political science classes that by 1994 trust in government among Americans had dropped to 19 percent, and 57 percent were dissatisfied with the political parties. When he asked why, the students responded "almost unanimously" that "our government has been 'purchased' by special interests. They believe that their elected representatives . . . pander to large donors."[71]

In general, the government tried to make the case that the ban on soft money constitutionally differed not at all from the limitations on hard money contributions upheld in *Buckley;* that it had been narrowly drawn so as to avoid First Amendment problems; and that the severity of the problem—corruption or its appearance in campaign financing—constituted the compelling governmental interest that the Court required whenever Congress or a state government attempted to legislate in the area of the First Amendment. The defendants, especially the interveners, did not believe this fear of corruption to be illusory, and in their brief they claimed that "the press documents the appearance of corruption on a daily basis." Congress had failed to act on prescription drug benefits, had defeated antismoking legislation, and had given big corporations massive tax breaks; whatever virtues these decisions may have had, all appeared to be the payoff for corporate soft money donations to key legislators.[72] If the government could get the court to agree to its basic premises—that corruption and its appearance were rampant and that the ban on soft money differed little from restrictions on hard money—then it might be able to get past the First Amendment problem.

In regard to Title II, where the plaintiffs concentrated on the provisions limiting electioneering advertisements in periods prior to elections, the defendants tried to downplay those and instead focus on what they claimed to be the underlying rationale—the effort to counteract corruption and its appearance. So the first argument they made involved the provision that corporations and labor unions finance electioneering communications by using segregated funds, and three of their four subheads related not to constitutional points, but to the argument that BCRA would prevent corruption. They maintained that the use of money by unions and corporations "distorted and influenced the electoral process," that companies and unions had "recently engaged in systematic evasion of FECA's restrictions," and that spending could be used to "create political debts."[73] Their fourth argument did relate to constitutional provisions, and essentially said that the BCRA electioneering provision had been narrowly tailored, met the *Buckley* requirements, and did not violate either equal protection or First Amendment strictures. The effort to control corruption, they argued, constituted a compelling governmental interest that the Supreme Court had recognized in prior decisions, and BCRA fully conformed to the rules on campaign speech laid down in the Court's earlier decisions.[74]

As for issue ads, the government conceded that some of BCRA's provisions might appear broad, but they did not go so far as to constitute overbroadness or vagueness. The law did in fact place incidental regulatory burdens on "a tiny percentage of genuine issue advocacy that might be broadcast in proximity to federal elections." But that resulted from a legitimate legislative decision based on extensive investigation into the evils of so-called issue ads. This judgment, which "Congress came to only after many *years* of deliberation" deserved the "considerable deference" that the courts had many times said the judicial branch owed to the legislature. This was all the more true when, as in the case of BCRA, Congress, "a coequal branch of government whose members take the same oath [judges] do to uphold the Constitution . . . specifically considered the question of [BCRA's] constitutionality."[75]

Whereas the government lawyers for the most part stuck to fairly formal arguments, the interveners concentrated on the history of campaign finance reform and the evils that BCRA redressed. Their brief quoted Justice Oliver Wendell Holmes, Jr.: "A page of history is worth a volume of logic."[76] The interveners' "page of history" detailed what had happened after *Buckley* and how political parties and special interests had perverted that decision. "*Buckley* never intended, and cannot reasonably be read, to establish 'express advocacy' (let alone 'magic words') as an inflexible constitutional constraint on Congress' ability to fashion workable campaign finance regulation." Congress and the courts had jumped on those phrases and fashioned statutory interpretations that allowed candidates, parties, and committees to run amok, and thereby ignore the spirit of *Buckley* and exploit the loopholes in the statutes that had been enacted supposedly to codify the *Buckley* rules.[77]

The brief then examined how Congress had investigated the issue of sham advocacy ads and the manner in which the sponsors of these ads managed to evade FECA rules and even to hide who actually paid for them. In page after page the interveners listed issue advocacy ads that managed to say, "Vote for X," without actually using the magic words, and showed how ads could present a negative impression of a candidate without actually saying, "Vote against Y."[78] In response to the briefs of the NRA and the AFL-CIO that alleged a loss of First Amendment rights, the interveners' brief detailed how both of them had exploited the loopholes in FECA to run sham issue ads.[79] The interveners tellingly quoted Tanya Metaska, the executive director of the NRA's Institute for Legislative Action:

Today there is erected a legal regulatory wall between issue advocacy and political advocacy. And the wall is built of the same sturdy material as the emperor's clothing. Everyone sees it. No one believes it. It is foolish to believe there is any practical difference between issue advocacy and advocacy of a political candidate. What separates issue advocacy and political advocacy is a line in the sand drawn on a windy day. We engaged in issue advocacy in many locations around the country. Take Bloomington, Indiana, for example. Billboards in that city read:

"Congressman Hostettler is right. Gun laws don't take criminals off Bloomington's streets. Call 334-1111 and thank him for fighting crime by getting tough on criminals."

Guess what? We really hoped people would vote for the Congressman, not just thank him. And people did. When we're three months away from an election, there's not a dime's worth of difference between "thanking" elected officials and "electing" them.

In all parts of their briefs, the government and especially the intervener-defendants kept hammering on the alleged corruption of the system, piling up one horrible example after another, in the hope that the court would agree and would acknowledge the compelling interest necessary to justify restricting speech.

In a similar manner, the defendants pointed to the issues that had led Congress to enact Title III—in particular, the so-called millionaire provision and restrictions on donations by minors. The government claimed that the millionaire provision had been closely drawn, and, rather than restricting free speech, actually enhanced it. The content-neutral provisions "neither impose uneven burdens among candidates nor 'abridge, restrict, or censor speech, but rather facilitate and enlarge public discussion and participation in the electoral process.'"[80] The provisions would do this by leveling the playing field, and allowing poorer candidates, when confronted by a very rich, self-financing opponent, to secure sufficient funds to make their voices heard. Moreover, rich candidates could accept the limits imposed under the law, nullifying the provisions as they applied to their particular federal races. The provisions placed no limit on how much money a rich candidate could raise from others; they merely said that, if he or she dug into his or her own deep pockets, then the law would help to make sure that both voices would be heard.

The ban on contributions by children also met constitutional standards. It had been narrowly drawn to meet a real problem as perceived by Congress: the use of minors as a conduit of campaign contributions to evade FECA requirements. As in the earlier sections of their brief, the government lawyers focused more on legal issues, whereas the interveners drew attention to examples of what Congress had deemed corruption when it passed these provisions. In addition, both the government and the interveners raised questions about whether certain of the plaintiffs attacking just these provisions had standing to do so.[81]

With regard to Title V, the government made a fairly short and simple argument. The type of reporting that the act required of radio and television stations was not much different, nor more onerous, than the types of material that they had been required to keep for years under the basic Communications Act. As for the provision ensuring the lowest available rates to those who obeyed the law, this also did not depart from earlier FCC practices. In addition, the government argued that none of the plaintiffs had standing to challenge these provisions, since none of them could show that they would in fact be harmed by them. Only Senator McConnell claimed a potential harm, and since he would not be running for reelection for several years, that made the harm too attenuated to warrant standing.[82]

The government defendants and their intervener allies had based their case on assumptions that *Buckley* had been misinterpreted and that its provisions had never been intended as a blanket prohibition against any and all regulation of campaign finance by the Congress. *Buckley* and other First Amendment cases merely required that the government present a compelling interest as to why speech should be regulated and then show that the legislation had been narrowly drawn so that it corrected that evil without being either overbroad or vague. This, the government claimed, had been done.

★ ★ ★ ★ ★

The procedure in court allowed each group, after presenting its main case, to file a response brief to that of the other side, after which the court would hear oral arguments and then reach its decision. For the most part, the reply briefs, although shorter than the initial arguments, followed the same general scheme; only this time each side tried to rebut or shred the arguments of the other. The plaintiffs hammered at the theme that nothing presented by the defendants negated their claim that important sections of BCRA violated the First Amendment and other sections of the Constitution. The main points can be found in the introduction, in which the plaintiffs claimed that the "metes and bounds that govern this Court's consideration of BCRA could hardly be clearer. . . . Congress cannot limit robust and uninhibited debate about public figures and public issues —most particularly during election campaigns—under the guise of enacting campaign finance 'reform.'"[83] Moreover, they charged that, contrary to the defense's assertion that BCRA just refined the older FECA, in fact the new statute, by its sponsors' own admission, constituted a "landmark" law, because "real and meaningful campaign finance reform" could not be achieved under the older powers vested in the FEC.[84]

The Republican National Committee acknowledged that "Congress may legislate to prevent corruption or its appearance in federal elections, but not so far as to trample the federal system of dual sovereignty." The defendants, it declared, "have a fundamentally different view of federal campaign finance regulation: it is the paramount good, the overriding interest, the goal to which all constitutional values must yield." But, the RNC went on, the defense had it backward. The aim of closing "loopholes" (a word used 70 times in the defense brief) or avoiding "circumventions" (109 times) or "evasions" (128 times) of existing laws, although commendable, nonetheless turned the constitutional order on its head. The primary consideration ought to be the fact that the Constitution and the Bill of Rights do "not allow the *exception* of federal campaign finance regulation to swallow the *rule* of constitutional governance."[85] Like the other plaintiffs, the RNC reply dismissed the extensive factual allegations of corruption and its appearance as unconvincing, and insisted on a strict observance of constitutional—especially First Amendment—guarantees. In short, for all the stories the defendants told about supposed corruption, they had failed to prove the one thing needed to justify restrictions on political speech: a situation so bad that correcting it constituted a compelling governmental interest. Moreover, the means chosen failed the second part of the test, a law narrowly drawn to solve the problem without affecting other speech. Title I, according to the RNC, ought to be seen as a meat cleaver; the First Amendment required a scalpel.

As in their main brief, the plaintiffs kept referring to *Buckley*, downplaying the factual materials submitted by the defense, and emphasizing that the Constitution could not be sacrificed for allegations that did not add up to a convincing portrait of actual corruption or even its appearance. As the ACLU put it, the defense, by focusing so much on stories of alleged corruption, had "lost sight of the forest for the trees." The Supreme Court had established rules that forbade limits on expenditures, with the sole exception of corporate and union treasury funds going directly to candidates. To try to do what BCRA intended—place severe and unjustified limits on political speech—required the Court to utilize a strict scrutiny rule, which BCRA clearly failed.[86]

The defendants, as in their main brief, emphasized that corruption and its appearance existed and posed a severe threat to the integrity of the political system, and therefore constituted the compelling governmental interest necessary to meet the strict scrutiny standard of the First Amendment. In addition, despite characterizations of BCRA as a meat cleaver, in fact Congress had drawn it very narrowly. Although conceding that *Buckley* and its progeny remained guiding law, the defendants claimed that the cases should be interpreted liberally, that the Supreme Court could not have intended to handcuff Congress permanently or limit it to regulation of the "magic words." According to the plaintiffs' reading of *Buckley*, the defendants charged, "the First Amendment affords Congress no flexibility to prevent the distortion and corruption, despite a substantial factual record—both legislative and legal—demonstrating the need for such regulation, and despite controlling precedent that clearly establishes Congress's authority to legislate in the face of such compelling interests."[87] The court, according to the interveners' brief, "need not venture beyond established constitutional jurisprudence," because existing case law "amply supports" congressional power to limit soft money, sham issue ads, and other abuses.[88]

In their introductory section, the interveners claimed that after two rounds of briefing, the positions of the parties posed a stark contrast:

> If plaintiffs are right, then the Constitution condemns the Nation to endure a campaign finance system that is rife with influence-peddling, ridden with loopholes that mock existing law, encourages evasion on a massive scale, and causes over seventy percent of the American people to believe their government is corrupt. The First Amendment renders Congress impotent to solve these problems, say the plaintiffs, even if an unanswered "perception of impropriety . . . jeopardized the willingness of voters to take part in democratic governance."
>
> If defendants are right, then Congress has the power to protect the integrity of federal elections and federal officeholders from the insidious assaults of actual and apparent corruption, to reinvigorate longstanding bans on the use of corporate and union money in connection with federal elections, to close loopholes in longstanding (now increased) contribution limits and in the presidential public financing system, and to restore respect for the law by abandoning unworkable and easily evaded distinctions that have had some currency in the life of the law but have had no viability in the real world life of American politics.[89]

Ignoring the hyperbole, the contrast is in fact quite clear. For those attacking McCain-Feingold, the allegations of corruption rested primarily on anecdotal evidence, and did not prove the system corrupt. If some misconduct existed, there was very little of it, and certainly not enough to launch a broad-scale attack on the First Amendment, which protected free speech—especially political speech—and constituted part of the democratic bedrock. For those defending BCRA, the abstractions of free speech, although important, could not be allowed to hinder a desperately real problem, one so dangerous to democratic politics that it justified the relatively mild and straight-forward measures aimed specifically at that misconduct.

The briefings, of course, did not boil down to theory on one side and fact on the other. Both sides appealed to jurisprudence and to life, but Senator McConnell and his allies believed that the greatest ill lay not in allowing alleged corruption to continue, but in undermining the protection given by the Constitution to free speech in the political marketplace. Senator McCain, the other interveners, and the government believed that if one did not clear up what they considered real abuses, real corruption, then there would be no meaningful political marketplace left.

★ ★ ★ ★ ★

One aim shared by both sides involved the building of a factual record that would be the basis for an appeal. The rules of civil procedure normally do not allow a party to either introduce new factual material or raise new legal issues on appeal that have not been part of the record of the original trial. Whatever else they may have accomplished, the opponents and the defenders of McCain-Feingold had built an appeal. The various parties had submitted briefs totaling 1,676 pages by the court-ordered deadline of November 25, 2002. On the following day the two sides submitted 576 recommended findings of fact, statements of the issues that they hoped the court would accept as part of the decision. In addition, the court received 41 boxes of evidentiary material as well as 13 thick binder notebooks that contained the testimony and depositions of more than 200 expert witnesses, all adding up to more than 100,000 pages of materials. Floyd Abrams, one of the attorneys for the McConnell group, described the record developed for the case as "elephantine," and in its decision, the court noted, "We agree."[90] The three judges had little more than a week to try to peruse this enormous written record before hearing the case on December 4, 2002.

7 / Interlude: Confusion in the District Court

SOMETIMES a lower court opinion is so well crafted that even if the Supreme Court were to overturn it, the issues would have been clarified, the constitutional questions made evident, and the central questions for the High Court to decide made manifest. There is little positive to be said, however, about the 774-page district court opinion in *McConnell v. Federal Election Commission*.[1] Even recognizing the many complex issues involved in the case, the opinion is so incomprehensible that the three judges had to insert a chart and table of contents to show where each of them stood on particular issues.[2] All the litigants agreed, however, that the decision and the resulting orders were so unhelpful and confusing that a stay should be sought so that the orders would not go into effect until the Supreme Court had heard the case.[3]

★   ★   ★   ★   ★

The three-judge panel that heard *McConnell* consisted of Karen LeCraft Henderson, Richard J. Leon, and Colleen Kollar-Kotelly. Henderson, after earning her law degree at the University of North Carolina, had served for 10 years in the office of the South Carolina attorney general before entering private practice in that state. In 1986 President Reagan named her to the federal district court for South Carolina, and President George H. W. Bush elevated her to the influential Circuit Court for the District of Columbia in 1990. Richard Leon, a graduate of Suffolk Law School in Boston, had served in several governmental agencies and as a senior trial attorney in the criminal section of the Justice Department's Tax Division. He had taught for a while at St. John's Law School, and in 1989 he entered private practice in Washington, D.C. President George W. Bush named him to the District Court for the District of Columbia in 2002, and while on the bench Leon also taught as an adjunct professor at Georgetown. After both her undergraduate and legal education at the Catholic University of America, Colleen Kollar-Kotelly had been an attorney in the Justice Department's Criminal Division, and then became chief counsel to Saint Elizabeth Hospital. President William J. Clinton named her to the District Court for the District of Columbia in 1997. In May 2002 Chief Justice William Rehnquist appointed her to serve as presiding judge of the newly created U.S. Foreign Intelligence Court.

As a member of the Circuit Court of Appeals for the District of Columbia, Judge Henderson presided over the panel. Although she, Leon, and Kollar-Kotelly had seemed to agree on the procedural issues eight months before the trial, the three would be far from collegial in the five months between the time they heard arguments and the day they handed down the decision on May 1, 2003. Their disagreements boiled over into angry and quarrelsome footnotes in the opinion, but that future wrangling had not yet appeared when batteries of the nation's top lawyers showed up in the federal courthouse on Constitution Avenue on Wednesday, December 4, and Thursday, December 5. Some 24 attorneys spoke for six hours the first day and an additional three hours on the second.

Kenneth W. Starr, a former solicitor general and the special prosecutor in the Whitewater investigation of President and Hillary Clinton, led off the attack on BCRA.[4] He urged the court to declare the law unconstitutional. "In addition to federalism and freedom of speech [issues]," Starr declared with references back to the Constitutional Convention of 1787, "it had the practical effect of anoint[ing] winners and declar[ing] losers." Republican National Committee attorney Bobby Burchfield told the panel that the RNC had already laid off 25 percent of its staff less than one month after the BCRA ban on soft money went into effect, and that the layoffs would undoubtedly increase. BCRA, he claimed, unconstitutionally cripples the national parties' abilities to participate in state and local politics. He dismissed out of hand the concern about apparent corruption, calling it "exaggerated," and said any wrongdoing could easily be handled simply by restricting federal officeholders from soliciting unlimited funds. Deborah Kaplan, representing the California Democratic Party, said her party would have to forego 50 to 75 percent of the funding it normally used for electoral activities where federal candidates appeared on the ballot, even though the state party's work focused solely on state and local—not federal—candidates.

Lawyers for McConnell and his allies kept hammering at the theme that BCRA abridged First Amendment guarantees of free speech. Running television or radio ads about important issues or campaigns constituted an important form of political speech that had to be protected. Moreover, the new law divorced national parties from their state and local affiliates because state groups remained free to collect and spend soft money. A bill supposedly designed to limit special interest influence, they charged, actually increased it, because such groups would not be bound by the same restrictions that applied to the national parties.

Both sides played video tapes of so-called attack ads of the type forbidden under the law. Floyd Abrams, a longtime defender of civil liberties in general and the First Amendment in particular, acknowledged the negative tone of many ads run by interest groups, but pointed out that the First Amendment clearly prohibits regulation of speech based on content. "Attack ads," he told the court, "are deeply protected by the First Amendment."

BCRA's defenders tracked the arguments they had made in the briefs about the dangers of corruption in the political system. Roger Witten of the Wilmer, Cutler firm, appearing for the intervening senators and House members, told the court that "this law is designed to repair a thoroughly broken campaign finance system that has been brought to its knees by massive cheating." He pointed to the depositions in the record by former Democratic and Republican party chairs as well as by longtime members of Congress, all testifying about the problems of the system prior to BCRA. "They're all telling this court that money corrupts," he said, "that unions, corporations, and wealthy individuals . . . pay to play." In a newly disclosed example, Witten cited a memorandum from the Pharmaceutical Research and Manufacturers Association discussing a meeting with BCRA's leading foe, Senator McConnell. The memo indicated that the group wanted to explain its position on drug price controls, and noted that it had recently given $200,000 to Republican Party committees.

Although the defenders of BCRA emphasized the problems they saw in the political system, they did not neglect the constitutional issues. The facts had been organized to prove one thing: that corruption and its appearance had become so endemic in U.S. politics that cleaning it up constituted the compelling governmental interest required to limit speech. Measures included in BCRA, former solicitor general Seth Waxman told the court, had one purpose: to limit the disproportionate influence of money in the political process. These measures, he declared, are needed "to safeguard the integrity of the political process."

Throughout the hearings the three judges paid close attention and interrupted often with sometimes sharp questions. There seemed to be little common ground between the two sides, leading Judge Henderson to compare them to "ships passing in the night." It appeared that the judges would not be able to forge any opinion that would be acceptable to both sides. In fact, they would have trouble writing any opinion at all.

*   *   *   *   *

Both proponents and opponents of BCRA hoped that the district court would hand down its opinion before the end of January, which would have given the Supreme Court time to hear and decide the appeal before its term ended in June. In fact, during the trial Judge Henderson asked Kenneth Starr when he thought a decision would be needed so that it could go to the High Court in its current term. He responded late January or early February, and she indicated it could be even sooner than that. By the time the panel released the opinion in May, given the time needed to file for certiorari, prepare briefs and responses, hear arguments, reach a decision, and then write an opinion (and potential dissents), it was clear that the Supreme Court would be unable to take the case before the justices went on their summer hiatus at the beginning of July.

The three judges could agree on little, not even on a single majority opinion. Instead, they issued four opinions—a per curiam opinion and separate opinions from each judge. For decisional purposes, only the per curiam (a memorandum opinion summarizing the findings on which two or more of the judges agreed) matters, but since the three agreed on so little, they could not provide a coherent jurisprudential rationale for the Supreme Court to utilize. Moreover, Judge Henderson refused to sign the per curiam even on those points with which she agreed. The first paragraph of section IA, dealing with part of Title I, provides a sense of the internal dissension on the bench:

Section 323(a) of BCRA bans national parties from soliciting, receiving, directing, transferring, and spending nonfederal funds (i.e., soft money). Judge Henderson strikes this section down as unconstitutional in its entirety. Judge Leon, for different reasons, files a concurrence, joining with Judge Henderson, except with respect to the ban on national parties from using (i.e., "directing," "transferring," and "spending") nonfederal funds (i.e., soft money) for "federal election activity" of the type defined in Section 301(20)(A)(iii). As to that type of conduct, Judge Leon upholds the constitutionality of Congress's ban on the use of nonfederal funds by national parties for Section 301(20)(A)(iii) communications. Judge Kollar-Kotelly upholds Section 323(a) in its entirety. Accordingly, Judge Leon's decision regarding Section 323(a) controls.[5]

In addition to the 83-page per curiam opinion, Judge Henderson submitted a 166-page opinion, Judge Kollar-Kotelly wrote for 324 pages, and Judge Leon added an additional 191 pages. Each judge found it necessary to include a table of contents as a guide to his or her opinion, but because they agreed on so little, even a careful reader will be unable to find commonality on basic issues. Judge Henderson found BCRA "unconstitutional in virtually all of its particulars; it breaks faith with the fundamental principle—understood by our nation's Founding Generation, inscribed in the First Amendment and repeatedly reaffirmed by the United States Supreme Court—that 'debate on public issues should be uninhibited, robust, and wide-open.'"[6] Judge Kollar-Kotelly, on the other hand, after detailing the history of congressional efforts to keep the political process free of corruption, argued that this "thoughtful and careful effort . . . deserves respect." Claiming that her constitutional approach "is rooted in the record of this case and guided by the constitutional boundaries established by the Supreme Court's campaign finance jurisprudence . . . I have only found three of the challenged sections unconstitutional."[7] Like the defenders of the law, Judge Kollar-Kotelly relied heavily on a factual record showing corruption or its appearance, and, far more than Judge Henderson, she indicated her willingness to defer to Congress.[8] Judge Leon also deferred to Congress, but to a far lesser extent than Kollar-Kotelly. Where the government could show that it had a legitimate reason for a rule, and that that rule did not violate First Amendment principles, he would uphold the BCRA.[9]

Judge Leon had the swing vote on almost every issue, and although he frequently joined Judge Henderson in the result, he often differed with her reasoning. Thus he rejected her view that soft money regulation must be subject to strict scrutiny, and agreed with Kollar-Kotelly that such restrictions need be only "closely drawn" to pass constitutional muster, a standard of review less rigorous than strict scrutiny. But, like Henderson, he found that most of BCRA's soft money provisions failed to meet even this lower standard. According to one commentator, Judge Leon took "an unusually creative approach to the judicial role." He "literally rewrote" two key sections of the law in order to make them conform to his constitutional analysis. Congress had provided for a complete ban on national party soft money, and in a more limited way, required state and local parties to use only hard money to pay for specific activities. Leon, and along with him the court, held the complete ban on soft money overbroad, and then in narrowing the allowable uses of the soft money by local parties, upheld that portion of the soft money ban. When it came to the provision on electioneering communication, he struck down the primary definition, then rewrote in effect the backup definition and upheld it.[10] The two main themes of Leon's opinion, and thus of the court, are (1) that Congress has broad authority to regulate the funding of communications by both party and nonparty participants that refer to federal candidates, but that (2) otherwise Congress may not restrict party finances.

Not only did the district court divide deeply in its analysis, but it had a great deal of trouble even agreeing on findings of facts. Each of the three judges made different factual findings. Altogether the three sets of factual findings add up to 320 pages, and although some findings were common to at least two of the judges, very rarely did all three agree. As a result the Supreme Court would derive little if any benefit from the lower court's findings; it would, for all practical purposes, have to review the record from scratch. Even in their opinions, according to one critic, their work "is distressingly sloppy."[11]

In terms of Title I, the section dealing with soft money, Judge

Henderson found all of its provisions to be unconstitutional, except for the section barring federal candidates from soliciting or transferring nonfederal funds for use in any local, state, or federal election. Because Judge Kollar-Kotelly found all of the Title I provisions constitutional, the swing vote belonged to Judge Richard Leon. He joined Kollar-Kotelly in upholding some of the provisions regulating soft money, but joined Henderson in striking down several others. The court dealt with six provisions of Title I, invalidating some in toto, upholding another, and finding others partially void and/or partially valid.

With regard to national party soft money, the court for the most part invalidated BCRA §323(a). Under Judge Leon's interpretation, this became a ban on national parties' use of soft money only on expenditures for public communications that either favored or attacked a clearly identified candidate. Leon and Kollar-Kotelly agreed that the criterion for donations of soft money should be whether the provision is "closely drawn" to prevent corruption or its appearance.[12] However, Leon also ruled that national party communications fell into the restricted category even if they managed to avoid the "magic words" listed in *Buckley*. Therefore, contributions to national parties that help to fund these communications raise precisely the specter of corruption and its appearance that the Supreme Court had indicated could justify restrictions. But the provision that national parties fund all of their communications with hard money went too far, since activities such as national party support for state and local candidates in off-year elections did not relate to federal activity.

Leon, and thus the court, took a similar approach to state and local party use of soft money under §323(b). Communications that directly promote or attack a federal candidate, even if they avoid the magic words, have a direct effect on federal elections, and thus can be banned. However, he ruled unconstitutional the requirement that state and local parties use only hard money to pay for other federal election activities, such as voter registration campaigns within four months of an election, voter mobilization, or generic party activities just because a federal candidate is on the ballot. He conceded that although some of these activities would bear on federal elections, and that the FEC could regulate some local behavior that affected federal elections, the bulk of the direct benefit goes to state and local candidates, and only indirectly to federal candidates. As a result, Congress cannot limit the use of soft money in this area. Judge Henderson would have banned this provision in its entirety, since she could find no evidence that it created any danger of corruption, while Judge Kollar-Kotelly believed sufficient evidence of corruption existed to uphold the entire provision.[13] Thus Judge Leon's differentiation as to how the money would be used, and his perception of whether it would or would not create an appearance of corruption, determined the outcome.

In a third section, §323(c), dealing with party fund-raising, it is unclear just what the court decided. Judge Henderson believed that since this section related so closely to provisions limiting state and local party federal election activities, it should be considered along with that provision.[14] Kollar-Kotelly noted that since the section had not been challenged by any plaintiff, the court need not deal with it. Leon's opinion does not mention it, and neither does the per curiam opinion. As a result, with one negative vote and two silences, one might be tempted to conclude that the restriction survived. However, with Judge Henderson finding so many parts of the related provisions unconstitutional, it might not have. The section is not listed in the per curiam chart, and thus winds up in a sort of judicial limbo.

With regard to the provision regulating party solicitation for and donations to tax-exempt groups, §323(d), Judges Henderson and Leon voted over Kollar-Kotelly's objection to invalidate this section. Both judges believed the statutory language overly broad, especially the part denying *all* transfers to tax-exempts, whether the funds would be used for federal election purposes or not.[15]

In a rare unanimous vote, all three judges found the ban on raising soft money by federal candidates or officeholders for use in connection with any federal, state, or local election (§323(e)) to be constitutional. This provision turns out to be the only part of BCRA that all three judges thought met constitutional requirements. However, both Henderson and Leon found different parts of the provision unconstitutional, and so one could not tell what status—legitimate or void—the provisions enjoyed as a result. Leon disapproved of the ban on candidates or officeholders soliciting funds for party use, while Henderson voted to invalidate a section that read raising funds "for any federal election activity," since she had already voted to invalidate the BCRA definitions of federal activity as too broad. Otherwise, this is the only section of the act that Henderson found legitimate.

Finally, Kollar-Kotelly and Leon voted to sustain §323(f), requiring that when state candidates spent money on electioneering communications that clearly identified federal candidates, they had to use hard money. Henderson would have thrown the provision out as inseverable from the rest of the ban on soft money, which she believed unconstitutional.

All told, the court, with regard to the soft-money provisions of Title I, awarded better than half a loaf to supporters of McCain-Feingold. Although striking down several provisions, the court did uphold the bans on fund-raising by federal candidates and office-holders and on the use of soft money by parties for candidate advocacy, which many saw as the key provisions of the attack on soft money. Candidate advocacy constituted the chief use of party soft money. On the other hand, opponents of reform also got some things. The court allowed the continued use of soft money for voter registration, party activities, and voter mobilization. Although reformers attacked issue ads as the most blatant and largest use of soft money, it actually accounted for less than half of all soft-money expenditures. As a result, the decision allowed the flow of soft money into parties—for specific party usages—to continue unabated.[16]

The Title II provisions dealt primarily with regulation of electioneering communications, so-called issue advocacy advertisements. Because Congress had worried that in this area it had, indeed, overstepped First Amendment bounds, it provided two definitions of electioneering communications, a primary definition, and in case that should be struck down, a backup. The primary definition had four parts. It defined a regulated communication, one subject to federal disclosure rules and the ban on corporate or union treasury funds, as (1) a broadcast, cable, or satellite communication that (2) referred to a clearly identified candidate for public office, that (3) was broadcast within 60 days of a general election or 30 days of a primary, and that (4) was targeted on the candidate mentioned by being aired in that candidate's constituency. The backup definition had three parts. First, it specified too that the ad had to be a broadcast, cable, or satellite communication. Second, the ad had to promote or oppose a candidate whether or not it used *Buckley's* magic words, and third, the communication had to be "suggestive of no plausible meaning other than an exhortation to vote for or against a specific candidate."[17]

The court, again with Leon's decisive vote, held the primary definition unconstitutional, but upheld the backup definition. However, Leon deleted the third element of the backup definition, so that the remaining parts were actually far broader in scope than not only the backup but even the primary definition. Henderson would have struck it down as unconstitutional, but Kollar-Kotelly would have upheld it in deference to Congress. Leon actually wound up closer to Kollar-Kotelly, since, as he wrote, *Buckley*'s express advocacy test, the so-called magic words, had been intended only to cure the vagueness in the original Federal Election Campaign Act. It had never been intended, he believed, "to be a constitutional rule of law limiting the power of Congress to regulate expenditures for certain uncoordinated advocacy that directly affects federal elections."[18] The primary definition, he wrote, reached too far, and as a result it did not distinguish between true issue ads, which could not be regulated, and candidate advocacy. Moreover, the time limits meant that important communications could not be made before elections; the backup definition, however, lacked this impediment since it contained no time constraints.

There is no doubt that this section had the potential to be the most significant part of the decision when appealed to the High Court. Along with Kollar-Kotelly, Leon had reinterpreted *Buckley* so as to give Congress the right to regulate electioneering communications whether or not they contained the magic words. In fact all three judges, although they reached different conclusions, agreed that the express advocacy/magic words test utterly failed to distinguish between election-related speech (the support or opposition of a candidate) and non-election-related issue speech, which the First Amendment clearly protected. Congress could regulate the former, but only if it crafted those regulations in a careful and narrowly tailored manner.

Regarding Title III, the court found the millionaire provision, as well as the sections dealing with lowest unit charges and indexing of contribution limits, to be nonjusticiable, because the plaintiffs had failed to show any injury had occurred to them or that any might reasonably be expected. These matters, the court decided, were not yet ripe, and plaintiffs could not attack them facially, that is, without proof of real or potential harm. They did uphold, by a 2–1 vote, §311, requiring sponsors of electioneering communications to identify themselves, but unanimously struck down the provision barring political contributions by minors.

Also by a unanimous vote, although for different reasons, the court struck down the Title V provision requiring extensive reporting by broadcasters of any request by a political entity to purchase time.

★   ★   ★   ★   ★

The decision, aside from its confusing muddle of legal points, made quite clear the tensions and animosities that had beset the three judges during the five months of their deliberations. Judge Henderson, who normally sat on the Court of Appeals for the District of Columbia, blamed her colleagues from the lower court for the delay and the failure to meet the expedited schedule that Congress had set, and thus they had "ill-served the strong public interest in election law and clarity." She suggested that if Congress wanted to move things along, it should assign these cases only to appellate courts in the future.[19] Henderson also attacked Judge Colleen Kollar-Kotelly, claiming that several parts of her opinion were so flawed that it had left Henderson with "the definite and firm opinion that a mistake had been committed."[20]

Kollar-Kotelly responded in a footnote of her own, using italics to claim that Henderson had been the one in error. "I am compelled to respond to Judge Henderson who, *without any elaboration,* has criticized three of my findings. I have . . . discussed in great detail the foundation and basis for the particular findings she cites. Judge Henderson does not assail that analysis nor does she in any way indicate a reasoned basis for her disagreement."[21] As for Henderson's claim that they had "all agreed" to deliver the case no later than the first week of February, Kollar-Kotelly and Leon reminded Henderson that she had been the only one to make such a promise. Leon also noted that it had taken the lower court that had decided *Buckley* just about the same amount of time after arguments to prepare its decision; the real delay had occurred because of the six months to which all members of the court had agreed for discovery.

Some of the disagreement might be attributed to the different courts on which the three judges sat, even though both the district court and the court of appeals share offices and courtrooms in the same building. The Court of Appeals for the District of Columbia routinely handles much of the litigation involving the constitutionality of federal laws, and is regarded as the second most influential court in the country. Since 1969 it has sent four members to the U.S. Supreme Court, whereas no member of the D.C. district court has been elevated to the appellate bench since 1966. In addition, the older custom of civility in opinion writing seems to be losing ground, especially if one looks at the attacks launched by Justice Antonin Scalia, whose opinions are often harshly critical or even dismissive of his colleagues. The three judges may not have been able to agree on jurisprudence, but they made their dislike for one another perfectly clear.

*   *   *   *   *

In all, the district court held 10 sections of the Bipartisan Campaign Reform Act of 2002 unconstitutional, but it appeared that no one—plaintiffs or defendants—liked the entire opinion. Both sides tried to put the best face on it by seizing upon a section that had gone their way. Senator Feingold, one of the chief sponsors of BCRA, declared that "by and large, the ruling accepts the premise of McCain-Feingold, which is that certain kinds of soft money can be prohibited and that does not violate the First Amendment." Similarly, some of the Republicans who had challenged the law claimed that the decision had gone largely in their favor. "We believe the court has fully vindicated the rights of political parties to participate in state and local elections and to work with state and local parties in furtherance of the mission of the Republican Party," said Bobby R. Burchfield, the RNC lawyer.

Officials from both parties, however, admitted that they remained uncertain about what the ruling actually meant, and what leeway they would have in raising funds and carrying out activities. Larry Noble, the executive director of the Center for Responsive Politics, summed it up best: "Candidates and parties should tread carefully." Fred Wertheimer, the president of Democracy 21, a Washington, D.C.-based group that had defended the law, said that although overall the ruling pleased him, he remained troubled over allowing soft money donations for alleged party-building activities.[22] Although the

American Civil Liberties Union liked the decision in general, Stephen R. Shapiro, the group's legal director, acknowledged, "We know that the fate of this legislation is not yet settled."[23] Columnist George Will wrote, after reviewing the decision, a piece titled, "Who Knows What McCain-Feingold Says?"[24] One of the leading scholars of campaign finance thought that the opinions would have little impact, since they would not greatly affect what the Supreme Court would do. Despite virtues in Kollar-Kotelly's opinion, Dan Ortiz of the University of Virginia Law School felt sure that it would "in no way manage to present the case in a way that will structure the Supreme Court's decisionmaking. For that matter, neither do the other judges' opinions."[25]

Because the exact impact of the district court's ruling could not easily be ascertained, and because parts of its decision could be overturned when the case reached the Supreme Court, nearly all the parties managed to agree on one thing—actual implementation of the ruling had to be stopped. Under the schedule promulgated by the court, parties had until noon on May 9 to request a stay, and groups ranging from the National Rifle Association (NRA) to the American Civil Liberties Union (ACLU), to the sponsors of the bill themselves all filed petitions for stays of implementation. Many followed the line articulated by the ACLU in its petition. As long as the current ruling regarding issue advertisements remained in place, "we are without any guidance defining how far these planned ads can go in criticizing the proposed legislation [on civil liberties issues] and members of Congress who support it. We can only assume that the more aggressive we are in our criticism and rhetoric, the more likely our statements will fall within the definition of speech that is now prohibited."[26] Several groups also wondered how the time frame on acceptable or unacceptable issue ads would be determined, since theoretically an ad run 18 months before an election might very well fall within the ban.[27] Ten days later, the court unanimously granted the stay, pending review by the U.S. Supreme Court.[28]

* * * * *

On June 5, the Supreme Court accepted the case on appeal and in a surprise move set an accelerated schedule for the parties. Initial briefs would have to be filed by 3:00 P.M. on July 8; and reply briefs, by August 21. Instead of the usual one hour of oral argument allotted by the Court to cases before it, this time it would hear four hours of oral argument beginning at 10:00 A.M. on Monday, September 8, 2003.[29] For the first time in decades the Court would cut short its summer recess. Clearly the justices wanted to have a decision handed down in time for the 2004 presidential election.[30]

8 / The Supreme Court Decides

Concentrated wealth is nothing if not creative.
As this Court has observed, the history of
campaign finance reform has been a cycle of
legislation followed by the invention and
exploitation of loopholes, followed by more
legislation to cut off the most egregious
evasions.
—Solicitor General Olson, during oral argument

IN THE END, it would come down to what five members of the Supreme Court would say—whether the Bipartisan Campaign Reform Act (BCRA) and its limits on the activities of political parties violated the Constitution or not. The fact that the justices agreed to meet in September and allotted four hours to oral argument heightened interest in the decision. Although the sponsors of the bill hoped the Court would put its imprimatur on their efforts, and opponents hoped that their constitutional arguments would prevail, cynics took the view that it did not really matter what the Court said. Political campaigns need money the way a car needs gasoline, and one way or another the parties and willing donors would manage to keep the dollars flowing. But the Court's decision would be important for the future. In the years following *Buckley* the Court's equating of money with speech had seriously hampered reformers, since they believed that except for limits on contributions, all other measures would run afoul of the Court's First Amendment views. If in *McConnell* the Court took a similarly restrictive position, it would be almost impossible to pass any legislation that substantially changed the way Democrats and Republicans financed election campaigns. On the contrary, if the Court took a more expansive view of congressional power over federal campaigns, then even if BCRA did not work as effectively as its sponsors hoped, reformers might come back and attempt to amend the act and tighten its provisions. Both sides recognized that the case could be a watershed event in the history of campaign finance reform.

★   ★   ★   ★   ★

Anticipating that the district court would, in all likelihood, not give total victory to either the proponents or critics of BCRA, both sides began preparing appeals to the Supreme Court even before the three district judges handed down their mammoth opinion. The district court released its opinion on Friday morning, May 2, 2003; that evening lawyers for Senator Mitch McConnell delivered a 25-page petition to the nation's highest court asking for review. The brief, signed by former independent counsel Kenneth W. Starr, urged the Court to strike down the law's ban on unregulated "soft money," the provisions regulating issue advertisements, and limitations on coordinated expenditures. The law, Starr claimed, "constitutes a frontal assault on First Amendment values, the likes of which have not been seen since the Republic's infancy. . . . Rarely has Congress acted with such utter disregard for so many constitutional limitations on its power." The fact that McConnell had gone forward without consulting any of his partners irked several of the coplaintiffs. James Bopp, Jr., who represented 10 of the plaintiffs in the case, complained that "it was done without consultation, and that's troubling."[1]

Although all parties wanted the district court's orders stayed pending a ruling by the High Court, some of the parties could barely restrain themselves. The National Rifle Association (NRA), even before the district court could rule on motions to stay, petitioned Chief Justice William H. Rehnquist to issue an order halting execution of the lower court opinion. Rehnquist turned down the request without comment, but said the NRA could return if the lower court had not ruled on motions to stay by May 20. The National Right to Life Committee and the Club for Growth also asked Rehnquist to lift the law's restrictions on political advertisements until the High Court could decide, but the chief justice refused. "An act of Congress is presumed to be constitutional," he noted, and the BCRA "should remain in effect until the disposition of this case by the Supreme Court."[2] Well before then the various parties had begun talking among themselves about strategy. The government apparently disliked the district court opinion as much as the law's critics. Solicitor

General Theodore Olson, in asking the Supreme Court for review, charged that "in invalidating key provisions [of BCRA], the district court substituted its own judgment for that of Congress, which has firsthand experience with the electoral process and a unique understanding of the concerns to which campaign finance laws are addressed."[3] Not just the litigants wanted the Court to move forward expeditiously. In an editorial representing a broad spectrum of opinion, the *New York Times* urged a stay of the district court opinion, "leaving McCain-Feingold in place as the law of the land and preventing the political parties from resuming the corrupting behavior the new law was meant to stop." Then the Supreme Court should act as quickly as possible, so that confusion surrounding the law could be resolved.[4]

The district court granted its stay orders on May 19, and on June 5, 2003, the Supreme Court granted review, too late for it to hear and decide the case before its summer recess.[5] Even before the justices granted certiorari, lawyers for the different parties had begun lengthy meetings to iron out procedural details in order to facilitate the appeals process. Jan W. Baran, a Washington, D.C. lawyer on McConnell's team, predicted that "there will be consultations between the plaintiffs and defendants to see if procedurally we can agree on something to recommend to the Court so we don't have appeals, cross-appeals, and four flights of briefing."[6]

The rules of briefing and argument in the Supreme Court are much tighter than those that prevail in the lower courts. By the time an issue has reached the nation's highest tribunal, the justices expect —and insist—that its essential questions be posed in a minimal amount of space and time. Schedules for filing briefs are usually very tight, and the size of the briefs is governed by an elaborate code. Most cases are given no more than one hour for oral argument, each side getting just 30 minutes to convince the Court of the rightness of its arguments. Since several of the justices have a penchant for continuous questioning of counsel, trying to make a point in the limited time available is quite difficult.

Because of the complexity of the lower court ruling, there was not a clear winner and loser when the sides appealed. Normally, the losing side in the lower court files the appeal and frames the legal questions it wants the Court to review. The winner in the lower court can then respond, usually urging the High Court to affirm the lower court's ruling. In this instance, however, both sides wanted the Supreme Court to reverse different parts of the district court decision.[7] Solicitor General Theodore B. Olson, who would lead the government's defense of BCRA on behalf of the Federal Election Commission, asked the Court for permission to file both an opening brief and a second one replying to the opponents' arguments—an arrangement that would have given defenders of the law the last word before oral argument. The Court rejected Olson's proposal, but it did agree with his contention that the law's opponents should have to file their briefs first, as the losing party in the lower court generally must. Lawyers for McConnell and the other plaintiffs deemed this inappropriate, since they considered the results of the lower court largely a victory for them. Requiring them to go first, Kenneth Starr wrote, "would deprive them unfairly of their hard-won victories below."[8]

Despite the maneuvering over procedural details, both sides professed pleasure at the speed with which the Supreme Court agreed to hear the case. Floyd Abrams, representing McConnell, said the Court's scheduling meant the case would in all likelihood be settled before the 2004 presidential primaries and caucuses. "It's very important," he said, "to know what the rules of the game are going to be." Representative Christopher Shays (R-Conn.), one of the bill's authors, declared himself "thrilled." He believed that Congress had written "a very good law. We know it meets the constitutional test."[9]

★　★　★　★　★

Then in one of its last opinions for the term, the Supreme Court handed down a decision regarding campaign finance law that might —or might not—be a clue as to how it would decide the challenge to BCRA that fall. The existing federal election law (FECA) barred corporations from making direct contributions to federal elections, but did allow them to establish separate funds—namely, political action committees—that could expend moneys in political campaigns. A nonprofit group, North Carolina Right to Life, and others challenged the applicability of the corporation rule to nonprofit groups, claiming that it violated their First Amendment rights.

The Supreme Court, in *Federal Election Commission v. Beaumont*, held that Congress had sufficient power to regulate the political process to extend that ban to any group without violating the group's constitutional rights.[10] By a vote of 7–2, the Court, speaking through Justice Souter, said that the right to free speech does not trump Congress's goal of limiting the corrosive effects of corporate money in politics. The government had argued that permitting non-profit advocacy groups to ignore the corporate ban would allow their members to circumvent the limits on individual campaign contributions and to do so with little public disclosure about the source of the money. "Any attack on the federal prohibition of direct corporate political contributions goes against the current of a century of congressional efforts," Souter wrote.[11]

All of the justices except Antonin Scalia and Clarence Thomas joined in Souter's opinion, fueling speculation as to how the individual justices would align themselves in the upcoming and all-important *McConnell* case. In prior cases, Justices John Paul Stevens, Ruth Bader Ginsburg, David H. Souter, and Stephen G. Breyer had shown the most sympathy for campaign finance regulation, while Scalia, Thomas, and Anthony Kennedy had been the most skeptical. In the middle, and the key voters in the case, would be Chief Justice William H. Rehnquist, who as an associate justice had supported the limit on campaign contributions in *Buckley*, and Sandra Day O'Connor. Three years earlier they had voted with the liberals to sustain a Missouri law setting limits on campaign contributions, reaffirming that the *Buckley* rationale preventing the appearance of corruption constituted a sufficient rationale for regulation.[12]

O'Connor, it is important to note, had been the Court's leading centrist for well over a decade, and in the previous term had been the key voter as well as the chief author of the 5–4 opinion upholding affirmative action.[13] She had also given the swing vote in the final determination of majority-minority districting.[14] Unlike the redistricting and affirmative action cases, in which O'Connor had been deeply engaged, campaign finance issues "didn't seem to motivate her," according to Professor Richard L. Hasen, an election law specialist at Loyola Law School in Los Angeles. "We never knew where she stood."[15]

For Rehnquist, often characterized as an archconservative, to be considered a potential swing voter showed that the issue of campaign finance reform, on the Court as in Congress, cut across traditional conservative-liberal lines. In prior cases the chief justice had voted to uphold bans on corporate and union contributions, on the grounds that Congress had the power to decide what needed to be done to prevent corruption or its appearance in the world of politics. In 1990, he had joined with liberal justices William J. Brennan and Thurgood Marshall in upholding a Michigan law banning the Michigan Chamber of Commerce from using its corporate treasury to support a candidate for the state assembly.[16] Four years earlier, in a dissenting opinion, he had argued for regulation of spending by nonprofit corporations that had been organized for ideological purposes, declaring that he "would defer to the congressional judgment that corporations are a distinct category with respect to which this sort of regulation is constitutionally permissible."[17] At the same time, Rehnquist also balked at laws that hobbled political parties. In 2001 he joined Scalia, Thomas, and Kennedy in dissenting from a 5–4 ruling that upheld federal limitations on amounts political parties could spend in coordination with the campaigns of their federal candidates. He saw no possibility of parties corrupting their own candidates; parties are linked to candidates, he reasoned, and "breaking this link would impose significant costs on speech."[18]

Although the range and complexity of issues in *McConnell* far exceeded the question in *Beaumont*, commentators took the Court's decision as an omen that a majority of the justices did not oppose regulation of federal campaign finance out of hand. Fred Wertheimer of Democracy 21, a group that favored BCRA, noted that "this is the third time since 2000 that the Supreme Court has rejected challenges to the constitutionality of campaign finance laws," and predicted that the High Court would find BCRA constitutional. Professor Elizabeth Garrett of the University of Southern California Law School, a well-known scholar of campaign finance law, agreed. The role of nonprofit advocacy groups had become increasingly important in campaign finance, and the *Beaumont* decision provided a green light for government efforts to regulate their political activities.[19] The *New York Times*, a leading advocate of campaign finance reform, cautiously noted that although *Beaumont* did not necessarily foretell how the judges would vote in *McConnell*, "its reasoning, including its deference to Congress on when contributions carry a threat of corruption, and the size of the majority, are reasons for optimism."[20]

★ ★ ★ ★ ★

Even though the Court agreed to allow each side two hours for oral argument, lawyers considered this barely enough time to get across their views regarding the wide range of issues that had been decided by the lower court and then appealed. The government side seemed to get its ducks in a row fairly quickly. Solicitor General Theodore Olson, Deputy Solicitor General Paul Clement, and former Solicitor General Seth Waxman were to handle the defense of BCRA.[21]

The large number of litigants challenging the law, however, found themselves squabbling over who would get to share the two hours. The McConnell group, the lead plaintiff, proposed to the Court that its two hours be divided among former Solicitor General Kenneth W. Starr; the noted First Amendment lawyer Floyd Abrams; Bobby Burchfield (representing the Republican and Democratic National Committees); and Laurence Gold, former general counsel of the AFL-CIO, now representing the union. This left the other plaintiffs, including the powerful NRA, out in the cold, and they wanted the Court either to alter the arrangement or to add a half-hour to oral argument for them (as had been done in *Buckley*). Charles Cooper, the chief lawyer for the NRA, filed a motion on July 14 seeking argument time, noting that the NRA had not been consulted in the plaintiffs' request for time allotment. John Bonifaz, a founder of the National Voting Rights Institute and lawyer for some of the plaintiffs, claimed that his group had been given short shrift by the high-profile lawyers who wanted to control the case. "If we were part of the club," he lamented, "they might have allowed us time."

In response, Jan Baran, a Washington, D.C., lawyer who had played a major role in the district court case but who had not asked for time before the Supreme Court, offered an explanation as to why some of the plaintiffs had been excluded. The lead plaintiffs, McConnell and the political parties, had focused on certain constitutional arguments that they wanted the Court to adjudicate. Other plaintiffs had different concerns, some of which went against the direction that the McConnell group wanted to take. Charles Cooper, representing the NRA, acknowledged that "we make arguments that are positively unhelpful" to corporations and media organizations. Bonifaz had attempted, in the lower court, to make an equal protection argument against the individual contribution limit, but supported other parts of the law that McConnell and his allies opposed.[22] In the end the McConnell group brought in one more lawyer, Jay

Alan Sekulow of the American Center for Law and Justice, a legal agency established by evangelist Pat Robertson in order to defend conservative groups and causes; in this instance Sekulow represented the Echols plaintiffs, individuals who objected to the provisions of BCRA that governed individual contributions and expenditures as opposed to candidate and party activities.

★　★　★　★　★

At 10 o'clock on the morning of Monday, September 8, 2003, the clerk of the U.S. Supreme Court ordered all persons in the great courtroom to rise, and—as the nine justices filed in from behind the velvet curtains to take their seats—to come forward if they had business with the Court. Then, after he had intoned the ritual "God save this honorable court," Chief Justice William H. Rehnquist banged his gavel, and called the only case on the docket for that special session, *McConnell v. Federal Election Commission.*

Then followed four hours of intense questions and answers, at the end of which even experienced Court watchers could not determine whether five votes existed to uphold the law or to strike it down.[23] Uncharacteristically, Justice O'Connor asked few questions and seemed mainly concerned about how to draft a ruling that could strike down parts of the law in a way that would not overturn *Buckley v. Valeo.* As expected, Justice Scalia attacked the law at every opportunity, at one point stopping to read the text of the First Amendment out loud and declaring that "it's a very simple text," the meaning of which ought to be obvious to all. Justice Breyer seemed to support the law, suggesting that its total ban on soft money could be justified on the basis of administrative convenience—not normally a winning argument in First Amendment cases—but that here it would in fact be too difficult to sort out portions that could legally go to state parties.

That in turn prompted the chief justice to comment that he did not find administrative reasons good enough to justify speech restrictions. Such regulations might be acceptable under the tax code, Rehnquist said, but not under the First Amendment. If there was any surprise, it was in Rehnquist's seeming hostility to BCRA and in intimations that perhaps he had been wrong in his earlier votes upholding campaign finance regulations. Under the *Austin* decision, the Court had held that huge corporate treasuries have little correlation to the public's support of the corporation's political views, an idea that had been used as a rationale for parts of BCRA. Rehnquist now seemed to cast doubt on that reasoning, suggesting that the "whole purpose" of the First Amendment was to allow expressions of unpopular views.

Neither side got a free ride, as can be seen from these two excerpts from the transcript of the oral argument. First, speaking for the law, Solicitor General Olson:

> MR. OLSON: The issues the Court considers today, every single one of them in connection with Title I, are not new. For a century, with the overwhelming support of the public, Congress has struggled to curb the corrupting influence of corporate, union, and large, unregulated contributions in federal elections. Time and again this Court has agreed that achievement of that goal is critical to avoid erosion of public confidence in representative government to—and I'm using the Court's words—to a disastrous extent.
>
> JUSTICE SCALIA: General Olson, is every problem soluble?
>
> MR. OLSON: Well, this Court hasn't found every problem to be solvable.
>
> JUSTICE SCALIA: If for example, the executive should make a compelling case that it is really impossible to eradicate crime if we continue with this silly procedure of having warrants for searches of houses? We wouldn't entertain that argument, you know, [that] this is the only way to achieve this result.
>
> MR. OLSON: Of course not.
>
> JUSTICE SCALIA: There are certain absolutes, aren't there, even if problems subsist? There are just some things the government can't do?
>
> MR. OLSON: Of course, Justice Scalia . . . but this Court has said over and over again, not only is it a critical problem that is fundamental to the integrity of our election system, but that the solutions that the legislature has enacted before, the central principles of which are embodied in BCRA, are constitutional solutions to that problem. . . .

CHIEF JUSTICE REHNQUIST: But the reason for upholding the contribution limits restriction was because of the corruption or the appearance of corruption between the contribution and the candidate. I don't think *Buckley* supports the proposition that Congress can willy nilly regulate any sort of contributions in connection with an election campaign.

MR. OLSON: Of course not, Mr. Chief Justice. What this Court has said over and over again, [is] that Congress can regulate contributions from corporations—the treasuries of corporations and unions.

JUSTICE O'CONNOR: Is there any evidence in the record of access corruption, so to speak, using soft money to fund purely state and local elections, as opposed to Federal?

MR. OLSON: The evidence—

JUSTICE O'CONNOR: Is there evidence of that?

MR. OLSON: What the evidence [is], if I understand your question correctly, is that the money was going from, through the national parties and at the direction of the national parties to the state subordinate committees in order to fund various activities that had to do with Federal elections, and that's what, they were—

JUSTICE O'CONNOR: If I understand, evidence that the money [is] being used to fund purely state and local election activities?

MR. OLSON: No, that was not what Congress was concerned about. Congress was concerned—

JUSTICE O'CONNOR: But the ban extends to that, apparently?

MR. OLSON: The—the ban—no. In the sense that the state parties can raise money that's not regulated, provided that it's not used in conjunction with Federal election activity. So in that sense, the states are free to continue to do that and spend all they wish.

Then, speaking against the law, Floyd Abrams urged the Court to strike down any regulation that went further than *Buckley* and its "magic words" formula:

MR. ABRAMS: As we turn from Title I to Title II, we turn to

efforts by Congress to limit, to regulate, and ultimately to punish what are only expenditures, expenditures not made in coordination with parties or candidates. . . . I think we are all agreed that this is a content-based restriction on speech, [and] whether we're all agreed or not, it is a content-based restriction on speech. I'd like to start with a just a few observations of—

JUSTICE O'CONNOR: Do you take the position that no effective regulation of electioneering communication is permissible?

MR. ABRAMS: I take the position that electioneering communications as defined in the statute is so overbroad that the totality of what is encompassed in it is not regulatable. Electioneering communications includes within it express advocacy, what is now or what had been subject to regulation, and to that extent it is subject to regulation.

JUSTICE SOUTER: Beyond express advocacy, do you concede that anything can be regulated?

MR. ABRAMS: I thought very hard about that, Justice Souter, to see if there was something I could give you in that respect. No, I do not concede that there is anything beyond express advocacy.

JUSTICE GINSBURG: Do you also recognize that express advocacy is the easiest thing in the world to avoid? You just say everything about how great your candidate is or how terrible the opponent is, except, and go to the polls and vote for X.

MR. ABRAMS: I understand that happens. I understand what this Court in *Buckley* understood just as well, when it said almost the same thing. The *Buckley* Court did not say that express advocacy was going to catch most, not to say all—

JUSTICE GINSBURG: But, but *Buckley* was dealing with two words, relative to. It was not confronted with this problem at all.

MR. ABRAMS: But [the] *Buckley* Court was prescient in understanding that what has happened was going to happen. . . . And when they balanced the First Amendment against that—

JUSTICE KENNEDY: I understand why you would want to keep what one of the briefs calls this impregnable line because you are within *Buckley*, but it seems to me this distinction is just meaningless. . . . Why don't we just junk it and . . . begin anew?

MR. ABRAMS: It seems to me that there are only two choices that I would urge on you at least as constitutional choices. One is to adhere to *Buckley* and to do so, understanding that, or accepting, excuse me, that express advocacy is as far as the First Amendment will allow you to go in terms of allowing regulation.

JUSTICE STEVENS: But shouldn't you at least be able to answer the question, Why should a speech urging expressly to elect a particular candidate . . . be entitled to less constitutional protection than a speech urging the ratification of the Panama Canal Treaty, for example?

MR. ABRAMS: The only reason and the only justification is that the speech becomes, as it were, so much like a contribution, so much like a final act of saying, "Vote for the candidate."

The intensity and length of the argument eventually began to wear down some of the participants. For most of his time at the lectern, Olson referred to his predecessor as "Mr. Starr," but, after a series of sharp questions from the bench, suddenly began calling him "Justice Starr." The members of the Court began to laugh, and when Olson realized his error, he smiled at Starr, now in private practice, and said, "I guess we'll have to wait for that."

At another point, when AFL-CIO associate general counsel Laurence Gold rose to speak, Scalia looked at him quizzically. "You're Laurence Gold?" he asked, as if some stranger had suddenly arisen in the courtroom. As it turned out, Gold had been subjected to this form of mistaken identity before, as he would often be confused with another lawyer by the same name, a frequent advocate before the High Court who used to be AFL-CIO general counsel and who now worked for a private firm. Supreme Court rules bar lawyers from identifying themselves in detail, and Scalia finally seemed to realize what had happened, saying, "You're not the Laurence Gold I expected."

There has been a great deal of debate—all of it inconclusive—as to whether oral arguments really affect the final decisions of the Court. Some justices practically ignore it; on the present bench Justice Clarence Thomas hardly ever asks a question. A generation earlier, William O. Douglas would listen to oral argument with part of one ear while he answered correspondence. Others say that although the briefs are the key source of arguments pro and con, a good lawyer can help the bench to focus on important matters, and will occasionally raise a point not cited earlier. How effective the four hours of give-and-take were in changing any of the justices' minds is impossible to determine. At the end, Chief Justice Rehnquist banged his gavel and declared, "The case is submitted." Now the justices would have to sift and weigh the competing constitutional arguments, and in order to achieve at least some of the expedited treatment Congress had requested, they would have to move a good deal faster than the district court. They did, handing down their decision just three months later.

★ ★ ★ ★ ★

Unlike many laws, even those with multiple parts, all of which focus on the same object, the BCRA's different titles addressed multiple issues that, despite the relation all bore to campaign finance, rested on different constitutional grounds and needed to be addressed separately. A justice might well vote to uphold the ban on soft money but not the restrictions on electioneering communications. It surprised no one when the Court handed down eight separate opinions, nor when only five justices formed the majority in the vote on some key provisions.

Back when the Court heard *Buckley*, the justices of that era had divided the ruling into sections, each assigned to a different member of the Court. There had been four hours of oral argument on November 10, 1975; the justices met in conference within a day or two, voted, divided up the work, and handed down their joint opinion on January 30, 1976—a rather remarkable 81-day turnaround. A similar division of labor may well have occurred in *McConnell*. Three separate opinions dealing with the major titles, each commanding a majority, constituted the opinion of the Court.

Justices Stevens and O'Connor coauthored the lead opinion, dealing with BCRA Titles I and II, joined by Souter, Ginsburg, and Breyer.

Chief Justice Rehnquist wrote the opinion with respect to Titles III and IV, joined by O'Connor, Scalia, Kennedy, and Souter, and in part (all except for one provision) by Stevens, Ginsburg, and Breyer, and also in part (except for four provisions) by Thomas.

Justice Breyer dealt with Title V, joined by Stevens, O'Connor, Souter, and Ginsburg.

Justice Scalia, although concurring in Titles III and IV, dissented with respect to Title I and part of Title II, and concurred in part and dissented in part regarding Title V.

Justice Thomas, joined by Scalia, concurred with various parts of the Rehnquist opinion, dissented in part regarding Title II, and dissented fully from the Court's holding on Titles I and V.

Justice Kennedy, joined by Rehnquist, and in most parts by Scalia and Thomas, dissented as to the holding on Titles I and II.

Chief Justice Rehnquist, joined by Scalia and Kennedy, dissented with respect to Titles I and V.

Justice Stevens, joined by Ginsburg and Breyer, dissented on the ruling on standing regarding one section, and would have upheld §305 on its merits.

Examining the main opinions and seeing how the justices voted on them reveal the same division in approach that we noted in the original briefs (Chapter 7) and in the district court's ruling (in this chapter). On the one hand, some justices took a more theoretical approach to the problem, setting up First Amendment standards and then asking whether or not BCRA violated them. This view—a First Amendment jurisprudence based on strict scrutiny—had been the theory that Senator McConnell and his allies had pushed in their briefs and arguments in both the district court and High Court, and that Judge Henderson had championed in her lower court opinion. On the other hand, several justices adopted the view of the defenders of BCRA—namely, that real political-world facts indicated that the pre-BCRA regulatory scheme failed to prevent corruption or its appearance, and that the law had been narrowly tailored to address this problem, the position taken by Judge Kollar-Kotelly. Those justices taking this stance also showed a very large deference to Congress and its judgment regarding the severity of the problem of corruption or its appearance in campaign finance, a deference unusual in cases involving the First Amendment.

The lead opinion, coauthored by Justices Stevens and O'Connor, followed this latter approach, and upheld most of the provisions in BCRA Titles I and II. With regard to the soft-money and related provisions of Title I embedded in different parts of §323, the majority chose not to apply the strict scrutiny standard often associated with the First Amendment, but adopted the less rigorous standard that had been utilized in *Buckley*—namely, whether the regulations had been "closely drawn." Just as in *Buckley*, the Court drew a distinction between campaign contributions and expenditures, and held that contribution limits imposed only a marginal restraint upon the contributor's right to engage in communication. Beyond that, the majority accepted congressional reasoning: that the government had an important interest in preventing "both the actual corruption threatened by large financial contributions and the eroding of public confidence in the electoral process through the appearance of corruption."[24] Finally, because Congress in its lengthy deliberations had properly relied on *Buckley* and its progeny, the Court had powerful incentives to adhere to *stare decisis* considerations—that is, letting the rulings in earlier cases guide the Court's current deliberations. The majority saw the issues in the light of *Buckley*, and therefore rejected the plaintiffs' claims that the type of speech and associational burdens imposed by BCRA were substantially different from the burdens imposed earlier by *Buckley*.

Section 323(a), the key provision of Title I, met with approval because the governmental interest in preventing corruption or its appearance in federal races provided sufficient importance to justify contribution limits. This interest is so important that it can support not only restrictions on contributions themselves, but also laws designed to prevent the circumvention of these limits. Conceding that it would be difficult to establish explicit quantitative measures of corruption, the Court essentially said Congress did not have to do so. "The idea that large contributions to a national party can corrupt or, at the very least, create the appearance of corruption of federal candidates and officeholders is neither novel nor implausible."[25] Sufficient evidence had been presented to show that the uses of soft money could lead to actual corruption or its appearance, and Congress met First Amendment requirements by closely drawing its restrictions to meet its goal.

Because §323(a) carried such importance, the Court answered each argument that had been brought up against it. It rested upon a sufficient governmental interest, and had been narrowly drawn. It was not impermissibly overbroad because it subjected all funds raised to FECA's hard money limits. Because the record showed the close relationship between national parties and state and local parties, Congress could legitimately conclude that party activities connected to a federal election at any level could be regulated in order to prevent corruption and its appearance. By the same token, the ban on national parties soliciting or directing soft money contributions could not be characterized as overbroad; the committees remain free to solicit unlimited amounts of hard money. Although conceivably the ban might adversely affect the speech and associational rights of minor parties, no evidence had been presented to show that this would actually happen, so the Court would not strike down the provision on a facial challenge.[26] Similarly, the claim that BCRA unconstitutionally interfered with the ability of national committees to associate with state and local committees failed to persuade the Court. Nothing in the law prevented them from cooperating, except in regard to the uses of soft money.

The Court also found §323(b), prohibiting state and local parties from using soft money for activities affecting federal elections, to be closely drawn to confront an important objective, and therefore constitutional. This section, perhaps more than any other, highlighted the deference the majority showed to Congress. Looking at the record, the Court pointed out what Congress and everyone knew— close ties and a high level of coordination existed between national parties and their state and local affiliates. Congress thus had justifiable reason to ban the use of soft money by state and local party committees for a variety of purposes that could affect federal elections.[27] Congress had legitimately worried that, given this close connection, soft money could work its way into the political process from the state and local levels upward just as effectively as from the national parties downward:

> Congress both drew a conclusion and made a prediction. Its conclusion, based on the evidence before it, was that the corrupting influence of soft money does not insinuate itself into the political process solely through national party committees. Rather, state committees function as an alternate avenue for precisely the same corrupting forces. Indeed, both

candidates and parties already ask donors who have reached the limit on their direct contributions to donate to state committees. There is at least as much evidence as there was in *Buckley* that such donations have been made with the intent—and in at least some cases the effect—of gaining influence over federal officeholders. Section 323(b) thus promotes an important governmental interest by confronting the corrupting influence that soft-money donations to political parties already have.[28]

The plaintiffs, aware that the section might be upheld, had proposed an alternative argument: that even if this provision served legitimate interests, it had not been closely drawn, and therefore unjustifiably burdened associational interests protected by the First Amendment. The Court rejected this argument out of hand, noting that although the rules affected some state campaigns for nonfederal offices, these activities had already been brought under the umbrella of acceptable federal regulation by the Federal Election Commission's pre-BCRA allocation rules. State campaigns already had to be funded in part by hard money because the activities affected federal as well as nonfederal campaigns.

The Court found that the ban on political party committees at any level soliciting funds for, or making direct contributions to, nonprofit groups, §323(d), was not facially invalid. No evidence had been presented to show that a real transgression of associational rights would take place, and Congress had ample reason to draft this provision to prevent circumvention of the soft-money rules. Stevens and O'Connor, the chief drafters of this opinion, clearly recognized the validity of the government's insistence that one had to look at the law not in the abstract, but in light of the conditions and practices that made up the real political world. In a footnote to this section, they pointed out that these groups, although qualifying for nonprofit status, were far from politically neutral. Indeed, the record showed that "many of the targeted tax-exempt organizations engage in sophisticated and effective electioneering activities for the purpose of influencing federal elections, including waging broadcast campaigns promoting or attacking particular candidates and conducting large-scale voter registration and GOTV [get out the vote] drives." They cited in particular an effort in the final weeks of the 2000 presidential campaign, when the NAACP's nonprofit National Voter Fund registered more than 200,000 people, promoted a GOTV hotline, ran three newspaper print ads, and made several direct mailings, funded primarily by a $7 million contribution from an anonymous donor.[29]

The Court upheld two other parts of §323—the ban on federal officeholders or candidates from soliciting soft money in connection with a federal election, §323(e); and the ban on state and local candidates or officeholders from using soft money to fund ads promoting or attacking federal candidates, §323(f). Neither provision violated the First Amendment, and both constituted a logical and closely drawn effort by Congress to prevent circumvention of the general ban on soft money.

Several of the plaintiffs argued, "unpersuasively," as the Court described it, that Title I exceeded Congress' Election Clause authority to "make or alter" rules governing federal elections, or that it violated basic principles of federalism by impairing the states' authority to regulate their own elections. The proper test, the majority found, was whether the federal government had commandeered state officials to carry out a federal policy.[30] Title I did not regulate state conduct, but that of private entities, candidates, and party committees. Moreover, Title I left states free to impose their own restrictions on state campaign finance procedures.

The Court also dismissed the equal protection argument, in which plaintiffs claimed that political parties had been discriminated against in favor of special interest groups that remained free to raise soft money for voter registration and similar activities. The Court noted that BCRA actually favored the parties by raising the limits on the amount of hard money they could receive for party-building activities. In a passage that clearly showed how the majority favored the arguments of fact over those of theory, and that also indicated the deference paid to Congress, the opinion noted:

> Congress is fully entitled to consider the real-world differences between political parties and interest groups when crafting a system of campaign finance regulation. Interest groups do not select slates of candidates for elections. Interest groups do not determine who will serve on legislative committees, elect congressional leadership, or organize leg-

islative caucuses. Political parties have influence and power in the legislature that vastly exceeds that of any interest group. As a result, it is hardly surprising that party affiliation is the primary way by which voters identify candidates, or that parties in turn have special access to and relationships with federal officeholders. Congress' efforts at campaign finance regulation may account for these salient differences. Taken seriously, appellants' equal protection arguments would call into question not just Title I of BCRA, but much of the pre-existing structure of FECA as well. We therefore reject those arguments.[31]

So far, defenders of BCRA could not have asked for more. A majority of the Supreme Court had reversed those portions of the lower court opinion invalidating parts a, b, and d of the §323 ban on soft money, and had confirmed the lower court's ruling on the constitutionality of parts e and f. They would also be pleased with how the majority treated Title II, with its controversial ban on issue advertisements and the timing of certain types of "electioneering communications." In dealing with Title II, however, although the justices could look at the facts, they could not ignore the vast body of First Amendment jurisprudence that the Court had developed over the previous half-century.

Title II dealt with various issues of electioneering speech, including strict reporting requirements, controls on time, and the mandate that sponsors of issue ads identify themselves. The Court upheld the detailed reporting requirements of BCRA as well as its broad definition of what constituted an electioneering communication—"any broadcast, cable, or satellite communication that clearly identifies a candidate for federal office," is targeted to a relevant electorate, and that airs within a specific time period (60 days before a general election and 30 days before a primary).

The plaintiffs complained that the new law, by failing to draw the *Buckley* distinction between contributions and expenditures, violated their First Amendment right to speech, and especially to this type of speech, political communication. If they avoided *Buckley*'s "magic words" as well as the similar conclusion the Court had drawn in *FEC v. Massachusetts Citizens for Life (MCFL)* (1986), then issue ads fell outside the limits of congressional power to regulate.[32]

The First Amendment trumped even important considerations regarding campaign rules.

The majority rejected this claim, and in words reminiscent of Judge Leon's lower court opinion, held that the express advocacy provisions (the magic words of *Buckley* and *MCFL*) had never been a constitutional ruling, but merely part of the Court's statutory interpretation of FECA. In that footnote, and in *MCFL*, the Court had simply tried to fix a potential problem of vagueness and overbreadth in the statute by refining the general idea with some specific suggestions:

> A plain reading of *Buckley* makes clear that the express advocacy limitation, in both the expenditure and the disclosure contexts, was the product of statutory interpretation rather than a constitutional command. In narrowly reading the FECA provisions in *Buckley* to avoid problems of vagueness and overbreadth, we nowhere suggested that a statute that was neither vague nor overbroad would be required to toe the same express advocacy line. Nor did we suggest as much in *MCFL*, in which we addressed the scope of another FECA expenditure limitation and confirmed the understanding that *Buckley*'s express advocacy category was a product of statutory construction.[33]

The "magic words," so long interpreted by nearly everyone as a hard and fast *constitutional* rule had been, at least according to five justices, little more than a suggestion on how to refine a vague law and avoid nullifying it. Congress, therefore, had the power to regulate at least some additional types of political speech even if it passed the magic words test.

The majority then had to face the basic First Amendment challenge—namely, that the phrase "electioneering communication" was both overbroad and underinclusive in how it dealt with different types of political speech. To begin with, using their new interpretation of what the *Buckley* magic words test had been, the Court announced that its consideration of the plaintiffs' challenge would be "informed by our earlier conclusion that the distinction between express advocacy and so-called issue advocacy is not constitutionally compelled." Given that assumption, the Court found that the government did, in fact, have the necessary interest to regulate both types of speech, namely, the prevention of corruption or its appearance in the political process.

The five justices engaged in what surely must be considered judicial sleight of hand:

> In light of our precedents, plaintiffs do not contest that the Government has a compelling interest in regulating advertisements that expressly advocate the election or defeat of a candidate for federal office. Nor do they contend that the speech involved in so-called issue advocacy is any more core political speech than are words of express advocacy. . . . Rather, plaintiffs argue that the justifications that adequately support the regulation of express advocacy do not apply to significant quantities of speech encompassed by the definition of electioneering communications.
>
> This argument fails to the extent that the issue ads broadcast during the 30- and 60-day periods preceding federal primary and general elections are the functional equivalent of express advocacy. The justifications for the regulation of express advocacy apply equally to ads aired during those periods if the ads are intended to influence the voters' decisions and have that effect.[34]

In fact, plaintiffs had never conceded any such thing. They operated within the context of *Buckley*'s magic words test, but had never conceded that issue advocacy fell into the same category. Moreover, the Court failed to deal with true issue advocacy. If the NRA ran an ad that said, "A right to bear arms is protected by the Second Amendment, and cannot be abridged by Congress. When you go to vote this fall, consider how valuable this right is to you," that constituted true advocacy of an issue that stood beyond a candidate's effort to get votes. It would be equally as true if the American Association for Retired Persons ran an ad that detailed the rising cost of prescription drugs for seniors, and then said, "Isn't it about time Congress acted on this issue?" Whether one agrees with the NRA's interpretation of the Second Amendment or the AARP's plan for subsidizing prescription drugs, these are in fact true issue ads and ones that bear directly on the political process. If this is not the core political speech that the Court and scholars have proclaimed to be especially protected by the First Amendment, then what is?

The Court proceeded to uphold the ancillary parts of Title II that implemented the main provision regarding electioneering communications. It upheld section 202, which held that disbursements made in coordination with candidates or parties had to be treated as contributions to the candidate or party, and therefore subject to other limits within the act. It reversed the district court's invalidation of part of §203, which the lower court had seen as a total ban on corporate or union spending. In fact, the Supreme Court said, corporations and unions could still set up segregated funds (PACs), which would then be subject to the regulations contained in other parts of the law.[35]

In an important decision affecting nonprofit entities, the Court upheld the district court's ruling that BCRA §204 extended the ban on using general treasury funds to pay for electioneering communications to nonprofit groups, a ruling that followed directly from the *Beaumont* decision earlier in the year.[36]

In one of the few victories for the plaintiffs in this part of the opinion, the Court agreed with the district court's invalidation of §213, requiring political parties to choose between coordinated and independent expenditures in the period after the convention and before the election. This provision, according to the Court, placed an unconstitutional burden on the parties' right to make unlimited expenditures. Even though the amount of speech involved here was relatively small, it was still core political speech, and the government did not have a sufficiently compelling interest in regulating it.[37]

Finally, the Court affirmed the district court's ruling upholding §214, extending to political parties the rule that expenditures controlled by or coordinated with a candidate will be treated as contributions. The Court observed that ever since *Buckley* it had protected truly independent expenditures, but at the same time it had noted that "independent expenditures may well provide little assistance to the candidate's campaign and indeed may prove counterproductive." Thus there was little danger that such expenditures would lead to any form of quid pro quo or other improper commitment from the candidate.[38] This rationale, that wholly independent expenditures posed little danger of corruption, nonetheless could pose problems if there was "a wink or nod" that a certain type of seemingly independent expenditure would be useful to the candidate. This could easily be done through the political party rather than the candidate, but the result would be the same. Nor does the absence of any explicit agreement matter, since there had never been a requirement that coordination between candidates and others be overt or in the form of a contract. Congress had sufficient justification to extend the same strictures that existed on candidates and allegedly independent expenditures to political parties.[39]

In conclusion, the five justices noted:

> Many years ago we observed that "to say that Congress is without power to pass appropriate legislation to safeguard . . . an election from the improper use of money to influence the result is to deny the nation in a vital particular the power of self-protection."[40] We abide by that conviction in considering Congress' most recent effort to confine the ill effects of aggregated wealth on our political system. We are under no illusion that BCRA will be the last congressional statement on the matter. Money, like water, will always find an outlet. What problems will arise, and how Congress will respond, are concerns for another day. In the main we uphold BCRA's two principal, complementary features: the control of soft money and the regulation of electioneering communications.[41]

The paragraph is noteworthy in that it makes no mention of the First Amendment, but rather focuses on the power of Congress to prevent corruption in the electoral process. There is a sense of realpolitik in its rather bleak assumption that no matter what Congress has done in BCRA, it will not be the last word on reform, since people with money will always find new and innovative ways to get that money into the system, where willing candidates and parties will be eager to accept it. The justices had no idea how soon this prediction would be borne out.[42]

★   ★   ★   ★   ★

Although the majority opinion regarding Titles I and II did not go unchallenged, let us look at the other sections of the decision that conveyed the views of five or more justices in reference to Titles III, IV, and V.

Chief Justice Rehnquist delivered that part of the opinion dealing with Titles III and IV, and here he had a far larger majority than did the five justices who prevailed on I and II. Justices O'Connor, Scalia, Kennedy, and Souter joined in his entire opinion; and Stevens, Ginsburg, and Breyer joined in all but one section of it. Justice Thomas joined in regard to most of the sections. This is the shortest of all the opinions, with the chief justice allotting at most two paragraphs to most sections, one stating the complaint and the other dismissing it. The Court reaffirmed the district court and dismissed one complaint after another on the ground that the plaintiffs lacked standing to bring the suit in a facial challenge to the law.

The problems of facially challenging a law manifested themselves almost immediately as the chief justice dealt with §305 of Title III. It required broadcast stations to provide the lowest unit charge to political advertisers beginning 45 days before a primary and 60 days before a general election, once the candidate promised that there would be no reference to another candidate for the same political office, and that the candidate identified himself or herself at the end of the ad and stated approval of the ad. Senator McConnell claimed that since he intended to run advertisements critical of his opponents in the future, and that he had run them in the past, he had sufficient standing to challenge the law.

"Standing" simply means that a party bringing suit has the right to participate in the litigation. For example, a business owner whose real estate taxes are raised in what he or she considers an unfair manner can challenge the law because he or she could suffer material losses if the tax hike goes into effect. The parent of a child injured in an automobile accident may bring suit on behalf of a daughter who, as a minor, may not be permitted to sue. A person who philosophically opposes the death penalty may not, however, enter a case in which a convicted murderer sentenced to death is appealing the punishment; that person has no direct interest—other than his or her views on capital punishment—and these are insufficient to give him or her standing.

When bringing a facial challenge to a law—that is, a challenge to a law before it goes into effect, on the grounds that it violates some provision of the Constitution—standing is very important. The person bringing the suit must be able to show that he or she, because of their position, or holdings, or beliefs (if the law regulates expression), will be directly harmed once the law is implemented. Standing must be specific; a direct nexus must be shown between the person's plans or holdings or beliefs and the operation of the law. To use the death penalty example again, if a state passed a law changing the method of execution from the gas chamber to beheading, a person who opposed capital punishment—no matter how sincere that belief— could not challenge the law; on the contrary, an inmate on death row would certainly have standing to claim that the new method violated the Eighth Amendment ban on cruel or unusual punishment.

The fact that McConnell had run ads critical of his opponents before and planned to do so again did not, in the eyes of the justices, give him the requisite standing. After briefly summarizing how important the Court considered standing under the provisions of Article III of the Constitution, Rehnquist pointed out that Senator McConnell's current term would not expire until January 2009, so that the earliest §305 would apply to him would be in the primary and general election of 2008. "This alleged injury in fact is too remote temporarily to satisfy Article III standing. . . . Because we hold that the McConnell plaintiffs lack standing to challenge §305, we affirm the District Court's dismissal of the challenge to BCRA §305."[43]

Similarly, in a challenge to §307 of BCRA, which increased, and indexed for inflation, the FECA contribution limits, the Court dismissed the claims of the Adams and Paul plaintiffs for lack of standing. The Adams group consisted of individual voters, groups of voters, and some candidates who claimed that the indexing provisions constituted electoral discrimination based on economic status. By increasing the contribution caps, they argued, people with limited means would be put at a disadvantage, since they lacked the ability to increase their donations. Secondly, the candidates in this group claimed that they wanted to base their campaigns on small donations, and that increasing the contribution limits put them at a disadvantage. The Paul group, representing groups who ran extensive press campaigns, complained that §307 violated the First Amendment Freedom of the Press Clause, and that the contribution limits in effect deprived them of editorial freedom of expression.

The Court practically dismissed these claims out of hand. As to the Adams voters, the Constitution guaranteed them equal access to the ballot; nothing promised them an equal voice in the electoral process. As a result, they had no claim on which to base their standing. As for the Adams candidates, they had chosen how they wished to finance their campaigns. The fact that §307 allowed their opponents to raise more money grew out of their own choices. The Paul plaintiffs also lacked standing because they could not show a "substantial likelihood that the requested relief will remedy their alleged injury in fact." Since it appeared they were actually attacking any and all contribution limits, they were in the wrong court. Such suits had to start in designated lower courts.[44]

Rehnquist also made short work of §§304 and 316, the "millionaire provisions" that allowed differential contribution limits for opponents of self-financed wealthy candidates. Once again, this challenge had been brought by the Adams candidates, and once again the Court could find no "cognizable injury that was 'fairly traceable' to BCRA." Moreover, as the district court had noted, none of the Adams plaintiffs was a candidate in an election in which the millionaire provisions would apply, and so the Court affirmed the lower tribunal's dismissal of the complaint.[45]

Standing did not play a role in the McConnell group's challenge to §311, which required that communications authorized by a candidate or political committee clearly identify the sponsor, and that if the ad had not been authorized by the candidate, and did not announce who paid for it, it lacked authorization. McConnell had claimed that this and all other limits on communication violated the First Amendment. The Court disagreed. It considered that providing this information bore "a sufficient relationship to the important governmental interest of 'shedding the light of publicity' on campaign financing."[46]

The only part of Title III that the Court struck down involved the prohibition against contributions by minors, §318. The Court noted that minors enjoy the protection of the First Amendment, and although the Court had upheld some limits on contributions, as in *Buckley,* as well as a total ban on direct contributions by corporations and unions, it had never approved a total ban on contributions by individuals. To justify such a ban the government would have to show a "sufficiently important interest," and that the remedy had been "closely drawn," in order to avoid an "unnecessary abridgement" of the First Amendment. The government claimed that §318 prevented wealthy parents from using their children as conduits to circumvent federal contribution limits. The government had shown no evidence that this actually occurred, and the Court believed that existing state and federal laws prevented adults from circumventing the limits. Children, therefore, retained the right to make contributions.[47]

In the only challenge to a Title IV provision, the Court dismissed the National Right to Life's argument that the district court had erred in granting intervener-defendant status to Senators McCain and Feingold and others under §403(b) because they lacked standing. The opinion did not really address this issue, but neatly sidestepped it. "It is clear," wrote the chief justice, "that the Federal Election Commission has standing, and therefore we need not address the standing of the intervener-defendants, whose position here is identical to the FEC's."[48]

The brevity of the disposition of the Title III provisions reflected the fact that none of them, with the exception of the ban on contributions by minors, really struck at the core political speech guaranteed by the First Amendment. Assuring lowest rate schedules in a specific time period, indexing contribution limits to reflect inflation, and the identification of sponsors of political advertisements could be seen primarily as technical adjustments to laws previously upheld. As to the millionaire provision, the Court followed a long-standing policy of not deciding an issue until ripe—that is, until it had a plaintiff with standing who could show actual injury. Compared to the far more substantive issues in Titles I and II, the Court found Title III matters easy.

★　★　★　★　★

Justice Stephen Breyer wrote that part of the opinion dealing with Title V of BCRA, requiring broadcasters to keep detailed records of political advertisements and requests for time. In upholding the provisions, Breyer was joined by Stevens, O'Connor, Souter, and Ginsburg, the same five who comprised the majority regarding Titles I and II. Section 504 required broadcasters to maintain public records of requests for air time for politically related advertisements. The McConnell plaintiffs, including the National Association of Broadcasters, claimed that §504 imposed onerous administrative burdens that had no justification, and therefore violated the First Amendment. The lower court had accepted this argument and had found §504 facially unconstitutional. The slim five-justice majority, however, disagreed and reversed the district court, holding §504 valid.

Section 504 had three separate provisions. Broadcasters had to keep records of "candidate requests"—that is, requests made by or on behalf of a candidate; "election message requests"—advertisements that either referred to a candidate or to any election for a federal office; and "issue requests," made by anyone in which the content related to a "national legislative issue of public importance," or otherwise relating to a "political matter of national importance."

The Court found no problem in upholding candidate requests, since the Federal Communications Commission (FCC) had required similar records in one form or another since 1938.[49] McConnell and the National Association of Broadcasters called this revised rule "intolerably burdensome and evasive"; Breyer said that the majority could not understand this claim. The FCC had over the years reported on what effort it took for licensees to comply with its rules, and estimated that the candidate request report imposed a burden of no more than six to seven hours of work per year on regular radio and television outlets and less than one hour on cable systems. "That burden means annual costs of a few hundred dollars at most," Breyer wrote, "a microscopic amount compared to the many millions of dollars of revenue broadcasters receive from candidates who wish to advertise."[50] Moreover, the candidate records were not unique; broadcasters had to keep many other types of records to comply with FCC regulations.

As for the McConnell claim that §504 failed to further any important governmental interest, the Court disagreed. Such reports not only allowed the FCC to determine if broadcasters had complied with other provisions of the Communications Act relating to political advertising, but also informed the public of which candidates sought air time, and how much they spent on it, information that would help the public evaluate candidate behavior. Similarly the election message requirement "can help both the regulatory agencies and the public evaluate broadcasting fairness, and determine the amount of money that individuals or groups, supporters or opponents, intend to spend to help elect a particular candidate."[51] Again, the claim that such reporting constituted an onerous burden on broadcasters received no sympathy from the Court.

With regard to the issue request, the McConnell plaintiffs argued that the terms "political matter of national importance" or "national legislative issue of public importance" were unconstitutionally vague or overbroad. The Court, however, found this language no more vague or overbroad than Congress had used to impose other reporting obligations on broadcasters. (Unlike the print media, which enjoy extensive, in fact almost total, protection from Congress under the Freedom of the Press Clause, the broadcast media, at least constitutionally, have been treated quite differently, with Congress able to impose wide-ranging controls.[52]) The Court admitted that the recordkeeping might be more burdensome than some FCC requirements, but also less problematic than others. In addition, §504 only required reporting the fact of a request, and the name and address of the person or group making the request; it did not ask for information about the content of the proposed ad. As a result, the Court found no First Amendment bar to §504 in terms of a facial challenge, but once the law went into effect, should there be an actual damage, then plaintiffs remained free to raise a constitutional argument on whether §504, as applied, violated their First Amendment rights.[53]

Chief Justice Rehnquist dissented from this opinion, and Breyer took a few paragraphs to rebut his argument. Rehnquist charged that the majority "approached §504 almost exclusively from the perspective of the broadcast licensees, ignoring the interests of the candidates and other purchasers, whose speech and association rights are affected." The chief justice also claimed that the government, had "proffer[ed] no interest whatever to support §504 as a whole." The fact that the FCC imposed other regulations did not compel the conclusion that §504, because it imposed no greater burden, was therefore constitutional.[54]

Breyer answered that although Rehnquist certainly was right in emphasizing the speech interests of the candidates, the majority did not ignore them. Rather, the Court saw the interests of the candidates and the broadcasters as substantially similar, and neither suffered under the requirement. The only separate claim advanced by McConnell that differed from that of the broadcasters involved strategy—that is, by having their requests made public, their broadcast advertising strategy would be given away to their opponents. The majority had rejected that argument, because §504 "can be applied, in a significant number of cases, without requiring any such political-strategy disclosure—either because disclosure in many cases will not create any such risk or because the FCC may promulgate rules requiring disclosure only after such risks disappear, or both." As to Rehnquist's second argument, that the existence of other burdensome rules did not support the constitutionality of §504 rules, Breyer responded that a long history of the Court's upholding federal rulemaking had made it unnecessary for the government to enter an extensive defense of these rules, which in so many ways merely tracked other regulations. Moreover, this had been a facial attack on §504, and the fact that the other rules had been upheld provided enough justification to sustain the new ones. "The Chief Justice's contrary view would lead us into an unfortunate—and at present unjustified—revolution in communications law. And that is why we disagree with his dissent."[55]

★ ★ ★ ★ ★

The dissents regarding §305 of Title III (as to the justiciability of its provisions) and to §504 of Title V (dealing with broadcaster record-keeping) have already been mentioned, but the heart of the dissents by Chief Justice Rehnquist and Justices Scalia, Kennedy, and Thomas focused on the majority opinion concerning the Title I ban on soft money, and the Title II ban on certain types of electioneering communication.

As we have seen, the central issue for the majority was: defining the type of political corruption that Congress could properly address. Definition mattered, because in *Buckley* the Court had sustained regulations impinging on First Amendment rights in order to curb corruption or the appearance of corruption. Given the recent experience of Watergate, "corruption" and "the appearance of corruption" meant something concrete, and brought to mind images of people with cash-stuffed satchels going in and out of the Nixon campaign headquarters. Defenders of BCRA, however, wanted the Court to expand that notion, to look at the subtle but nonetheless corrupting effects that soft money had on the political process.

The four dissenters rejected this view, and stood by the notion that corruption had to be overt—the trading of votes for dollars or something close to such a quid pro quo. They found the alleged proof of corruption offered by BCRA defenders insufficient to justify such major inroads on First Amendment rights. The majority rejected that view as "crabbed," and said that it "ignores precedent, common sense, and the realities of political fund-raising exposed by the record in this litigation." Corruption no longer meant a simple trade of votes for dollars, Stevens and O'Connor wrote, but "the manner in which parties have sold access to federal candidates and officeholders that has given rise to the appearance of undue influence. It is not unwarranted for Congress to conclude that the selling of access gives rise to the appearance of corruption."[56] But the dissents, especially the lead opinion by Justice Anthony Kennedy, which the other three signed in whole or in part, raised serious questions about the First Amendment and the degree to which it could be curtailed by Congress in an effort to cure the political system of alleged corruption. If the majority had deferred to Congress and accepted the fact-based view of the defenders of BCRA, the dissenters proved far less willing to allow Congress, just because it said a problem existed, to interfere with the traditional protections of free speech. Kennedy wasted no time in invoking the First Amendment:

> The First Amendment guarantees our citizens the right to judge for themselves the most effective means for the expression of political views and to decide for themselves which entities to trust as reliable speakers. Significant portions of Titles I and II of the Bipartisan Campaign Reform Act of 2002 constrain that freedom. These new laws force speakers to abandon their own preference for speaking through parties and organizations. And they provide safe harbor to the mainstream press, suggesting that the corporate media alone suffice to alleviate the burdens the Act places on the rights and freedoms of ordinary citizens. . . .
>
> Today's decision upholding these laws purports simply to follow *Buckley v. Valeo* (1976), and abide by *stare decisis*; but the majority, to make its decision work, must abridge free speech where *Buckley* did not. *Buckley* did not authorize Congress to decide what shapes and forms the national political dialogue is to take. To reach today's decision, the Court

surpasses *Buckley*'s limits and expands Congress's regulatory power. In so doing, it replaces discrete and respected First Amendment principles with new, amorphous, and unsound rules, rules which dismantle basic protections for speech.[57]

Until this case, Kennedy claimed, the Court had accepted but two principles to determine the validity of campaign finance restrictions. The first had been that of countering corruption, which he defined as an agreement for a quid pro quo between officeholders or candidates on the one hand and donors seeking to influence them on the other. The second had been the existence of large sums of money in corporate form—namely, companies and unions—and by accepting the corporate form these entities had been blocked from contributions. These two rationales had been the basis for the Court's decisions in *Buckley, Austin,* and *National Right to Work Committee.*

Kennedy and the other dissenters did not want to expand the definitions that the Court had handed down in these cases, all of which required that Congress show that the provisions clearly supported the anticorruption rationale expounded in *Buckley,* and had been closely drawn to do so. "The perception of corruption that the majority now asserts is somehow different from the quid pro quo potential discussed" in those opinions, and the majority, Kennedy charged, had expanded that definition in violation of the clear commands not only of the First Amendment but of past precedents as well. Kennedy found these new definitions far too vague and amorphous, so elastic as to allow almost any form of regulation that Congress chose to impose.[58]

Kennedy spent a fair amount of time pointing out the obvious—namely, that the majority had in fact abandoned the quid pro quo basis that he found in *Buckley.* The majority said that it had done so, and explained why—that new conditions indicated that the old idea no longer sufficed; that instead of an out-and-out trade of votes for dollars, a new problem had arisen, access to the candidate or officeholder only by those who could contribute the large amounts of soft money that evaded FECA limits. Kennedy did not find the majority reasoning persuasive, nor did he accept their so-called commonsense view of modern political reality. "Access in itself," he wrote, "shows only that in a general sense an officeholder favors someone or that someone has influence on the officeholder. There is no basis, in law or in fact, to say favoritism or influence in general is the same as corrupt favoritism or influence in particular." By making that unwarranted conclusion, the majority "dismantles basic First Amendment rules."[59]

Kennedy's dissent reflected, at least in part, the problems that had plagued the lower courts as well as Congress in passing BCRA. There had actually been very few instances of outright corruption; the quid pro quo type of deal had, fortunately, been relatively rare in recent U.S. history. Watergate, which triggered the FECA amendments that eventually led to *Buckley*, had in many ways been a fluke. Although the defenders of BCRA had piled up thousands of pages of anecdotal material, their basic argument had been a sort of, "If there's smoke then there has to be fire," and the fire they attacked involved access to the men and women in office who could enact policies that would affect their interests. Those without money would have no access, and therefore be shut out of the process.

But did this constitute corruption or its appearance? BCRA said yes, and it would be wiser to close off the spigot of soft money before the situation reached an actual quid pro quo situation; purchasing access provided enough appearance of corruption. The majority accepted this reasoning, the dissenters did not, and the dissenters had a strong argument in claiming that this new definition of corruption imposed greater limits on the First Amendment than had *Buckley*. Their dissents reflected their bitterness at what they believed to be an abandonment not only of the rules developed in prior decisions, but of basic First Amendment principles as well.

Justice Kennedy—"This new definition of corruption sweeps away all protections for speech that lie in its path; [the decision] leaves us less free than before."[60]

Justice Scalia—"If the Bill of Rights had intended an exception to the freedom of speech in order to combat this malign proclivity of the officeholders to agree with those who agree with him, and to speak more with his supporters than his opponents, it would surely have said so."[61]

Justice Thomas—"Apparently, winning in the marketplace of ideas is no longer a sign that the ultimate good has been reached by free trade in ideas. It is now evidence of 'corruption.' This conclusion is antithetical to everything for which the First Amendment stands."[62]

Justice Scalia especially hit hard on what he perceived as the majority's betrayal of the First Amendment:

> This is a sad day for the freedom of speech. Who could have imagined that the same Court which, within the past four years, has sternly disapproved of restrictions upon such inconsequential forms of expression as virtual child pornography, tobacco advertising, dissemination of illegally intercepted communications, and sexually explicit cable programming, would smile with favor upon a law that cuts to the heart of what the First Amendment is meant to protect: the right to criticize the government. For that is what the most offensive provisions of this legislation are all about. We are governed by Congress, and this legislation prohibits the criticism of Members of Congress by those entities most capable of giving such criticism loud voice: national political parties and corporations, both of the commercial and the not-for-profit sort. It forbids pre-election criticism of incumbents by corporations, even not-for-profit corporations, by use of their general funds; and forbids national-party use of "soft money" to fund "issue ads" that incumbents find so offensive.
>
> To be sure, the legislation is evenhanded: It similarly prohibits criticism of the candidates who oppose Members of Congress in their reelection bids. But as everyone knows, this is an area in which evenhandedness is not fairness.[63]

The heart of Scalia's dissent consisted of his attack on what he considered three fallacies inherent in the majority opinion: (1) money is not speech, (2) pooling money is not speech, and (3) speech by corporations can be abridged. Scalia made plain what everyone on the Court knew—namely, that in politics money buys expression, whether directly through the purchase of advertisements in one's own name, or less directly by contributions to a campaign or candidate who will then speak out on issues. For the majority, soft money, because of its potential for corruption, deserved less First Amendment protection than did other types of campaign expenditures. For the dissenters, political speech of any kind, made directly or purchased indirectly, constituted the core values protected by the First Amendment. The debate in *McConnell v. Federal Election Commis-*

sion was hardly new—it had appeared in the district court opinions, in the briefs before both courts, and in the debate that had gone on in Congress leading up to the passage of McCain-Feingold.

★　★　★　★　★

Judge Henderson had complained in the district court that judges had been like ships passing in the night, never touching one another, never actually coming to grips with the key issues. In fact, all three judges had touched upon the salient questions, but because they differed so much they had been unable to forge a coherent judicial response to BCRA. That was less true of the Supreme Court. The five who made up the majority agreed that in trying to prevent corruption or its appearance, Congress had the compelling governmental interest to restrict some forms of political speech through campaign finance reform, and that it had done so in an appropriate, closely drawn manner. The majority also expanded the meaning of corruption beyond the quid pro quo that had been at the heart of *Buckley* and its progeny and accepted the government's contention that soft money purchased access, a new but equally virulent form of corruption. This soft money paid for attack-issue advertisements that, for all practical purposes, rendered the magic words test of *Buckley* obsolete and therefore could be proscribed. The dissenters argued with these conclusions, and in each of the opinions there was a give-and-take in which the majority responded to some claim by the dissenters, or the dissenters attempted to take apart the basis for the majority conclusion.

But the themes that emerged from the beginning went on to dominate the arguments before and within the Court. On the one hand, those who looked at what they saw as the real world of politics attempted to devise a scheme that, although perhaps circumscribing some First Amendment rights, could be justified because it would purify the political process. It would make election campaigns more honest and open in that they would not be distorted by millions of dollars of soft money and the appearance of attack advertisements that depended on those dollars.

On the other hand stood those who believed that the political process always involved a give-and-take between candidates and those interests seeking to present their case. Although conceding that any deal involving cash for votes should be illegal, they did not see soft money, issue advertisements, or other recent developments in the campaign process as necessarily bad. Certainly they did not view them as sufficient to warrant any limitation on political speech protected by the First Amendment.

In the end, five justices deferred to congressional findings and agreed with the defenders of the law that sufficient evidence existed to warrant the restrictions placed on campaign finance and on political speech. Their opinion emphasized what they saw as real evidence and common sense. Four did not see it that way, and their opinions upheld what had been the Court's devotion to the basic principle that under the First Amendment, political speech in any form is a core value that should not be restricted.

*   *   *   *   *

The academic and legal reaction to the decision proved almost unanimously negative. Lillian BeVier of the University of Virginia, a longtime advocate of political speech as the core of the First Amendment, found herself "largely dismayed" by the majority opinion, and admitted, "One has, after all, been quite thoroughly vanquished."[64] Robert F. Bauer, a lawyer specializing in election law, lamented the decision as a signal of how little the Court valued another First Amendment right. The decision, he declared, "signals the effective demise of the right of association in campaign finance jurisprudence."[65] James Bopp, Jr., and Richard E. Coleson, who represented several socially conservative groups in the case, angrily charged that the Court had abandoned "its role as guardian of free speech where and when it counts the most, while giving the unenumerated abortion right a highly protected status." The Court, they claimed, had shown Congress far too much deference, not in protecting the rights of the unborn, but in "protecting incumbent politicians from the people."[66] Other authors also complained that the Court had been too deferential to congressional findings, all to the detriment of core First Amendment values of speech and association. Two lawyers who represented the NRA charged that Title II of BCRA had been cut from the same cloth as the infamous Sedition Act of 1798, aimed specifically at stifling criticism of government and its elected members.[67]

Although one might have expected such criticisms from lawyers on the losing side, the analysis by the distinguished law professor Richard A. Epstein proved equally critical. He denounced the decision as "yet another backward step in the march of constitutional law." Even if one conceded that Congress had the power to enact laws aimed at preventing corruption or its appearance in electoral campaigns, it had done so in a heavy-handed manner that deserved not the acquiescence of the Court but "an instant and merciless repudiation." Although Epstein believed that judges should normally show deference to legislative policy judgments, he argued that courts also had an independent role to play, a role the Supreme Court had completely abandoned in the *McConnell* case. The "dense network of regulations" under BCRA promised full employment for a generation of lawyers, but the bottom line "is less political speech." For that the Court would have to bear much of the blame.[68]

Would BCRA work now that it had the blessing of the highest court in the land? Elizabeth Garrett, director of the University of Southern California's Center for the Study of Law and Politics, thought that the disclosure aspects of the law would probably be fairly effective, but they were the act's least controversial aspects. Moreover, by affirming BCRA's requirements, the Court had put its stamp of approval on other forms of campaign financial disclosure, and these rules "are the most widespread regulation of the campaign finance system, and they are the sole regulation in several electoral arenas," such as state and local elections.[69] Beyond that, Professor Samuel Issacharoff of Columbia University expected few positive results in straightening out the morass that campaign finance had become. If history were any guide, all BCRA would do is "prompt new forms by which money seeks to influence, cajole, inform, capture, and even corrupt." Although the law banned soft money and attempted to limit hard money, in fact the law opened the gates to all sorts of hard money contributions, and in his view hard money could be just as corrosive an influence on the political process as soft.[70]

On the other hand, Professor Robert C. Post of the Yale Law School suggested that one ought to look at the opinion as part of the ongoing dialogue between Congress and the Court over the extent of congressional powers. There had been several high-profile cases in which the Court had told Congress that it had no power to intrude on functions traditionally within the ambit of the states. "Things were getting pretty explosive," he noted, and he had little doubt that Justice O'Connor had been moved, at least in part, by "her political antennae. . . . The tension was too high, and she understood that the rhythm of the Court's relationship with Congress had to be attended to, the pace of the conversation had to be lowered." In effect, "the Court gave Congress space to breathe."[71]

★   ★   ★   ★   ★

Supporters of McCain-Feingold rejoiced. For example, Thomas Mann and Norman Ornstein, academics who had been involved with the bill from the beginning and who had testified in its defense, believed that the Court had acted properly. They conceded that perhaps they did not understand all of the doctrinal implications of the Court's decision, but what mattered was that they now had a bill with teeth in it.[72] The bill's authors and advocates had won far more than they had expected to, in that the majority had upheld the ban on soft money and all its ancillary provisions, allowed regulation of issue ads, and required the media to keep public records of who asked for and purchased political advertising time. But in their celebration, perhaps they forgot the line in the majority's last paragraph: "Money, like water, will always find an outlet."[73] The truth of that prediction would manifest itself far sooner than anyone had expected.

Epilogue
McCain-Feingold:
Requiescat in Pace

I can assure all Americans that no longer can a
member of Congress or a senator pick up the
phone, call a trial lawyer, a corporate head, or a
union leader and say, 'Write me a six- or
seven-figure check. And by the way, your
legislation is coming up soon.'
—Senator John McCain

This law will not remove one dime from
politics. Soft money is not gone, it has just
changed its address.
—Senator Mitch McConnell

IN THE DAYS following the High Court's decision in the *McConnell*
case, one heard the expected joyful statements from the bill's backers and the regretful ones from those who had opposed it. The
national political parties had already begun their preparations for the
2004 election campaigns to conform their fund-raising and campaign
expenditure programs to the new law. Although some optimists predicted that a new era in political democracy would be ushered in
with the elimination of soft-money and false-issue ads, realists predicted that money—lots of money—would easily find its way into
the political system through some other avenue. Before long not one
but several outlets opened, and campaign money poured through
them at a rate equal to or even greater than the floods of soft money
in the 1990s. Well before American voters went to the polls in
November 2004 to choose between George W. Bush and John Kerry,
it became clear that this campaign would be—despite the best efforts
of BCRA—the most expensive in the nation's history. The Court's
decision in *McConnell* may hold more relevance for future First

Amendment jurisprudence than for the never-ending efforts to reform the campaign finance system; in the short run, for most Americans at least, it appeared that in terms of campaign finance, nothing had really changed.

⋆　⋆　⋆　⋆　⋆

The day after the Court's decision, the *Washington Post* ran a story with the headline "McCain, Feingold and Co. Laugh Last." It began, "For nearly a decade, they were the Don Quixotes of Capitol Hill, whose crusades against the influence of big money in politics caused colleagues to snicker at their relentless optimism and zeal in the face of repeated defeats." But now that small band of reformers—John McCain, Russell Feingold, Christopher Shays, and Martin Meehan— had the last laugh. McCain, who had made campaign finance reform the centerpiece of his bid for the Republican presidential nomination in 2000, was visiting the U.S. Naval Base at Guantánamo Bay, Cuba, when an aide called to inform him about the ruling. When a reporter asked him if he had ever lost hope after years of congressional obstruction, delays, presidential vetoes, and court challenges, he laughed and said no. "Did Don Quixote ever despair?"

In his official statements, McCain reiterated that the bill reflected longtime citizen revulsion at the abuses in the system. "For years, poll after poll revealed the public's strong support for genuine campaign finance reform. These polls clearly marked the progress of public sentiment on this question." The polls, according to McCain, indicated that voters had lost faith in the basic integrity of the system. "That faith was shaken and it was imperative that Congress act."[1] In an interview on the *Today Show*, McCain said that he could "assure all Americans that no longer can a member of Congress or a senator pick up the phone, call a trial lawyer, a corporate head or a union leader and say, 'Write me a six- or seven-figure check. And, by the way, your legislation is coming up soon.'"[2]

His cosponsors echoed this theme. According to Christopher Shays, "We believed the cause was noble, it was worth fighting for, and we trusted each other." Senator Russ Feingold claimed that "the system had careened so far out of control that even members of Congress didn't want to be part of the system." Scandals involving corporate giants such as Enron gave them an added impetus. "We knew the bill would ultimately pass," Shays said, "because the system was going to get worse. . . . There would always be some new abuse."[3]

Other defenders of BCRA and of the Court decision upholding it could not have been happier. Fred Wertheimer, president of Democracy 21 and a longtime champion of reform, declared: "In the end, it was the combination of extraordinary leadership on the part of the congressional leaders of this battle and the will of the American people that forced this legislation through an extremely resistant Washington establishment."[4] The Public Citizen, another reform advocacy group, issued a statement signed by its president, Joan Claybrook, and by Alan B. Morrison, the lawyer who headed the Public Citizen Litigation Group. Morrison had worked on drafting BCRA and had been one of the lawyers representing McCain and Feingold in the case. They praised the decision as a "home run," and a "magnificent vindication" of more than a decade's work. It would ensure "the removal of the corrupting influence of 'soft money' from elections." As for the Court's warning that money would find new outlets, Public Citizen gave its solemn assurances that it would "be on guard to be sure that corrosive influences on the political process are brought to the public's attention, and that Congress remains ever-vigilant in safeguarding our democracy and the electoral process."[5]

Common Cause, which had over the years served as a gadfly in efforts to get the Federal Election Commission to enforce election finance law, termed the decision "a major victory for democracy and all Americans. The American people wanted this law, Congress enacted it, and now the Supreme Court has ruled it constitutional," exulted president Chellie Pingree. "The toxic link between donors who write six-figure checks and people in power at the highest levels of government has been severed for good." Praising the bill's congressional sponsors, Pingree noted that "this struggle took more than a decade, but it proves that citizens can trump the power of special interests."[6]

The foundation that had underwritten many of the studies used by the BCRA defense team, the Pew Charitable Trusts, "commended" the decision. Rebecca W. Rimel, the president of Pew, declared that BCRA and its "subsequent affirmation by the Supreme Court are important first steps to mending the broken campaign finance system." Repairing that system "is vital for restoring Americans' trust in democracy," and she promised that Pew would continue supporting efforts "to shine light on campaign finance activities."[7]

Newspapers around the country in general praised the ruling. The *Alameda Times-Star* had just about given up hope that there would be meaningful reform, but Congress had acted and now the Court had validated McCain-Feingold. The ruling "counters that pessimism and raises hope for such other proposed reforms as increased public financing of elections. . . . It also opens the door to further refinements as politics finds other streams through which its mother's milk—money—may flow." The California paper opined that campaign finance reform—"the Rodney Dangerfield of American political policy—finally got some respect, and it came from the U.S. Supreme Court of Chief Justice William Rehnquist and justices Antonin Scalia and Clarence Thomas, even though none of the conservative justices approve" of the law.[8]

On the East Coast, an op-ed piece in the *Boston Globe* by law professor Spencer Overton praised the decision, but warned that if Americans truly wanted to reform the system, other steps remained, especially empowering the average citizen by increasing the influence of the smaller contributor. To do this, Overton urged that two critical steps be taken. First, reward contributions of $100 or less by providing a 4–1 match from public funds. In the proposed revision to the presidential campaign funding law, candidates who emphasized small gifts would reap significant rewards and thus could avoid the fat cats looking for favors or access. Second, Overton wanted this system extended to *all* federal elections, for the House and Senate as well as the presidency.[9]

The Knight-Ridder papers carried similar editorials praising the *McConnell* decision, but they also warned that enacting McCain-Feingold and securing the Court's blessing did not automatically reform the system: "The nation will have to keep a close watch to see if the campaign finance reform law restores people's faith in democracy and actually limits the undue influence money has on politics, without making it too hard for political groups to make themselves heard."[10]

Not everyone praised the ruling, and as a reporter for the *Washington Post* commented, "It's not every day the National Rifle Association and the American Civil Liberties Union are outraged by the same Supreme Court decision."[11] An angry Anthony D. Romero, executive director of the ACLU, condemned the ruling. "The notion that the government can tell an organization like the ACLU when and how it should address important civil liberties issues is a form of censorship masquerading as campaign finance reform. The fact that those restrictions have now been upheld by the Supreme Court is extremely disappointing." Romero predicted that the decision "will do far more to restrict political speech than to curtail the influence of money on politics. More speech should not be seen as a threat to our democracy, but sadly, that is the message of the Court's decision."[12] A longtime supporter who had often argued on the ACLU's behalf in defense of the First Amendment, Floyd Abrams, denounced the ruling as "incomprehensible," and charged that the justices had missed the fundamental importance of political speech. "It almost reads like a tax case rather than a First Amendment case. In style, tone and nature, it reads like an opinion about regulation by government of some sort of improper activity."[13]

Wayne LaPierre, head of the NRA, shared Romero's anger, calling the ruling "the most significant change in the First Amendment since the Alien and Sedition Act of 1798, which tried to make it a crime to criticize a member of Congress. This whole thing from the start has been an inside deal among politicians to stop criticism, whether it comes from us or from the Sierra Club." LaPierre's analysis of BCRA as a means of protecting incumbents resonated with other critics of the law and the decision. James Bopp, Jr., the general counsel at the James Madison Center for Free Speech, denounced the law as "an orgy of incumbent protection." Like other critics of the ruling, he noted the irony that a law designed to limit the influence of money in politics left one class of citizens almost entirely unregulated—the superrich. People willing and able to spend their own money on political ads could say whatever they wanted, whenever they wanted.

LaPierre promised, however, that the NRA would not be silenced. "We're going to be heard, and they're going to be surprised how loud we're going to be heard." Like the corporations and unions that had to establish independent committees to air their political ads, the NRA would also create a PAC. LaPierre said that the organization would immediately ask its 4 million members and 28 million affiliated members to donate $20 each, so that the organization's voice could be heard. (The ACLU, on the other hand, dismissed the idea that it should have to form a political committee to promote issues that it saw as nonpartisan.)[14]

An "obviously disappointed" Kenneth Starr expressed his views in an online discussion run by the *Washington Post* on the very afternoon the Court handed down its decision. Starr pointed out that his clients had facially challenged the law, and that given the close vote, it would not be inconceivable that in the future an "as applied" challenge, showing all of the law's defects, might lead to another result. Beyond that, he predicted that many of the law's supporters, enamored by the idea of "reform," would actually be appalled at its "draconian practical consequences."[15]

★   ★   ★   ★   ★

On the day the decision came down, Democrats, Republicans, and political commentators speculated on just what the new rules would mean. Under BCRA, an individual could give no more than $2,000 to a candidate and no more than $25,000 to a political party in an election cycle. Both parties had three major committees, the National Committee that dealt with presidential campaigns, and both a House and a Senate committee. Bob Bauer, a Democratic campaign finance lawyer, told a reporter that in his view, *McConnell* "was not a good decision for the parties," since it would make it much more difficult for them to raise money.[16]

Initially, it appeared that the Democrats, who had relied far more than the GOP on soft money, would be hardest hit by BCRA. The Democrats, according to political scientist and campaign finance scholar Gary Jacobson of the University of California at San Diego, "are going to be in trouble, and unless they could find—and quickly —alternatives to soft money, they are going to be at a major disadvantage." Representative Thomas M. Reynolds (R-N.Y.), chair of the National Republican Congressional Committee, practically crowed in declaring, "Today's ruling breaks the Democrats' back." Even Jim Jordan, former director of the Democratic Senatorial Campaign Committee, conceded the decision is "particularly a blow to the Democratic Party."

John McCain just scoffed at predictions that the political parties would be worse off because of his bill; such suggestions, he declared, are "ridiculous on their face." The parties would now be free of the "corrupting" influence of large contributions, an addiction, he charged, that had rendered them "irrelevant." Now they could concentrate on rebuilding their bases, bringing more people into the political process, people who had hitherto shunned the system since they considered it corrupt.

In the end, BCRA did not appear to have affected the fund-raising abilities of either party, although the deep ideological divisions and high passions of the 2004 presidential campaign may have induced more people to donate than might have done so at other times. Although Democrats, as usual, lagged behind Republicans in overall fund-raising, they did not do badly. As of June 30, a benchmark period for measuring campaign contributions, the Democratic National Party had collected $230 million in hard money, more than double the $102 million they had raised at the same time in 2000. The Republicans also doubled their intake, receiving $381 million, up from $178 million four years earlier.[17] By October the DNC, RNC, and the various congressional committees tied to the national parties had all exceeded the amounts raised in the 2000 election cycle.[18]

Conditions for both parties were certainly not as bleak as the pessimists had predicted. McCain-Feingold had been on the books for nearly two years by the time the Supreme Court handed down its decision in *McConnell*. During that time party leaders collected millions of dollars in contributions, some of which would be prohibited after the law took effect. But the parties also looked at what other choices they had. Liberal Howard Dean's success on the Internet and Richard Viguery's mass mailings for conservative groups showed that although it might take greater effort, money could still be raised. The Internet especially offered parties a relatively inexpensive way to advertise as they raised money. Anyone who opened their Web browser from March 2004 onward—that is, after John Kerry secured the Democratic nomination—probably found an appeal, such as, "Buy George W. Bush a one-way ticket back to Crawford." This technique seemed to work very well for Kerry, who raised record amounts of money in the spring quarter, mostly from small contributors. At the same time, mass mailings are also profitable. The executive director of a national rights protection group once explained that all he needed was *a 2 percent response* to bring in more money than it cost for the mailing.

In the immediate aftermath of *McConnell*, one particular type of activist suddenly gained prominence on the political stage. In the past, candidates and parties had valued not only the wealthy individual who could write a six- or even seven-figure contribution, but also the person, probably well-to-do but not necessarily rich, who could get other people to open their wallets. Under the new law, a campaign volunteer who got 25 people to give the maximum individual amount of $2,000 brought in $50,000 to the candidate's coffers, all legitimate "hard money." George W. Bush had, early on, recognized the value of these people, and had created a special club of so-called Rangers, each of whom had raised at least $200,000 for his campaign.[19] In 2004, he expanded this category and created new ones.

Adding further to the confusion, backers of BCRA, flush with their victory in the Court, announced that their next target would be the Federal Election Commission itself. Senator Russ Feingold said that he, John McCain, Christopher Shays, and Martin Meehan had, as one of their top priorities, replacing the agency that had proven so ineffective in enforcing campaign finance laws. Instead of six members, three from each party, the reformers wanted a three-person commission, a chair and two other members—the latter two from different parties—appointed by the president and confirmed by the Senate. In addition, no member of the new agency could come from the current FEC, have been a party employee, a candidate, an officeholder, or have worked for a candidate or officeholder. Current FEC chair Ellen Weintraub, a Democrat, called the new proposal a "pipe dream." Whoever held the White House, she noted, would be able to name a majority of the commission.[20]

Although she did not go into details, Weintraub pointed out one of the basic problems with the FEC. So long as it stood evenly balanced with six members of each party, it could not or would not act, except when confronted by so egregious a violation that it had no choice, or when groups like Common Cause called on the courts to make the FEC do its duty.[21] Although a three-member panel would not be tied, one of the parties would always have a majority. Beyond that, the restrictive rule for membership on the panel eliminated just about everyone in the country who had any practical experience with politics. Although this new FEC might have been more pure, at least in its sponsors' eyes, one wonders just how it would function in the real political world, where its members had no clue about how things worked.

Instead of worrying about reconstituting the FEC, McCain and company might well have paid attention to plugging some of the loopholes in the law they had so laboriously crafted. The Supreme Court had itself approved one such activity under the BCRA , noting that certain independent groups, organized under §527 of the tax code, "remain free to raise soft money to fund voter registration, get-out-the-vote activities, mailings, and broadcast advertising."[22] Both Democrats and Republicans recognized the importance of this ruling. Republican lawyer Jan Baran said that *McConnell* "makes the world a safer place for billionaires and 527 organizations. Nonparty interest groups under the current law may raise and spend soft money and the political parties may not." Steve Rosenthal, chief executive of the pro-Democrat Americans Coming Together (ACT), one of the most prominent 527 groups, took the decision as a green light for his organization to inform, register, and turn out voters, and by "inform" he meant telling voters "about the failed policies of the Bush administration."[23] Well before the Supreme Court handed down its decisions, some of these 527's had started preparing for the 2004 presidential campaign.

★   ★   ★   ★   ★

In the summer of 2002, Democratic and Republican strategists began planning how to get their hands on a resource they knew lay waiting for them—millions of dollars in soft money that would, theoretically, be barred by BCRA. As a *Washington Post* article noted, "White House political operatives, high-profile lobbyists, former aides of President Bill Clinton and staffers at the Democratic and Republican senatorial campaign committees are setting up tax-exempt organizations to raise and spend 'soft money.'" These new groups, such as the Republican-leaning Progress for America and the New Democratic Network, had no formal ties to either party, and thus came under the mantle of section 527 of the tax code—tax-exempt advocacy organizations. Although 527 committees have to make regular disclosures to the Internal Revenue Service and to the Federal Election Commission, BCRA explicitly exempted such groups from the ban on soft money.[24] Over the next two years the 527's became increasingly important in national politics.

Initially most of these groups seemed to identify with the Democratic Party. After John Kerry locked up the Democratic presidential nomination, he found himself with practically no money to combat the intensive television attack campaign launched by the Republicans, funded by the more than $100 million George Bush had raised during the primary season but had not spent. To counter the attacks on Kerry, groups like the Media Fund (headed by former Clinton aide Harold Ickes) and MoveOn.org began running "issue ads" such as, "George Bush's priorities are eroding the American Dream." Billionaire George Soros and his wife, Susan Weber Soros, gave $5 million to help start Americans Coming Together, and $1.46 million to MoveOn.org. Peter B. Lewis, CEO of the Progressive Corporation, gave $3 million to ACT and $500,000 to MoveOn.org. Linda Pritzker, of the Hyatt Hotel family, gave $4 million to the joint fund-raising effort.

Ellen Malcolm, president of Emily's List, which raises money to support candidates favorable to women's issues, explained that "we needed to have a message up on the air that tells the truth about the Bush record and defends the Democratic position on the issues." Bush, she said, had $100 million and Kerry at the time had nothing, so "it's very important that there are alternative voices out there talking about the Bush record." Asked about how much had been raised, Malcolm estimated it was about $75 million, although it was not clear that all of that money was already in hand.[25]

BCRA exempted 527 organizations because in the past they had been primarily one-issue groups, and it had been assumed that they would stay out of the electoral races and concentrate on their issues, such as abortion or the environment or gun control. But nothing in either the tax code or BCRA requires 527 groups to remain silent on candidates. The requirement is only that they may not be connected to, or coordinate their activities with, a political party or committee. One does not need a direct phone line to the DNC or RNC, however, to know what sort of ads will benefit a candidate or how to attack one. Moreover, BCRA placed no limits on how much 527's could raise or how much any individual could donate.

The general counsel's office of the Federal Election Commission immediately proposed new rules that would, as one commentator put it, bring the Democratic "shadow party" under BCRA regulation and impose hard-money requirements similar to those under which the regular political committees now had to function. The Republican Party, which had few 527's working on its behalf—and none as well financed as ACT—immediately applauded. Christine Iverson, the spokesperson for the Republican National Committee, described the proposed rules as a "warning shot across the bows of the 527s."[26] Common Cause also weighed in, applauding the proposed rules, and urging the FEC to adopt them to prevent the 527's from undermining the effort of the BCRA to clean up the system.[27]

The Republican National Committee, with the blessing of the Bush White House, especially wanted to close down the 527's, but found that the FEC, for a change, could not decide what to do. On Monday, February 16, the chair of the agency, Republican Bradley A. Smith (who had been highly critical of the *McConnell* decision and of BCRA), announced that he thought the 527 committees should remain free to raise and spend large sums of soft money.[28] In a 37-page memo to his colleagues, Smith argued that McCain-Feingold had been aimed at political parties and "does not apply to the regulation of political entities outside these specific provisions." Although, the *McConnell* decision "imposes numerous restrictions on the fundraising abilities of the political parties. . . . Interest groups, however, remain free to fund voter registration, [get-out-the-vote] activities, mailings, and broadcast advertising." In addition, he offered, as proof of his position, a letter from eight Democratic senators, including Minority Leader Thomas Daschle (S.Dak.), Christopher J. Dodd (Conn.), and Dianne Feinstein (Calif.), in which they asserted that the law had been aimed at political parties and did not impose similar restrictions on other types of political organizations or tax-exempt groups. House Democrats sent a similar letter signed by their leader, Nancy Pelosi (Calif.), and 50 others.[29]

Three days later, the FEC met and decided that at least some of the 527's were subject to regulation, but it could not agree on what those regulations should be. By a 4–2 vote, the agency warned Americans for a Better Country (ABC) that any activities that promoted, supported, or opposed a federal candidate had to be paid for with hard money. But then the commissioners apparently divided on what to do next, and delayed consideration of any specific regulations indefinitely. Ellen L. Weintraub, now the FEC vice chair, noted that the agency's actions that day meant little insofar as restricting 527 activities; they just had to act a little smarter. "I don't think sophisticated political actors," she said, "would have a hard time figuring out how to work within this framework."[30] When the final vote came in May, two of the Republican commissioners, Smith and David Mason, resisted White House pressure and, on philosophical grounds, voted not to impose restrictions on the 527's for the current campaign. The vote also reflected fears of the staff that it would be impossible to draft the necessary regulations and go through the elaborate rulemaking process in time. FEC General Counsel Lawrence H. Norton, a proponent of tough regulation, admitted that "even the most conservative approaches [to regulating 527's] raise issues that need to be thought through in a manner that the current schedule makes difficult."[31]

The FEC in the meantime had to defend itself in federal courts against attacks by both the Bush-Cheney campaign and two sponsors of BCRA, Representatives Christopher Shays and Martin Meehan. The lawyers for the president's campaign committee had sought an injunction against the FEC that they hoped would halt the work of Democratic-leaning 527's in their support of John Kerry. In September federal judge James Robertson agreed that the FEC was "notoriously slow" in investigating and acting on complaints, including the one that the Bush camp had lodged six months earlier. But he found that federal law did not give him the power to act independently on alleged campaign law violations, or demand that the FEC move more quickly. "The FEC moves with glacial speed," Robertson noted, "but that's the way Congress set it up, because that's apparently the way Congress likes it."[32]

In another case, district judge Colleen Kollar-Kotelly, who had been a member of the court initially hearing the challenge to BCRA, struck down more than a dozen FEC rules on political fund-raising just six weeks before the election. She declared that the rules, adopted by the commission after the passage of BCRA, essentially nullified provisions affecting how coordination between parties and other groups must be conducted. The FEC regulations, she found, would "create an immense loophole that would facilitate the circumvention of the act's contribution limits, thereby creating the potential for gross abuse," an outcome that the authors of the law had never intended. The case had originally been filed in October 2002, but had been held up until after the Supreme Court had decided BCRA's constitutionality in *McConnell.* The FEC had unsuccessfully asked Kollar-Kotelly to dismiss the suit, claiming that the commission had the authority to interpret the law, and that lawmakers had no standing to sue over rules implementing the legislation. She rejected both of the FEC's defenses outright.[33]

In the meantime, the 527's acted in exactly the same way as the soft-money committees of the pre-BCRA era, raising and spending millions of dollars in soft money. The Media Fund announced a fund-raising goal of $95 million for the year, and ACT reported that it paid 98 percent of its costs with soft money, raised primarily through large donations, and only 2 percent with what would be considered hard money—donations of $2,000 or less. ACT, which, along with the Media Fund, planned to conduct voter mobilizations in 17 "battleground" states, also announced plans to raise $95 million.[34]

By the end of June, filings with the FEC showed that large 527's had raised (cash in hand) nearly $242 million, and spent over $265 million. The Joint Victory Campaign led the way with $41.78 million, followed by the Media Fund with $28 million, and MoveOn.org at $9 million. In addition, several nonfederal 527s had raised large sums of money. The ACT NOW PAC's nonfederal account had nearly $27 million, and the Republican and Democratic Governors groups had $23.5 million and $14.4 million, respectively. The two largest donors had been Peter Lewis with $14 million and George Soros with $12.6 million. By way of comparison, George W. Bush at this time had raised $232 million, the largest war chest amassed by a presidential candidate in history, and this did not count the $75 million he would receive in federal funds after the GOP convention in September.[35]

Although Republicans had their own 527's, it appeared that the GOP had far more trouble establishing new ones than did the Democrats. A newspaper report indicated that Republican fund-raisers attempting to get businesses to donate to 527's had run into problems. Some people who had donated generously to George Bush's 2000 campaign, and had already given in 2004, refused to get involved with 527's because it would look suspicious. A key Republican 527, Progress for America, tried to recruit James Francis, Jr., to be its chair, and he refused. Francis had run the Bush 2000 campaign's "Pioneer" program, and he said, "It gets down to 'What does it look like?' And it might not look like I was independent." Although he could have complied with election law, he noted, appearances did matter and he decided the problems outweighed any benefits.

According to GOP lawyer Jan W. Baran, corporations, which could give money to 527's, had been very reluctant to do so. Kenneth A. Gross, a corporate lawyer specializing in election law and finance, told his clients "to proceed with caution" in regard to 527's, and to make sure that if they donated funds, to secure written assurances that the activities of the group would not be coordinated with political committees or candidates. A *Wall Street Journal* survey of the top 20 businesses giving soft money, before BCRA went into effect, showed more than half of them resisting pressure to give. In fact only one, Bell South, responded that it would make donations. For many business owners, the fact that President Bush had already raised more than $200 million provided a disincentive to give, since it seemed to them that he already had more than enough to wage a campaign.[36] In the end, however, 527 groups backing President Bush actually raised and spent more money than did those favoring John Kerry. In the final three weeks of the campaign alone, 527's supporting Bush spent nearly $30 million on television and radio ads, nearly three times what the pro-Democratic 527s spent.[37]

A few days before the Democratic convention in Boston, a news service headlined its story, "527 Groups Gain Political Clout." The article began with a story about Dave Leasure, who after working three decades in a steel mill in Canton, Ohio, found himself unemployed. He now worked for a 527—Americans Coming Together — knocking on doors in northern Ohio. "We have a petition here to protect the steel jobs," he told a woman who answered at one home, "and also we'd like to get your opinions on the direction of the country." He then asked her whom she had voted for in 2000, and what she thought of President Bush. He tapped her answers into his Palm Pilot, which he would later download, so his new bosses could analyze the data. Like his employer, Leasure wanted to see Bush defeated, and although he was not working directly for John Kerry, he and thousands like him—all employed by 527's—went around doing the foot soldier work necessary to get out the vote and win an election.

"Our goal," said ACT state spokesperson Jess Goode, "is to identify and mobilize progressive voters, people who are motivated by progressive values." If Goode spoke the language of an independent agency, the ACT Web site did not: "ACT needs you to help beat George W. Bush and elect Democrats up and down the ticket in 2004—in federal, state, and local elections."[38] By mid-July ACT claimed to have registered more than 31,000 voters in Ohio, a battleground state in the 2004 election. It also claimed to be registering tens of thousands of voters in other key states, including Florida, Missouri, and New Mexico, all considered to be tight races that were key to either a Bush or a Kerry victory.[39]

As of midsummer 2004, Democratic-leaning 527's were raising money at twice the rate of their GOP counterparts, and in doing so, clearly compensated for the huge lead in hard money raised by Bush. Their work certainly benefited the Kerry campaign, Mark Kornblau, a Kerry campaign spokesman, said, but it had a downside. "It helps to have friends, but you want to have friends who you can tell what to do. You can't do that with 527's." At the same time, if a 527 ran either an ad the candidate either did not agree with or an ad that crossed some self-imposed line, he could distance himself from it.

According to the Republicans, actual coordination was unnecessary. Most of the pro-Democratic 527's were run and staffed by former Democratic operatives clearly aware of the candidate's strategy. They did not have to consult, since they already knew what Kerry and the DNC wanted to do. "That's walking the line," said Reed Dickens of the Bush campaign.[40] The same, of course, could be said for Republican-leaning 527's, such as the Club for Growth. Its sole aim is to elect probusiness, antitax candidates, nearly all of whom tend to be Republican. Although the Club supported congressional and even local candidates, it planned to spend at least $15 million to elect George Bush. Manny Balar, a club member and real estate executive, said that although he would donate directly to the Bush campaign, he had more faith in the political clout of the club. Stephen Moore, the president of the club, also noted that 527's could sometimes do what the candidate could not. "If you're kicking John Kerry right between the legs with a hard-hitting TV ad," he explained, "we absorb the negative hit from it, and it doesn't do collateral damage to President Bush himself."[41]

How effective the 527's actually were is difficult to determine, although it is clear that they played an important role in the campaign. But in terms of BCRA, the 527's clearly managed to circumvent—legally—both the bans on soft money and the limitations imposed on issue ads. Although neither Bush nor Kerry, nor the RNC, nor the DNC could accept soft money; the 527's could. They "walked the line" in making sure that nominally they did not run a coordinated campaign, but that proved to be of little difficulty. Moreover, in some of their activities, such as get-out-the-vote campaigns, BCRA imposed absolutely no reporting requirements on the 527's. As William C. Miller, national political director of the U.S. Chamber of Commerce, candidly admitted, "We have no disclosures [to make]." Unlike the political parties, the 527's did not have to provide a list of donors and the amounts they gave, nor did the law impose any limits on how large of a check donors could write.[42] In two areas, at least, everyone agreed that the 527's had been effective. If it had not been for the Media Fund and other 527's responding in ads that defended Kerry or attacked Bush, Kerry would have been at an enormous disadvantage. On the other side, the Swift Boat Veterans for Truth launched what proved to be a vicious attack on John Kerry's record in Vietnam that many believed took away an advantage he might have had as a veteran who had served his country in combat.[43]

★ ★ ★ ★ ★

Other signs showed that the McCain-Feingold bill had not made that much difference. Both Bush and Kerry passed up federal financing in the primaries in order to raise record sums of money. Both parties raised hundreds of millions of dollars to underwrite the costs of their conventions, although neither convention would use up this fund, which could then be transferred to campaign expenditures.[44] Television ads saturated the airwaves, some paid for by the candidates and others by 527's. The NRA created another loophole by establishing a daily radio program and acting as a media entity, thus escaping BCRA regulation. Did anything change?

In terms of total spending, the 2004 presidential race proved the most expensive in history. Nine weeks before the election, total spending had topped $1 billion, twice the amount spent by the end of August 2000, and greater in fact than the entire cost of the 2000 presidential campaigns. The official postelection reports to the FEC at the beginning of December showed that the amounts raised by both parties exceeded everyone's projections. For the first time since the mid-1970s, the Democrats raised more money than the Republicans. The Democratic National Committee (DNC) reported that it had raised $389.8 million from January 1, 2003, through November 22, 2004, and the Republicans had, in the same period, garnered $385.3 million. In the comparable period for the 2000 election, the Republicans had raised $116.4 million more than the Democrats. Total spending from all sources seeking to influence the election exceeded $1.7 billion, and once again, the Democrats for the first time in nearly three decades had more to spend, with the DNC and other supporters of Senator John Kerry spending $925 million and the RNC and its allies laying out $822 million. By rejecting public financing for the primaries, Bush and Kerry together brought in more than $300 million they would not have otherwise been allowed to raise. Reports for congressional campaigns showed that both Senate and House races had become even more expensive than in 2000 and 2002.[45]

According to some commentators, BCRA did make a difference, but only as the first step in reforming a badly antiquated system. The candidates themselves no longer had to go soliciting large donors, the way Bill Clinton and others did, because of the limits placed on individual donations. Perhaps the most important result is that the donor base has been expanded, and more people have been involved in the process, a result that McCain and company clearly had in mind. Howard Dean's success in raising millions of dollars through small contributions over the Internet in many ways "democratized" the funding process. Kerry got this message and started peppering his speeches with references to "JohnKerry.com," asking for donations. Two months before the Democratic convention he had broken all Democratic Party records. The Kerry Web site in early June featured Cathy Weigel of North Kansas City, Missouri, who had become the one millionth online contributor. For her $50 donation, Weigel got a call from Kerry, a promise of a "great seat" at the inauguration and a visit to the White House. Although Ms. Weigel did not get her seat at a Kerry inauguration, as E. J. Dionne noted, "Such calls and promises used to go to big soft-money fundraisers who bagged a million or so in contributions."[46]

Thomas Mann and Norman Orenstein, both strong advocates of

BCRA, also believe it has done much good. They dismiss the argument that there is still a great deal of money in the campaigns. Reformers, they claim, "did not want to drain money out of politics." Rather, they wanted "to end the shakedown schemes and access-peddling officeholders and parties used to raise money from corporations, unions, and wealthy individuals." That happened, and the fact that candidates and parties now have more money to spend is not a failure but a success, since all of it came from relatively small hard-money contributions. Neither, they argue, has speech been stifled since "ad spots by independent groups still fill the airwaves." The fact that these come from 527's is acknowledged, but Mann and Ornstein neglect to mention that this development surely was not what McCain, Feingold, and others had intended.[47]

Self-financing, wealthy candidates fared badly in the 2004 elections. Of 12 candidates who spent more than $1 million of their own money in an effort to get elected to Congress, only one, Michael McCaul, a Republican, won—in the Texas district once represented by Lyndon Johnson. The amounts spent by the losers ranged from a little over $1 million to the $28.7 million expended by Blair Hull in the Democratic Senate primary race in Illinois; Hull lost to Barack Obama, who won the seat in November. The so-called millionaire provisions of BCRA apparently had little to do with the results; in nearly all of the cases the newcomers ran against incumbents such as Russ Feingold of Wisconsin, Barbara Mikulski of Maryland, and Christopher Dodd of Connecticut. Incumbency, and not the amount of money in play, determined these races.[48]

* * * * *

The claim that speech has not been constrained is one that is still to be determined. Certainly the 527's have not been intimidated by the *McConnell* decision, but shifting political speech from one actor to another is surely not what the framers of the First Amendment intended. The federal government has legislatively restricted speech only three times in our history—the Sedition Act of 1798, the Sedition Act of 1918, and BCRA in 2002. The first two laws—aimed at the criticism of government—have now been repudiated by both history and the courts. What exactly will happen with BCRA is hard to predict, yet one can foresee a number of difficulties.

The Court, in its decision on BCRA, paid much deference—too much, according to some critics—to congressional fact-finding that soft money, as well as soft money–funded issue ads, posed a danger of corruption or its appearance in the political process. The five-member majority found that this rationale provided the necessary justification for restricting speech. But they did so in the abstract. *McConnell*, despite the wealth of anecdotal material in the record, did not pinpoint a particular speaker whose constitutional rights had been limited by the government. One of the problems with a facial challenge, as noted earlier, is that it is often difficult to prove that a real injury will occur. The Court majority found no real injury, and in its opinion none would occur. But what will happen when some political speaker pays for and runs an advertisement in direct violation of the Title II ban on issue ads within two months of the election?[49] How will the Court rationalize that the message, which could clearly be true political speech aimed not at a candidate but at an issue, should be restricted?

The NRA appeared ready to test the limits of *McConnell* by airing a daily radio program to provide news and progun commentary to some 400,000 listeners. By styling "NRANews" as a media organization, the gun lobby claimed that it could not be regulated under BCRA, even if its news and commentary are political and endorse or attack specific candidates. As Larry Noble of the Center for Responsive Politics and former general counsel of the FEC, noted, "If the NRA is successful at this, we will definitely see other groups going down the same road."[50]

But why should the NRA, the ACLU, or any other group have to engage in such subterfuge? Although there has been some debate over how far the umbrella of the First Amendment extends, everyone agrees that political speech is at the core of First Amendment values. Such speech, as many commentators and jurists—both liberal and conservative—have explained, is often confrontational, excessive, and even rude. The same could be said for democracy itself, a system that is often sloppy, inefficient, and excessive. But the idea is that people should be able to speak their minds, and that those who choose to listen shall not have the government decide what messages can be sent.

The problem started with the *Buckley* decision that contributions can be limited, but expenditures cannot. The highly artificial reasoning that sustains that rationale has been under attack ever since, and in terms of cleaning up the system, all that the case, its progeny, and the laws they explicated did was to lead Americans to invent new ways to get around both the law and the opinion.

In *Buckley* the Court noted that the Federal Election Campaign Act restricts "the voices of people and interest groups who have money to spend and reduce[s] the overall scope of federal election campaigns . . . [since] the alleged 'conduct' of giving or spending money 'arises in some measure because the communications allegedly integral to the conduct itself are thought to be harmful.' "[51] The same can surely be said to be the result of BCRA and *McConnell*, and it is exceedingly troubling that the Court, which has been the bastion of free speech for the last half-century, has seemingly turned its back on those First Amendment values it once so ardently embraced.

It will take at least one case, and perhaps more, to see if the Court really means what it said in *McConnell*. Perhaps faced with a case involving a real governmental restriction on political speech, the justices will recognize that, as Louis Brandeis pointed out many years ago, in a democracy the cure for allegedly bad speech is not regulation, but more speech. One can only hope.

APPENDIXES

Appendix A:
Federal Election Campaign
Act of 1971

General

- Broadened definitions of *contribution* and *expenditure* as applied to a political campaign, but exempted monetary loans made in accordance with applicable banking laws.
- Prohibited the promise of employment or other political benefits by any candidate in exchange for support.
- Exempted communications, nonpartisan registration, and get-out-the-vote campaigns by corporations aimed at their stockholders or by unions aimed at their members.
- Exempted from the contribution and expenditure limits separate funds to be used by a corporation or a union solely for political purposes.

Contribution Limits

- Imposed a ceiling on contributions by any candidate or members of his or her immediate family to his or her own campaign of $50,000 for president or vice president; $35,000 for senators; and $25,000 for representatives.

Spending Limits

- Restricted the total amount that could be spent by federal candidates for advertising in communications media to 10¢ per eligible voter or $50,000, whichever was greater. The number would be determined annually by the U.S. Bureau of the Census.

- Defined "communications media" to include radio, television, newspapers, magazines, billboards, and automatic telephone equipment.
- Of this spending limit, no more than 60 percent could be spent on radio and television.
- During the presidential primary season, candidates for their party's nomination would also be subject to the 10¢-per-voter limit.
- Provided that the broadcast and nonbroadcast spending limits be increased in proportion to the annual increases in the Consumer Price Index over the base year of 1970.

Disclosure and Enforcement

- Required all political committees that anticipated receiving more than $1,000 during a calendar year to file an organizational statement listing the principal officers, scope of activities, names of the candidates it supported, and such other information required by law
- Named the appropriate federal officers to oversee this registration as the Clerk of the House for House candidates, the Secretary of the Senate for Senate candidates, and the Controller General for presidential candidates.
- Required each committee to report any individual expenditures of more than $100 and any expenditures aggregating more than $100 during a calendar year.
- Required each committee to report all contributions in excess of $100, with the name and address of the contributor and the date of the contribution.
- Required the supervisory officers to prepare annual reports based on the committee submissions and to make them available to the public.
- Required the reporting of the names, addresses, and occupations of any lender or endorser of any loan in excess of $100.
- Required any person who made any contribution in excess of $100, other than through a political committee or directly to the candidate, to report that to the supervisory officers.

- Prohibited any contribution to a candidate or a committee by one person in the name of another.
- Required that all reports filed with the federal government also be filed with the secretary of state in the state in which the committee operated or the election was held.

Miscellaneous

- Prohibited radio and television stations from charging political candidates a rate more than the lowest unit cost for the same advertising time available to commercial advertisers. This provision would apply only in the 45 days prior to a primary and in the 60 days prior to a general election.
- Provided that any amounts spent by an agent of the candidate and fees paid to an agent for services would be considered part of the expenses covered by the overall limits.
- No radio or television station could charge for advertising unless it received written consent from the candidate and unless the candidate certified that these charges would not exceed the legal expenditure limits.[1]

Appendix B:
1974 Amendments to FECA

Federal Election Commission

- Created a six-member commission, consisting of three Democrats and three Republicans, to enforce and monitor the law.
- The president, the speaker of the House, and the president pro tem of the Senate would each appoint two members, one from each party, all subject to confirmation by both houses of Congress.
- The secretary of the Senate and the clerk of the House, as the designated record keepers under the 1971 FECA, would serve as ex officio members, primarily to provide access to the records in their custodial care.
- The commissioners would serve staggered six-year terms, with a rotating one-year chair.

Contribution Limits

- Set a limit of $1,000 per person for each primary, run-off, or general election, with a limit of $25,000 per year to all candidates for federal office.
- Set a limit of $5,000 per organization, political committee, or national or state party organization for each election, but no limit on the aggregate amount they could spend in a campaign or the amount they could contribute to party organizations supporting federal candidates.
- Set limits on what candidates and their families could spend out of their own pockets—$50,000 for president or vice president, $35,000 for a Senate seat, and $25,000 for a House seat.

- Set a limit of $1,000 on independent expenditures by private persons on behalf of a candidate.
- Barred cash contributions of more than $100 and foreign contributions.

Spending Limits

- Presidential primaries—$10 million total per candidate for all primaries. In a state presidential primary, a candidate may spend no more than twice what a Senate candidate in that state would be allowed to spend.
- Presidential general elections—$20 million per candidate.
- Presidential nominating conventions—$2 million for each major political party, with lesser amounts for the minor parties.
- Senate primaries—$100,000 or 8¢ per eligible voter, whichever is greater.
- Senate general elections—$150,000 or 12¢ cents per eligible voter, whichever is higher.
- House primaries and general elections—$70,000 in each.
- National party spending—$10,000 per candidate in House general election; $20,000 or 2¢ per eligible voter, whichever is greater, for each candidate in Senate general elections; and 2¢ per voter (approximately $2.9 million) in presidential general elections. These expenditures would be above the candidate's individual spending limits.
- For those states where a House seat covers the whole state the House candidate would have the same spending limit as the Senate candidate.
- Repealed the media spending limitations in the 1971 FECA.
- Exempted expenditures of up to $500 for food and beverages, invitations, unreimbursed travel expenses by volunteers, and spending on "slate cards" and sample ballots.
- Exempted fund-raising costs of up to 20 percent of the candidate spending limits. Thus, the spending limit for House candidates would be effectively raised from $70,000 to $84,000, and for candidates in presidential primaries from $10 million to $12 million.
- Provided that spending limits be increased in proportion to annual increases in the Consumer Price Index.

Public Financing

- Presidential general elections—voluntary public financing. Major party candidates would automatically qualify for full funding before the campaign. Minor-party and independent candidates would be eligible to receive a proportion of full fund-raising based on past or current votes received. If a candidate opted for full public funding, no private contributions would be permitted.
- Presidential nominating conventions—optional public funding. Major parties automatically would qualify. Minor parties would be eligible for lesser amounts based on their proportion of votes received in a past election.
- Presidential primaries—matching public funds of up to $5 million per candidate after meeting fund-raising requirement of $100,000 raised in amounts of at least $5,000 in each of 20 states or more. Only the first $250 of individual private contributions would be matched. The matching funds were to be divided among the candidates as quickly as possible. In allocating the money, the order in which the candidates qualified would be taken into account. Only private gifts raised after 1 January 1975 would qualify for the 1976 general elections. No federal payments would be made before January 1976.
- Provided that all federal money for public funding of campaigns would come from the Presidential Election Campaign Fund. Money received from the federal income tax dollar check-off automatically would be appropriated to the fund.

Disclosures and Enforcements

- Each candidate has to establish one central campaign committee through which all contributions and expenditures on behalf of that candidate must be reported. In addition, each committee has to designate specific bank depositories for campaign funds.
- Full reports of contributions and expenditures must be filed with the Federal Election Commission 10 days before and 30 days after every election, and within 10 days of the close of each quarter, unless the committee expended less than $1,000 in that

quarter. In nonelection years, the committee must also file a year-end report.

- Contributions of $1,000 or more, received within 15 days before an election, must be reported to the FEC within 48 hours.
- Prohibited contributions made in the name of another.
- Loans would be treated as contributions and all loans had to have a cosigner or guarantor for each $1,000 of outstanding debt.
- Any organization that took any action or spent any money or committed any act for the purpose of influencing an election (including but not limited to the publication of voting records) must file a report as a political committee.
- Every person who spent or contributed more than $100, other than through or to a candidate or political committee, must report that sum.
- Permitted government contractors, unions, and corporations to maintain separate and segregated political funds.
- Provided that the FEC would receive campaign reports, make rules and regulations (subject to review by Congress within 30 days), maintain a cumulative index of reports (both filed and not filed), make regular and special reports to Congress and to the president, and serve as an election information clearinghouse.
- The FEC received the power to render advisory opinions, conduct audits, and investigations, subpoena witnesses and information, and go to court to seek civil injunctions.
- Criminal cases would be referred by the FEC to the Justice Department for prosecution.
- Increased existing fines for violation of the law to $50,000.
- Provided that a candidate for federal office who failed to file reports could be prohibited for the term of that office plus one year.

Miscellaneous

- Set 1 January 1975 as the effective date for the act, except that there would be immediate preemption of state laws.
- Removed Hatch Act restrictions on voluntary activities by state and local employees in federal campaigns if not prohibited by state law.

- Prohibited solicitation of campaign funds through the use of franked mail.
- Preempted state election laws for federal candidates.
- Permitted use of excess campaign funds to defray expenses of holding federal office or for other lawful purposes.[2]

Appendix C:
1976 Amendments to FECA

Federal Election Commission

- Reorganized the FEC as a six-person panel, all members of which were to be appointed by the president and confirmed by the Senate.
- Prohibited members of the FEC from engaging in any outside business activities, and gave them one year from the time they joined the commission to end such business interests.
- Gave Congress the power to veto individual sections of any regulation proposed by the panel.

Contribution Limits

- An individual could give no more than $5,000 a year to a political action committee and $20,000 to the national committee of a political party; this amplified but did not negate the 1974 provision that set a $1,000-per-election limit on individual contributions to a candidate and an aggregate limit for individuals of $25,000 a year.
- Limited a multicandidate committee to giving no more than $15,000 a year to the national committee; the 1974 limit of $5,000 per election, per candidate remained in effect.
- The Democratic and Republican senatorial campaign committees could give no more than $17,500 a year to a candidate.
- Permitted campaign committees organized to back a single candidate to offer "occasional, isolated, and incidental support" to another candidate; the 1974 law had not permitted any support by such a committee to anyone else.

- Attempted to stop the proliferation of political action committees by membership groups, corporations, and unions. All political action committees established by a company or an international union would be treated as a single committee for purposes of campaign limits, namely, $5,000 to the same candidate in any election.

Spending Limits

- Presidential and vice-presidential candidates could not spend more than $50,000 of their own or their families' money on their campaigns if they accepted public financing.
- Exempted from the spending limits payments by a candidate or a national committee for the legal and accounting services required to comply with the campaign law, but required that such expenditures still be reported.

Public Financing

- Presidential candidates who received federal matching funds and then withdrew from the prenomination campaign had to return unspent federal money.
- Cut off federal funds to any candidate who received less than 10 percent of the vote in two consecutive presidential primaries in which he or she had entered.
- Set out procedures by which an individual who became ineligible for matching federal funds could have eligibility restored through an FEC finding.

Disclosure and Enforcement

- Gave the FEC exclusive power to prosecute civil violations of the law and transferred to the commission jurisdiction over violations formerly in the criminal code, in effect giving it full jurisdiction over all types of violations of federal campaign election law.

- Required approval of four members of the FEC to issue regulations or advisory opinions or to initiate civil actions and investigations.
- Labor unions, corporations, and membership organizations had to report expenditures of $2,000 or more per election that had been used to communicate with their members or stockholders urging them to support or oppose particular candidates. Expenditures on issues would not have to be reported.
- Candidates and political committees had to keep records of contributions of $50 or more; the 1974 law had set the amount at $10.
- Candidates and political committees could waive the requirement for quarterly finance reports in a nonelection year if less than $5,000 had been raised or spent; the 1974 limit had been $1,000. Annual reports would still have to be filed.
- Political committees and individuals making an independent expenditure of more than $100 to advocate the election or defeat of a candidate had to file a report with the FEC, and the committee or individual state, under penalty of perjury, had to verify that the expenditure had not been made in collusion with a candidate.
- Independent expenditures of $1,000 or more made within 15 days of an election had to be reported within 24 hours.
- The FEC could issue advisory opinions relating only to specific factual situations, and such advisories could not be used to spell out commission policy. Such opinions had precedential value only for future situations where the factual situation was for all intents and purposes the same as the original.
- The FEC could initiate investigations only after it received a properly verified complaint or had reason to believe, based on information that came to it in the normal course of its business, that a violation had occurred or would occur in the near future. It could not launch an investigation based on anonymous complaints.
- The commission had to make an effort at reconciliation on allegations of campaign law violations before going to court. Violations of criminal law would still be referred to the Department of Justice, and the attorney general had to report back to the FEC within 60 days what action, if any, he or she had taken, and then

every 30 days thereafter until the matter had been fully resolved, either through trial or dismissal.

- If an individual knowingly violated the campaign law for a sum of money greater than $1,000, he or she would be liable under a criminal provision for a one-year jail sentence and a fine of up to $25,000, or three times the amount of the contribution or expenditure involved, whichever was greater.
- Civil penalties could be imposed for violation of the law in fines of $5,000 or an amount equal to the contributions or expenditures involved, whichever was greater. For violations knowingly committed, in addition to the criminal penalties there could be civil fines of $10,000 or an amount equal to twice the amount involved, whichever was greater. The civil fines could be imposed either by courts or by the FEC as part of a conciliation agreement.

Miscellaneous

- The law placed greater limits on the fund-raising abilities of corporate and union political action committees. Companies could seek contributions only from stockholders or from executive and administrative personnel and their families. Unions could solicit only from union members and their families. Twice a year, however, corporate and union PACS could seek contributions through mailings from all persons not included in this restriction. Such contributions would have to be anonymous and be received by a third party that would keep records, but would transfer the funds to the PACs without identifying the donors.
- Trade association PACs could solicit contributions from stockholders, executive and administrative personnel, and their families of member companies.
- Union PACs could use the same method to solicit campaign contributions as corporate PACs, and would then have to reimburse the company at cost for mailings and other related expenses.[3]

Appendix D:
1979 Amendments to FECA

Disclosure

- Candidates for federal office had to file finance reports if more than $5,000 was either received in contributions or expended. The earlier law required reports no matter the amount raised or spent.
- Local party organizations were excused from filing reports for certain voluntary activities, such as get-out-the-vote and voter registration drives, if the amount expended on these activities came to less than $5,000 a year. However, if expenditures on activities outside this area amounted to more than $1,000, a report had to be filed. Previously a report had to be filed when the costs for any types of expenditures exceeded $1,000.
- An individual could spend up to $1,000 on behalf of a candidate or $2,000 for a political party in the form of so-called voluntary expenses, such as use of his or her home, food, or personal travel, without it being counted as a reportable donation.
- Political committees would no longer have to have a chairperson, but would continue to have to have a named treasurer.
- Ten days, instead of the previous five, would now be allowed for a person who received a contribution of $50 or more on behalf of a candidate's committee to forward it to the treasurer of that committee.
- Committee treasurers had to preserve financial records for at least three years. Previously the FEC could set the time that records had to be kept.
- A candidate's campaign committee had to have the name of the candidate in its title, and political action committees had to have the name of its affiliated organization in its title.

- The law reduced the amount of information that political committees needed to provide in order to register from 11 to 6 categories. An important category the law removed was the requirement that political action committees name the candidates they supported. In effect this merely cured a problem of duplication, since the committees still had to report the names of candidates to which they contributed money.
- The law reduced the total number of mandatory reports candidates and committees had to file from 24 to 9, and set the dates for these reports on a schedule that gave the officials responsible for preparing reports a little more time to do so.
- Presidential campaign committees had to file monthly reports, plus pre- and postelection reports during an election year if they had received contributions of more than $100,000. Committees receiving less than this amount would file quarterly reports. During a nonelection year the committees could choose whether to file monthly or quarterly reports.
- Political committees not directly affiliated with a candidate had to file either monthly reports or a minimum of nine reports during a two-year election cycle.
- The FEC had to be notified within 48 hours of contributions of $1,000 or more made between 20 days and 48 hours before the election. Previously the window had been 15 days and 48 hours.
- Names of all contributors of $200 or more had to be reported; previously the amount had been $100.
- All expenses above $200 had to be itemized; the previous threshold had been $100.
- Independent expenditures of $250 or more had to be reported; the previous amount had been $100.

Federal Election Commission

- The law established a "best effort" standard by which the FEC would determine if a candidate or a committee had complied with the law. Committees had complained about the difficulty of meeting all of the minutia in the law and regulations, and this provision made compliance rest upon the spirit of the effort rather than complete attainment of all requirements.

- Extended the right to ask for an advisory opinion to any person who had a question about a specific campaign transaction; previously only officeholders, candidates, and committees could make such a request.
- Required the FEC to issue advisory opinions within 60 days of the request rather than the previous "reasonable time." If a request were made within 60 days of an election, the FEC had to respond in 20 days.
- Within five days of receiving a complaint about an election law violation, the FEC had to notify any person or committee accused of the violation. The accused then had 15 days to respond.
- Four of the six members of the FEC had to vote that there was "reason to believe" that a violation of the law had occurred in order for an investigation to begin, at which point the accused would be notified that an investigation was in process.
- If four members believed that probable cause existed that a violation had taken place, the FEC would be required to try to resolve the matter by conciliation within 90 days. Approval of the conciliation agreement required assent by four of the six members.
- The FEC would no longer serve a clearinghouse function on information on all elections, but only those for federal office.
- The FEC would no longer conduct random audits of committees, but would initiate an audit only after four members of the commission voted that evidence existed that a specific committee had not complied substantially with federal election law.
- The secretaries of state had to keep copies of FEC reports on file for public examination for two years; previously they had to keep reports on House candidates on file for five years, and reports on Senate and presidential candidates for 10 years.
- The law provided for an expedited procedure by which the Senate as well as the House could veto proposed FEC regulations.

Enforcement

- Extended the basic substance of both the civil and criminal provisions of the earlier law.
- Allowed PACs to include 10 pseudonyms on each report to protect against the illegal use of names of contributors. The true

identity of the 10 would be provided to the FEC but not made public.

- The law prohibited the use of FEC reports, particularly names of contributors, for commercial solicitation, but the names of PACs listed with the FEC could be used to solicit campaign contributions.

Political Parties

- State and local party groups could buy, without limit, buttons, bumper stickers, yard signs, and the like for voluntary activities.
- State and local party groups could conduct voter registration and get-out-the-vote drives on behalf of presidential tickets without any financial limit.

Public Financing

- The amount given to the Democratic and Republican Parties to help finance their nominating conventions was raised from $2 million to $3 million.

Miscellaneous

- Buttons and printed materials could promote one candidate and make passing reference to another candidate without that being considered a contribution to the second candidate. In commercial advertisements, whether in print or broadcast media, such references could not be made unless reported as a contribution to the second candidate.
- Leftover campaign funds (but not federal matching dollars) could be given to other political committees or to charities.
- Leftover campaign funds could not be converted to personal use, except by members of Congress at the time of the law's enactment.
- Members of Congress, candidates for Congress, and federal employ-

ees could not solicit campaign contributions from other federal employees; an inadvertent solicitation would not be a violation.

• Congressional employees could make voluntary contributions to members of Congress other than their own immediate employers.

• The law continued the ban on solicitation or receipt of campaign contributions in a federal building. It would not be a violation, however, if contributions received at a federal building (such as a check sent to a senator at her office) were forwarded within seven days to the appropriate political committee, and if instructions for sending contributions did not indicate that they should be sent to a federal office.[4]

Appendix E:
Bipartisan Campaign Reform
Act of 2002

Title I: Reduction of Special Interest Influence

BAN ON SOFT MONEY

- National parties and congressional committees may only raise and spend hard money received from individuals and political action committees (PACs).
- Labor and unions and corporations may not contribute to campaigns.
- State parties have to use hard-money contributions to pay for get-out-the-vote and voter registration drives in the 120 days preceding an election.
- State parties must also use hard-money to pay for any activities designed to influence a federal election during an election year (even-numbered years).
- A $10,000 individual contribution is made for specified state activities.
- Candidates may not raise soft money for get-out-the-vote, voter registration, or other federal election activities.

CONTRIBUTION LIMITS

- Individual limit for contributions to candidates are raised from $1,000 to $2,000, with primary and general elections considered two separate elections.
- Individual aggregate limit are raised from $25,000 to $37,500 per year.
- An individual may give $25,000 (up from $20,000) of the annual

aggregate to national political party committees, and $10,000 (up from $5,000) to state party committees.

- National party committees may give $35,000 (up from $17,500) to a party Senate campaign.
- These numbers are to be indexed for inflation in odd-numbered years, and are to remain in effect for the entire two-year election cycle.

REPORTING REQUIREMENTS

- National party committees (and any of their subordinate committees) as well as certain other types of political committees, must file reports with the Federal Election Commission (FEC) regarding the amount and sources of the moneys raised and expended during federal election activity.
- So-called building funds, originally permitted to manage soft-money expenditures, are abolished.

Title II: Noncandidate Campaign Expenditures

ELECTIONEERING COMMUNICATIONS DISCLOSURE

- Every organization not otherwise banned from making electioneering communications must report any expenditure of $10,000 or greater on broadcast electioneering communications.
- Such a communication is defined as any broadcast, cable, or satellite communication that clearly refers to an identified candidate, is run within 60 days of a general election and 30 days of a primary, convention, or caucus, and is designed to influence the electorate for that office.
- Should these previous provisions be struck down by the courts, then a secondary definition would come into play regarding advertisements that promoted, supported, attacked, or opposed a candidate. If a communication at any time during the election year is "suggestive of no plausible meaning other than an exhortation to vote for or against a specific candidate," then it is an electioneering communication and subject to the other provisions of the law.

- Within 24 hours of such a communication, a report must be filed with the FEC that details the name of the person buying the air time, the treasurer's name, organization contact information, the election, and the name(s) of the candidate(s) identified in the advertisement as well as the names and addresses of all donors contributing more than $1,000 and all disbursements over $200.

COORDINATED COMMUNICATIONS AS CONTRIBUTIONS

- Electioneering communications made in coordination with a candidate or party committee are regarded as contributions to the candidate or committee, and subject to all hard-money requirements and limits.

RESTRICTIONS ON CORPORATIONS AND LABOR UNIONS

- Corporations and labor unions are prohibited from running or indirectly financing electioneering communications identifying or targeting a federal candidate within 60 days of a general election. However, a corporate or union PAC may pay for such activities with hard money.

TARGETED ELECTION COMMUNICATION

- Nonprofit corporations exempt under sections 501(c)(4) and 527 of the Internal Revenue Code may not run targeted communications.
- A targeted communication is a broadcast, cable, or satellite communication run within 60 days of a general election or 30 days of a primary, featuring the name or likeness of a candidate whose audience consists primarily of the residents of the state associated with the candidate identified in the advertisement.

INDEPENDENT EXPENDITURE DEFINITION

- An independent expenditure expressly advocates the election or defeat of a clearly identified candidate and cannot be coordinated with candidates or their campaign committees.

DISCLOSURE SCHEDULE FOR INDEPENDENT EXPENDITURE GROUPS

- Sponsors of independent expenditures who spend more than $10,000 at any time during an election cycle must disclose details of that expenditure within 48 hours to the FEC. During the last 20 days before an election, independent expenditures exceeding $1,000 must be disclosed to the FEC within 24 hours.
- Each time these limits are exceeded within these time frames, the sponsor must file a new report to the FEC within 48 or 24 hours.

PARTY SPENDING

- Parties must choose either to make independent expenditures or coordinated expenditures on behalf of congressional candidates, but may not do both.

PARTY AND CANDIDATE COORDINATION

- Coordination between a party and a candidate occurs when payment is made in cooperation with, at the suggestion of, or per an understanding with a candidate, a candidate's agent or campaign, or party.
- The FEC is instructed to expand its current definition of coordination, taking into account factors such as republication of campaign materials, use of a common vendor, common employees, substantial discussion between an advertiser and a candidate or party, and coordination of corporate or union internal communications on get-out-the-vote, voter registration, or electioneering communications.

Title III: Miscellaneous

PERSONAL USE OF CAMPAIGN FUNDS

- Candidates are prohibited from using campaign funds for personal use.

FUND-RAISING ON FEDERAL PROPERTY

- Fund-raising on federal property, including the White House and the Capitol, is prohibited.

FOREIGN DONATIONS

- Candidates and parties may not receive donations from persons who are not citizens or permanent legal residents.

MILLIONAIRE OPPONENT

- In order to address the growing number of millionaires using their own personal wealth to seek federal office, the contribution limits for Senate candidates facing self-financing candidates are increased on a sliding scale.
- A threshold is established of $150,000 plus the number of eligible voters in the state times 4¢.
- If the personal spending of a wealthy candidate, minus that of the opponent, exceeds that threshold by a factor of two or three, the limit on individual contributions for the non–self-financing candidate is increased 300 percent to $6,000.
- If the threshold is exceeded by 4–20 times, the limit on individual contributions is increased 600 percent to $12,000.
- If the threshold is exceeded by a factor greater than 10, the limit on individual contributions is raised sixfold and the limit on all party-coordinated expenditures is removed.

TELEVISION MEDIA RATES

- Broadcast stations may not raise rates for campaign advertisements.
- Stations currently required to charge candidates their lowest unit cost may no longer bump campaign advertisements in favor of commercial ads paying a higher rate.
- In order to receive the lowest unit cost, candidates must certify to the stations that they will include in their ads an audio statement that the candidate and/or sponsor takes responsibility for the content of the ad. If the candidate makes this statement, he or she must identify themselves.

- A television ad must also include a picture of the sponsoring candidate.
- Parties may also avail themselves of the lowest unit cost rate if they follow the conditions in this section.

FEC SOFTWARE FOR DISCLOSURE

- The FEC is to develop standards for vendors to follow in developing software for campaign finance reporting that is user-friendly, transmits instantaneously, and is posted on the Internet immediately. Candidates for the presidency and for the House of Representatives will be required to file electronically beginning in 2001.

POLITICAL AD DISCOUNT FOR PARTIES IS CONDITIONED ON
COORDINATED SPENDING-LIMIT DONATIONS TO PRESIDENTIAL
INAUGURAL COMMITTEES

- All contributions to presidential inaugural committees have to be reported and posted on the FEC website. Foreign nationals or persons born overseas who are not U.S. citizens may not contribute to inaugural committees.

PUBLIC FINANCING STUDY

- The FEC is required to complete within one year after passage of the law a study of public financing of campaigns, as currently implemented in states such as Arizona and Maine.

CLARITY ON ELECTION-RELATED ADVERTISING DISCLAIMERS

- Existing requirements on sponsorship statements, to let viewers know who is paying for political advertisements, are extended to include all electioneering communications sponsored by political committees, parties, candidate committees, and PACs.
- The disclaimer must include the sponsor's name, website, or street address, and must be legible. Candidate-run television advertisements must include a picture of the candidate.

INCREASE IN PENALTIES FOR FECA VIOLATIONS

- For any violation where the sum involved is $25,000 or less, a person may be fined or imprisoned for no more than one year, or both. Where the sum is greater than $25,000, a person may be fined or imprisoned for no more than five years, or both.

STATUTE OF LIMITATIONS FOR FECA VIOLATIONS

- The statute of limitations for election law violations is extended from three to five years.

SENTENCING GUIDELINES FOR FECA VIOLATIONS

- The U.S. Sentencing Commission is directed to develop and/or amend FECA violation guidelines based on aggravating or mitigating circumstances, and make legislative recommendations to Congress within 90 days of the passage of BCRA.
- Penalties are to be enhanced for violations involving foreign money, large numbers of transactions, large dollar amounts, use of governmental funds, intent to achieve a benefit from government, and involvement of candidates and/or campaign officials.

CONDUIT CONTRIBUTION PENALTIES

- The civil penalty is increased to 300 percent of the amount involved in the violation, up to a maximum of 1,000 percent of $50,000. The criminal penalty is increased to at least 300 percent of the amount involved, up to a maximum of 1,000 percent or $50,000, and up to two years' imprisonment.

SEVERABILITY

- If the Supreme Court invalidates any part of BCRA, the remainder of the bill remains in force.

EFFECTIVE DATE

- This act will go into effect 30 days after enactment.

EXPEDITED COURT REVIEW

- Any constitutional challenges to this law will be heard in the federal district court for the District of Columbia, and any appeals from its decision will go directly to the U.S. Supreme Court. The courts are also to expedite any challenges "to the greatest possible extent."

FEC INTERNET POSTINGS OF DISCLOSURE

- Electronically filed disclosure notices must be posted by the FEC on its website within 24 hours of receipt; paper disclosures must be filed within 48 hours. All PACs, candidates, and campaign committees that raise over $50,000 must henceforth file all disclosure reports electronically.

FEC WEBSITE "CLEARINGHOUSE"

- The FEC is to create a centralized website of all reports filed under FECA, and any other "election-related information" disclosed to other agencies, such as the Internal Revenue Service (IRS) and the Federal Communications Commission (FCC).

DISCLOSURE SCHEDULE FOR PARTIES AND CANDIDATES

- Candidates must file monthly disclosure reports during the election year, and national party committees must file monthly reports at all times.

POLITICAL ADVERTISER DISCLOSURE TO
TELEVISION AND RADIO STATIONS

- Radio and television stations must make available to the public information on political advertising. The FCC already requires such records to be kept, but now they are to be public, and must include the name of the person buying the air time, contract information, a list of the sponsoring organization's executives and directors, the rate charged, the class of the time sold, and the date and times such ads ran on the air.

Notes

Chapter 1

1. Jeffrey H. Birnbaum, *The Money Men: The Real Story of Fund-raising's Influence on Political Power in America* (New York: Crown Publishers, 2000), 28.

2. Bradley A. Smith, *Unfree Speech: The Folly of Campaign Finance Reform* (Princeton, NJ: Princeton University Press, 2001), 18.

3. Dumas Malone, *Jefferson and the Rights of Man* (Boston: Little, Brown, 1951), 420–26.

4. Herbert E. Alexander, *Financing Politics: Money, Elections, and Political Reform*, 2nd ed. (Washington, DC: Congressional Quarterly Press, 1980), 4–5. During the height of the electioneering contest between the Federalists and the Republicans, one disenchanted voter in Charleston, South Carolina, complained, "We are so beset and run down by Federal republicans and their pamphlets that I begin to think for the first time that there is rottenness in the system they attempt to support, or why all this violent electioneering?"

5. Ibid., 5.

6. Birnbaum, *The Money Men*, 25.

7. For the politics of the era, see Richard P. McCormick, *The Second American Party System: Party Formation in the Jacksonian Era* (Chapel Hill: University of North Carolina Press, 1966).

8. Eugene H. Roseboom, *A History of Presidential Elections* (New York: Macmillan, 1957), 121. General Harrison, the hero of the army defeat of the Indians at the battle of Tippecanoe, proudly claimed that he had been born in a log cabin.

9. "Contributions often came in the form of cash packed in satchels or carpetbags, no questions asked. In 1839, Whig lobbyist Thurlow Weed raised $8,000 from New York merchants, and the money was delivered in a bandana handkerchief. No one appeared to think it unusual." George Thayer, *Who Shakes the Money Tree? American Campaign Financing from 1789 to the Present* (New York: Simon and Schuster, 1973), 29.

10. Smith, *Unfree Speech*, 19–20. Regarding Jackson and the Bank of the United States, see Robert V. Remini, *Andrew Jackson and the Bank War* (New York: Norton, 1967).

11. Lincoln's letter of 21 Nov. 1864, quoted in Birnbaum, *The Money Men*, 26.

12. Alexander, *Financing Politics*, 5. Alexander's Table 1-1 shows the amounts spent by the two major parties in each of the presidential campaigns from 1860 through 1976, but the amounts are given in the dollars of that year, and so do not provide a true comparison.

13. Tammany Hall, the Democratic Party organization in New York City, which apparently invented this means of financing elections, taxed all city employees 6 percent of their salaries. In post–Civil War America the practice was well-nigh universal, although the rates varied from state to state, and sometimes depended on the size of the salary. In Louisiana, all state employees had to pay 10 percent of their salary to the Democratic Party. Robert K. Goidel, Donald A. Gross, and Todd G. Shields, *Money Matters: Consequences of Campaign Finance Reform in U.S. House Elections* (Lanham, MD: Rowman and Littlefield, 1999), 19, 20.

14. Smith, *Unfree Speech*, 20.

15. Ari A. Hoogenboom, *Outlawing the Spoils: A History of the Civil Service Reform Movement, 1865–1883* (Urbana: University of Illinois Press, 1961).

16. Robert E. Mutch, *Campaigns, Congress, and Courts: The Making of Federal Campaign Finance Law* (New York: Praeger, 1988), xvi–xvii.

17. George Thayer, *Who Shakes the Money Tree?*, 40, 42.

18. Regarding the 1896 election, see Paul Glad, *McKinley, Bryan, and the People* (Philadelphia: Lippincott, 1964).

19. The $3.35 million figure is taken from Alexander, *Financing Politics*, Table 1-1 on p. 5. Smith, *Unfree Speech*, 22, claims that Hanna raised almost $7 million, a sum that would not be reached again until 1936.

20. Harold U. Faulkner, *Politics, Reform, and Expansion, 1890–1900* (New York: Harper and Row, 1959), 203–04. There is no modern biography of Hanna, and one must rely on the competent but outdated Herbert Croly, *Marcus Alonzo Hanna: His Life and Work* (New York: Macmillan, 1912).

21. Mutch, *Campaigns, Congress, and Courts*, 3.

22. This was not always the case, however. Cleveland outspent Harrison in 1892, and Wilson edged out Taft in 1912.

23. Frank J. Sorauf, *Inside Campaign Finance: Myths and Realities* (New Haven, CT: Yale University Press, 1992), 3.

24. *Santa Clara County v. Southern Pacific Railroad Co.*, 118 U.S. 394 (1886).

25. Elihu Root, *Addresses on Government and Citizenship* (1916), 143, quoted in *United States v. United Auto Workers*, 352 U.S. 567 (1957), 571.

26. Quoted in Mutch, *Campaigns, Congress, and Courts*, 2.

27. John A. Garraty, *Right-Hand Man: The Life of George W. Perkins* (New York: Harper, 1960), 182. Subsequent to the investigation, in a lawsuit to recover some of these funds to the policyholders, McCall testified that he had asked Perkins to make the donation to the Republican Party out of his own pocket, promising that the company would then reimburse him. This

way there would be no record of the company making a contribution to the GOP. *People ex rel. Perkins v. Moss,* 99 N.Y. 138 (1906), 139.

28. 40 *Cong. Rec.* 96 (5 December 1905).

29. Francis Butler Simkins, *Pitchfork Ben Tillman: South Carolinian* (Baton Rouge: Louisiana State University Press, 1944), 347–51.

30. 34 Stat. 864 (1907).

31. Smith, *Unfree Speech,* 24.

32. Mutch, *Campaigns, Congress, and Courts,* 166.

33. 36 Stat. 822 (1910).

34. *United States v. Newberry,* 256 U.S. 232 (1921).

35. Smith, *Unfree Speech,* 24–25; Mutch, *Campaigns, Congress, and the Courts,* 8–16.

36. Mutch, *Campaigns, Congress, and the Courts,* 19.

37. See Burl Noggle, *Teapot Dome: Oil and Politics in the 1920s* (Baton Rouge: Louisiana State University Press, 1962).

38. *Congressional Record,* 26 May 1924, S9507-08.

39. 43 Stat. 1070 (1925).

40. Louise Overacker, *Money in Elections* (New York: Macmillan, 1932), 271.

41. Mutch, *Campaigns, Congress, and the Courts,* 25.

42. Smith, *Unfree Speech,* 26–27.

43. 313 U.S. 299 (1941).

44. Alexander, *Financing Politics,* 14; for more on the financing of that election, see Michael J. Webber, *New Deal Fat Cats: Business, Labor, and Campaign Finance in the 1936 Presidential Election* (New York: Fordham University Press, 2000).

45. Alexander, *Financing Politics,* 5; Louise Overacker, *Presidential Campaign Funds* (Boston, MA: Boston University Press, 1946), 12, 14–15.

46. Ibid.

47. Christopher L. Tomlins, *The State and the Unions: Labor Relations, Law, and the Organized Labor Movement in America, 1880–1960* (New York: Cambridge University Press, 1985).

48. Birnbaum, *Money Men,* 30–31; Smith, *Unfree Speech,* 28.

49. Overacker, *Presidential Campaign Funds,* Table II, 15. In 1944, the percentage may have been even higher but because of intervening legislation (discussed below) the money from unions had to be listed as "unclassified."

50. 53 Stat. 1147 (1939).

51. 54 Stat. 767 (1940).

52. 57 Stat. 163 (1943). Roosevelt did not veto the bill because of the campaign provisions, but because it limited the flexibility of executive action in wartime labor disputes. During hearings on the bill, Lewis Hines, representing the American Federation of Labor, asked, Why "if it has been good over the years for the employers to elect Representatives to Congress— and there are many Representatives in Congress elected by employers—why is it not good for organized labor and the trade-union movement to put forth a little effort and financial support to help elect their friends?"

53. Smith, *Unfree Speech,* 28; Mutch, *Campaigns, Congress, and the Courts,* 155.

54. 61 Stat. 136 (1947); H.R. Rep. No. 2739, 79th Cong., 2nd Sess. 40 (1946), cited in Redacted Brief of Defendants, *McConnell v. FEC,* U.S. District Court for the District of Columbia, Civ. No. 02-0582, p. 15.

55. *United States v. Congress of Industrial Organizations,* 335 U.S. 106, 130 (1948).

56. *United States v. International Union of United Automobile, Aircraft, and Agricultural Implement Workers of America,* 352 U.S. 567 (1957).

57. Smith, *Unfree Speech,* 29–30.

58. In 1973, while working on a civic project in Albany, New York, I happened to go through a wrong door at City Hall on payday, to find municipal employees lined up making their contributions to the Albany County Democratic Party. How widespread this practice may have been is difficult to say, but according to Sorauf it did not apply at the federal level, due in large measure to the Hatch Act.

59. Frank J. Sorauf, *Money in American Elections* (Boston: Scott Foresman/ Little Brown, 1988), 21–24.

60. Alexander, *Financing Politics,* 5. This is equivalent to $270 million in 2005 dollars.

61. Goidel et al., *Money Matters,* 25.

62. 80 *Stat.* 1587 (1966). Although free-standing in its provisions, the Long Act was technically Title III of the Tax Code Revisions of 1966.

63. Sorauf, *Money in American Elections,* 31–32.

64. Alexander, *Money in Politics,* 185.

Chapter 2

1. Herbert E. Alexander, *Financing Politics: Money, Elections, and Political Reform,* 2nd ed. (Washington, DC: Congressional Quarterly Press, 1980), 5.

2. Gary C. Jacobson, *Money in Congressional Elections* (New Haven, CT: Yale University Press, 1980), 169.

3. 424 U.S. 1 (1976).

4. Herbert E. Alexander, *Money in Politics* (Washington, DC: Public Affairs Press, 1972), 201.

5. Ibid.

6. *New York Times,* 20 February 1956.

7. Robert E. Mutch, *Campaigns, Congress, and Courts: The Making of Federal Campaign Finance Law* (New York: Praeger, 1988), 26–27.

8. Alexander, *Money in Politics,* 202.

9. President's Commission on Campaign Costs, *Financing Presidential Campaigns* (Washington, DC: Government Printing Office, 1962).

10. Frank J. Sorauf, *Money in American Elections* (Glenview, IL: Scott, Foresman, 1988), 34.

11. Mutch, *Campaigns, Congress, and Courts,* 30–31.

12. Alexander, *Money in Politics,* 205.

13. "Message Transmitting Proposed Election Reform Act of 1966 (26 May 1966), *Messages and Papers of the Presidents: Lyndon Baines Johnson: 1966* (Washington, DC: Government Printing Office, 1967), 550.

14. Title III, Tax Code Revisions of 1966, 80 *Stat.* 1587 (1966).

15. For a list of actions and inactions, see Alexander, *Money in Politics,* 210ff.

16. Sorauf, *Money in American Elections,* 34.

17. Mutch, *Campaigns, Congress, and Courts,* 28.

18. The 1944 campaign had probably been limited by wartime financial restrictions, since it had cost less than the campaigns in 1936 and 1940, which were themselves limited by scarce resources during the Depression. Nonetheless, one might have expected more money to be spent in 1948. According to Bradley Smith, in inflation-adjusted dollars, the costs of the 1948 presidential election were the lowest since 1880. Smith, *Unfree Speech: The Folly of Campaign Finance Reform* (Princeton, NJ: Princeton University Press, 2001), 30.

19. Delmer D. Dunn, *Financing Presidential Campaigns* (Washington, DC: Brookings Institution, 1972), 60–61.

20. Alexander, *Financing Politics,* 10–11.

21. Ross K. Baker, *The New Fat Cats: Members of Congress as Political Benefactors* (New York: Priority Press, 1989), 7. In May, Askew withdrew from the race, claiming that he had to spend too much time fund-raising and not enough time campaigning.

22. Both quoted in Jacobson, *Money in Congressional Elections,* 184.

23. Ibid.

24. The dairy industry's pledge of $2 million to Nixon's reelection campaign in 1972 as well as smaller contributions to ranking members of the agriculture and finance committees supposedly helped to win an increase in price supports for milk worth more than $10 million to milk producers. But there is a question whether this was quid pro quo or merely support of people who already tended to favor such a policy. There is also a potential negative response, such as when Senator James Abourezk (D-S. Dak.) noted that he would have liked to support certain prodairy amendments to a finance bill, "but because I have received contributions from dairy farmers around the country, I am almost afraid to vote for them because it is set up now in the press that anybody who does vote for them who has taken money from the dairy farmers has been bought off."

25. U.S. Senate, 93rd Cong., 1st Sess., Committee on Rules and Administration, Subcommittee on Privileges and Elections, *Federal Election Reform* (Washington, DC: Government Printing Office, 1973), 185.

26. The bill in its entirety can be found in *Congressional Record,* 91st Cong., 2nd Sess. (23 November 1970), S18723-24. See Dunn, *Financing Presidential Campaigns,* 46–49.

27. "Veto of a Political Broadcasting Bill (12 October 1970)," *Messages and Papers of the Presidents: Richard Milhous Nixon: 1970* (Washington, DC: Government Printing Office, 1971), 837–39.

28. P.L. 92-178, 85 Stat. 562 (1971).

29. P.L. 92-225, 86 Stat. 3 (1972). Although Congress did not actually fin-ish passage of the bill until January 1972, it continues to be known as the act of 1971. It is codified at 2 U.S.C. §§431–455.

30. For fuller details of the 1971 FECA, see Appendix A.

31. Sorauf, *Money in American Elections*, 36.

32. Regarding Watergate in general, see Bob Woodward and Carl Bern-stein, *All the President's Men* (New York: Simon and Schuster, 1974), and Stanley I. Kutler, *The Wars of Watergate: The Last Crisis of Richard Nixon* (New York: Knopf, 1990). Regarding the effect on political campaigning, see Ralph K. Winter, Jr., *Watergate and the Law: Political Campaigns and Pres-idential Power* (Washington, DC: American Enterprise Institute, 1974).

33. Jeffrey H. Birnbaum, *The Money Men: The Real Story of Fund-raising's Influence on Political Power in America* (New York: Crown Publishers, 2000), 32–33; Alexander, *Financing Politics*, 73–81.

34. Kutler, *Wars of Watergate*, 355. Maurice Stans told CREEP treasurer Hugh Sloan, "I do not want to know and you do not want to know" why Liddy needed the money.

35. J. Anthony Lukas, *Nightmare* (New York: Viking, 1976), 128–29. Lukas drew on the little-noticed part of the Senate Select Committee on Presiden-tial Campaign Activities, chaired by Senator Sam Ervin (D-N.C.). After uncovering proof of wiretapping and misuse of federal agencies, and the evi-dence that led to Nixon's resignation, they also looked into some of the activities of the Committee to Re-elect the President.

36. Seymour Martin Lipset and William Schneider, *The Confidence Gap: Business, Labor, and Government in the Public Mind* (New York: Free Press, 1983) 16.

37. Mutch, *Campaigns, Congress, and Courts*, 42–43.

38. David W. Adamany and George E. Agree, *Political Money: A Strategy for Campaign Financing in America* (Baltimore, MD: Johns Hopkins Uni-versity Press, 1975), 5.

39. *Common Cause v. Democratic National Committee et al.*, 333 F. Supp. 803 (D.D.C. 1971).

40. Mutch, *Campaigns, Congress, and Courts*, 46.

41. Steven M. Gillon, *That's Not What We Meant to Do: Reform and Its Unintended Consequences in Twentieth Century America* (New York: Nor-ton, 2000), 203.

42. 88 *Stat.* 1263 (1974), codified at 2 U.S.C. 432 *et seq.* and 18 U.S.C. 591 *et seq.* The public financing provision is an amendment to the 1954 Internal Revenue Code, Subtitle H, and is codified at 26 USC 9001 *et seq.* For further details of the 1974 amendments, see Appendix B.

43. Jacobson, *Money in Congressional Elections*, 186–87.

44. A good example is Henry John Heinz, III, heir to the Heinz 57 food company, who put $2.5 million of his personal fortune into winning his Sen-ate race in Pennsylvania in 1976.

45. Ibid., 193–196.

46. Gillon, *"That's Not What We Meant to Do,"* 204–05.

47. *United States v. National Committee for Impeachment,* 469 F.2d 1135 (2nd Cir. 1972).

48. Joel M. Gora, "Dollars and Sense: In Praise of *Buckley v. Valeo,"* in Christopher P. Banks and John C. Green, eds., *Superintending Democracy: The Courts and the Political Process* (Akron, OH: University of Akron Press, 2001), 86. It should be pointed out that Gora served as the attorney for the American Civil Liberties Union in *Buckley v. Valeo,* discussed below.

49. *American Civil Liberties Union v. Jennings,* 366 F.Supp 1041 (D.D.C. 1975), vacated as moot in *Staats v. American Civil Liberties Union,* 422 U.S. 1030 (1975).

50. 2 U.S.C. 437(a).

51. For a more extended discussion of First Amendment decisions by the Warren and Burger Courts, as well as the development of free speech jurisprudence, see Melvin I. Urofsky, *The Continuity of Change: The Supreme Court and Individual Liberties, 1953–1986* (Belmont, CA: Wadsworth Publishing Co., 1991), Chapters 4 and 5. For the Rehnquist Court's speech-protection decisions, see Tinsley E. Yarbrough, *The Rehnquist Court and the Constitution* (New York: Oxford University Press, 2000), Chapter 7.

52. 274 U.S. 357, 372 (1927), Brandeis, J., concurring. For the best exposition of this opinion and its importance in the development of First Amendment jurisprudence, see Vincent Blasi, "The First Amendment and the Ideal of Civic Courage: The Brandeis Opinion in *Whitney v. California,"* 29 *William and Mary Law Review* 653 (1988).

53. Elizabeth Drew, *The Corruption of American Politics* (Secaucus, NJ: Carol Publishing Group, 1999), 49.

54. See Brief of Appellants in 84 *Landmark Briefs and Arguments of the Supreme Court of the United States* 37 (1977).

55. The "Valeo" in the case was Francis R. Valeo, then secretary of the Senate, to whom all reports required under the law had to be submitted. Valeo, of course, did not have to bear the costs of the case and was in fact only the nominal appellee. The solicitor general's office defended the act, as it does in all cases involving the constitutionality of federal laws.

56. *Buckley v. Valeo,* 519 F.2d 821 (D.C. Cir. 1975).

57. For an overview, see Christopher P. Banks, "The United States Supreme Court's Response to American Political Corruption," in Banks and Green, eds., *Superintending Democracy,* especially Tables 2.2, 2.3, and 2.4, 19–20, 26.

58. *United States v. Brewster,* 408 U.S. 501 (1972).

59. *United States v. Congress of Industrial Organizations,* 335 U.S. 106 (1948).

60. *United States v. International Union of Automobile, Aircraft, and Agricultural Implement Workers of America,* 352 U.S. 567 (1957).

61. *Pipefitters Local Union No. 562 v. United States,* 407 U.S. 385 (1972).

62. *Buckley v. Valeo,* 424 U.S. 1 (1976). There has been an enormous amount written on this case, but two articles that specifically address the

free speech aspects are Nelson W. Polsby, *"Buckley v. Valeo:* The Special Nature of Political Speech," *Supreme Court Review* 1 (1976), and Kathleen M. Sullivan, "Political Money and Freedom of Speech," 30 *University of California Davis Law Review* 663 (1997).

63. Ibid., 17–18, quoting *United States v. O'Brien,* 391 U.S. 367 (1968), 382.

64. Ibid., 19.

65. Ibid., 44, n. 52.

66. Ibid., 60 ff.

67. Ibid., 20–21.

68. Ibid., 28.

69. Ibid., 92–93. Chief Justice Burger concurred in finding the limits on expenditures unconstitutional, but dissented from that part upholding the limits on donations. Justice White would have found the limits on expenditures, as well as on the amount candidates themselves could spend, constitutional, and agreed with the limits on contributors. Justice Blackmun dissented from the ruling on donors, and Justice Marshall dissented from the part on wealthy candidates. Burger and Justice Rehnquist were the only dissenters from the public financing scheme, with Rehnquist charging that Congress had "enshrined the Republican and Democratic parties in a permanently preferred position." Ibid., 290, 293 (Rehnquist dissenting).

70. Anthony Corrado, "Money and Politics: A History of Campaign Finance Law," in Corrado et al., ed., *Campaign Finance Reform: A Sourcebook* (Washington, DC: Brookings Institution, 1997), 33.

71. The sole exception to contributions to party committees involved donations to building funds of national and state parties, which were exempt from all restrictions.

Chapter 3

1. The "congressional veto" over regulations and actions of federal agencies would be declared unconstitutional in *Immigration and Naturalization Service v. Chadha,* 462 U.S. 919 (1983).

2. P.L. 94-283, 90 Stat. 475. The main points are found in Appendix C.

3. P.L. 96-187, 93 Stat. 1339. The main points are in Appendix D.

4. Frank J. Sorauf, *Inside Campaign Finance: Myths and Realities* (New Haven, CT: Yale University Press, 1992), 13–14.

5. Quoted in W. Lance Bennett, *The Governing Crisis: Media, Money, and Marketing in American Elections,* 2nd ed. (New York: St. Martin's Press, 1996), 128.

6. Although some people complain that wealthy candidates have an unfair advantage in running for office, most studies indicate that personal wealth by itself is not a decisive factor. Nelson Rockefeller and the Kennedys did have private fortunes, but their political success resulted from other factors. In recent years we have seen rich candidates self-finance elections, and

in most instances they have lost. The so-called millionaire provision in the McCain-Feingold Act aimed not at reducing an individual's use of private wealth so much as allowing opponents, when faced by a rich candidate, to exceed certain guidelines in an effort to level the playing field. See Chapter 4.

7. Bennett, *The Governing Crisis,* 137.

8. *Buckley v. Valeo,* 424 U.S. 1 (1976), 24 n. 24 (emphasis added). Later in the opinion (p. 78) the Court again defined contributions as "contributions made directly or indirectly to a candidate, political party, or campaign committee.

9. 2 U.S.C. 431 (8)9Ao(i), (9)(A)(i).

10. Redacted Brief for Defendants, *McConnell v. Federal Election Commission,* U.S. District Court for the District of Columbia, Civ. No. 02-0582, 22-26; Expert Report of Thomas E. Mann, prepared for U.S. Department of Justice, 7ff.

11. Mann Report, 8–10.

12. Source: Anthony Corrado, *Campaign Finance Reform* (New York: Century Foundation Press, 2000), 70.

13. "Campaign Finance Chronology," *Washington Post,* 2 May 2003; Mann Report, 13.

14. Diana Dwyre, "Spinning Straw into Gold," cited in Robert K. Goidel, Daniel A. Gross, and Todd G. Shields. *Money Matters: Consequences of Campaign Finance Reform in U.S. House Elections* (Lanham, MD: Rowman and Littlefield, 1999), 146.

15. Herbert E. Alexander and Anthony Corrado, *Financing the 1992 Election* (Armonk, NY: M.E. Sharpe, 1995).

16. *Common Cause v. Federal Election Commission,* 692 F.Supp. 1391 (D.D.C. 1987).

17. Where Clinton and Morris got this idea is unknown, but the two must have been very much aware of the ads run by the health insurance industry in 1993 to sink the Clinton health care reform proposal.

18. Corrado, *Campaign Finance Reform,* 24–25.

19. *Buckley v. Valeo,* 424 U.S., 44. n 52.

20. Redacted Brief of Defendants, 30 n. 14.

21. Mann Report, 20.

22. Michael J. Malbin and Thomas L. Gais, *The Day after Reform: Sobering Campaign Finance Lessons from the American States* (Albany, NY: Rockefeller Institute Press, 1998), 11–12.

23. Ibid., 12.

24. Bradley A. Smith, *Unfree Speech: The Folly of Campaign Finance Reform* (Princeton, NJ: Princeton University Press, 2001), 37. Smith would later become chair of the FEC during the Bush administration.

25. Steven M. Gillon, *"That's Not What We Meant to Do": Reform and Its Unintended Consequences in Twentieth Century America* (New York: Norton, 2000). Chapter 5 deals with FECA and the 1974 amendments.

26. Edwin M. Epstein, "Business and Labor under the Federal Election Campaign Act of 1971," in Michael Malbin, ed., *Parties, Interest Groups,*

and Campaign Finance Laws (Washington, DC: American Enterprise Institute, 1979), 146–47.

27. Diana Dwyre and Victoria A. Farra-Myers, *Legislative Labyrinth: Congress and Campaign Finance Reform* (Washington, DC: Congressional Quarterly Press, 2001), 8.

28. This development astounded labor leaders. One labor lawyer who had lobbied for the 1974 changes confessed that it had been a mistake. "The way things have turned out, the labor movement would have been better off politically with no PACs at all on either side." Gillon, *"That's Not What We Meant,"* 214–15.

29. Ibid., 214; Jeffrey H. Birnbaum, *The Money Men: The Real Story of Fund-raising Influence on Political Power in America* (New York: Crown, 2000), 35–37. For more information on the number of PACs and their operations, see Brooks Jackson, *Honest Graft: Big Money and the American Political Process* (Washington, DC: Farragut Publishing, 1988), Chapter 5, and Robert Biersack, Paul S. Herrnson, and Clyde Wilcox, eds., *After the Revolution: PACs, Lobbies, and the Republican Congress* (Boston: Allyn and Bacon, 1999).

30. Ann B. Matasar, *Corporate PACs and Federal Campaign Financing Laws* (New York: Quorum Books, 1986), 4.

31. *Santa Clara County v. Southern Pacific Railroad Co.,* 118 U.S. 394 (1886). Corporations, it should also be remembered, are in essence made up of individual stockholders. When U.S. Steel, for example, through a PAC is lobbying for higher steel tariffs to protect its profits, it is in fact lobbying to protect the financial investment of its shareholders as well as the return on that investment.

32. The fact that business in this country developed prior to the growth of big business has also had an impact on how corporations view the political process. See Theodore J. Eismeier and Philip H. Pollock III, *Business, Money, and the Rise of Corporate PACs in American Elections* (New York: Quorum Books, 1988), 5–7.

33. Hugh Davis Graham, "Legacies of the 1960s: The American 'Rights Revolution' in an Era of Divided Government," 10 *Journal of Policy History* 267, 273–75 (1998).

34. Gillon, *"That's Not What We Meant,"* 216.

35. Dwyre and Farrar-Myers, *Legislative Labyrinth,* 8.

36. In practice, if the candidate had to enter a primary, that counted as another election, even if the candidate faced little or no opposition. So in a district where the incumbent faced only token opposition in the primary, he or she would not have to spend very much money, and could then transfer the balance for use in the general election. Of course, in those instances in which a competitive primary race occurred, then treating the primary and the general election as two separate elections made sense.

37. Dwyre and Farrar-Myers, *Legislative Labyrinth,* 13–16.

38. Congressional Quarterly, *Campaign Practices Reports* (11 February 1985), 1.

39. Herbert Alexander, *Financing Politics: Money, Elections, and Political Reform* (Washington, DC: Congressional Quarterly Press, 1976), 142–48. In 1981, Common Cause published a pamphlet on the FEC entitled *Stalled from the Start.*

40. Robert E. Mutch, *Campaigns, Congress, and Courts: The Making of Federal Campaign Finance Law* (New York: Praeger, 1988), 89.

41. Ibid., 96.

42. Brooks Jackson, *Broken Promise: Why the Federal Election Commission Failed* (New York: Priority Press, 1990), 23. Another critic described the FEC as "wielding a lash as stinging as a wet noodle."

43. Mutch, *Campaigns, Congress, and Courts,* 105.

44. David Magleby and Candice J. Nelson, *The Money Chase: Congressional Campaign Finance Reform* (Washington, DC: Brookings Institution, 1990), 127.

45. The Democrats then filed suit, and the FEC responded that the dismissal of the case was not justiciable, that is, capable of review by the courts. Since there had not been four affirmative votes, there had been neither a "dismissal" nor a "failure to act," but rather a "no-action" middle ground. Judge Stanley Sporkin of the federal district court for the District of Columbia, disagreed, and ruled the action could be maintained because there had been "absolutely no articulation of a rationale for the FEC's actions." The FEC appealed, but the Court of Appeals ordered the commissioners to provide written explanations of their vote. They did, and then the case was dismissed. Ibid., 128 n. 18.

46. Quoted in ibid., 128.

47. "Manufacturing the Next President," *Harper's Magazine* 275 (December 1987), 43–54.

48. Herbert E. Alexander and Brian A. Haggerty, *Financing the 1984 Election* (Lexington: D. C. Heath, 1987), 47; the authors include other examples of FEC delay and nonaction.

49. Jackson, *Broken Promise,* 14.

50. Magleby and Nelson, *Money Chase,* 133–34.

51. For examples of the housekeeping work done by the FEC—and such matters are administratively important—one should peruse the monthly *Record* published by the commission. In blatant matters, it has entered into enforcement and conciliation actions that have resulted in civil fines.

52. Ibid., 135.

53. Frank J. Sorauf, *Money in American Elections* (Glenview: Scott, Foresman, 1988), 31.

54. Alexander Heard, *The Costs of Democracy* (Chapel Hill: University of North Carolina Press, 1960), 344–57.

55. Louise Overacker, *Money in Elections* (New York: Macmillan, 1932), 295.

56. Ibid., 257.

57. Ruth S. Jones, "Campaign and Party Finance in the American States," in Arthur B. Gunlicks, ed., *Campaign and Party Finance in North America and Western Europe* (Boulder, CO: Westview Press, 1993), 44.

58. Ibid. 47–48; see also Joel A. Thompson and Gary F. Moncrief, *Campaign Finance in State Legislative Elections* (Washington, DC: Congressional Quarterly Press, 1998).

59. Malbin and Gais, *The Day after Reform*, 13.

60. Ibid.

61. Herbert E. Alexander, "Introduction: Rethinking Reform," in Herbert E. Alexander, ed., *Campaign Money: Reform and Reality in the States* (New York: Free Press, 1976), 4–7.

62. David S. Broder, "Assessing Campaign Reform: Lessons for the Future," in Herbert E. Alexander, ed., *Campaign Money: Reform and Reality in the States* (New York: Free Press, 1976), 307–10.

63. Ibid., 310.

64. J. Skelly Wright, "Money and the Pollution of Politics: Is the First Amendment an Obstacle to Political Equality?" 82 *Columbia Law Review* 609, 625 (1982).

Chapter 4

1. Association of the Bar of the City of New York, Commission on Campaign Finance Reform, *Dollars and Democracy: A Blueprint for Campaign Finance Reform* (New York: Fordham University Press, 2000), 1.

2. Thomas Mann, Report submitted as part of documentation in defense of BCRA to the federal district court (n.d.).

3. Austin Ranney, *Channels of Power* (New York: Basic Books, 1983), 53.

4. Elizabeth Drew, *Politics and Money* (New York: Macmillan, 1983), 77.

5. Dan Clawson, Alan Neustadtl, and Mark Weller, *Dollars and Votes: How Business Campaign Contributions Subvert Democracy* (Philadelphia, PA: Temple University Press, 1998), 22. Clawson and his colleagues note that if corporations paid the same share of total taxes in 1995 as they had in 1955, they would have paid an additional $213 billion, enough in one year to provide public funding for both House and Senate races for over a century.

6. Several scholars and institutes have kept track of campaign expenditures, and although some of their work is based on reports to the Federal Election Commission, their writings are far clearer than the FEC reports and provide a much easier way of assessing increases in campaign costs. For the late 1980s through the 2000 election, see Herbert E. Alexander and Monica Bauer, *Financing the 1988 Election* (Boulder, CO: Westview Press, 1991); Herbert E. Alexander and Anthony Corrado, *Financing the 1992 Election* (Armonk, NY: M.E. Sharpe, 1995); John C. Green, ed., *Financing the 1996 Election* (Armonk, NY: M.E. Sharpe, 1999); David B. Magleby, ed., *Outside Money: Soft Money and Issue Advocacy in the 1998 Congressional Elections* (Lanham, MD: Rowman and Littlefield, 2000); David B. Magleby, ed., *Financing the 2000 Election* (Washington, DC: Brookings Institution Press, 2002); and David B. Magleby, ed., *The Other Campaign: Soft Money and*

Issue Advocacy in the 2000 Congressional Elections (Lanham, MD: Rowman and Littlefield, 2003).

7. For an analysis of Bush and his fund-raising in 2000 and 2004, see "Building War Chest with Few Restraints" and "Fundraiser Denies Link between Money, Access," *Washington Post*, 15 and 16 May 2004.

8. Ibid., 21 October 1999. The amount of money paid out by the Presidential Election Campaign Fund has remained fairly constant, starting at $216 million in 1976 and going to $208 million in 2000 (in dollars adjusted for inflation). During that period it has spiked twice, to $257 million in the 1988 campaign and $256 million in the 1996 campaign.

9. Candice J. Nelson, "Spending in the 2000 Elections," in Magleby, ed., *Financing the 2000 Election*, 27–30.

10. FEC Press Release, 15 May 2001.

11. Ibid.

12. Cranston, it should be noted, had long been involved in such legitimate party-building activities; he had introduced bills in the Senate to support these activities, and over the years had raised considerable amounts of money for programs designed to enhance voter turnout.

13. Alexander and Bauer, *Financing the 1988 Election*, 79–80.

14. Ibid., 80–81.

15. *Washington Post*, 9 February 1997, A1.

16. Clawson *et al.*, *Dollars and Votes*, 199–200.

17. Ibid., 201.

18. Ibid., 202.

19. Ibid., 202–203. Burton, one of those who howled loudest at President Clinton's alleged improprieties, in 1997 became head of a U.S. House committee investigating the ways political money is used to secure access. Three weeks after taking over this committee, Burton played golf in the Pebble Beach National Pro-Am Tournament, courtesy of American Telephone and Telegraph. Burton had long wanted this invitation and admitted that "over the past several years, whenever I talked to anybody at AT&T, I told them that if they ever had a chance, I'd like to play in that tournament." The invitation came not because Burton headed an ethics committee but because he chaired a communications committee that oversaw at least $5 billion in telephone contracts with the government.

20. Ibid., 203.

21. Robert Biersack and Melanie Haskell, "Spitting on the Umpire: Political Parties, the Federal Election Campaign Act, and the 1996 Campaigns," in Green, ed., *Financing the 1996 Election*, 184.

22. Ibid., 184–85.

23. Herbert Alexander, "Epilogue: Shaping Election Reform," in Alexander and Bauer, *Financing the 1988 Election*, 111.

24. Ibid., 112–16.

25. Ibid., 118.

26. The members of the committee appointed by Dole were Herbert

Alexander of the University of Southern California, head of the Citizen's Research Foundation; Jan Baran, partner in a Washington law firm and former counsel to the RNC; and Larry Sabato of the University of Virginia, who had recently written a book on PACs. Mitchell appointed Robert Bauer, another Washington lawyer and counsel to a Democratic campaign committee; David Magleby of Brigham Young University; and Richard Moe, another Washington lawyer and veteran of several Democratic campaigns. For the politics surrounding efforts to enact the revised Boren bill, see Greg D. Kubiak, *The Gilded Dome: The U.S. Senate and Campaign Finance Reform* (Norman: University of Oklahoma Press, 1994), Chapter 10.

27. Ibid., 269–71; Alexander, "Shaping Election Reform," 119–121.

28. Ibid., 137–38.

29. *Congressional Record*, 23 May 1991, S12340.

30. *New York Times*, 1 May 1992; *Washington Post*, 1 May 1992.

31. *Public Papers of the Presidents of the United States: George Bush, 1992–1993* (Washington, DC: Government Printing Office, 1993), 736.

32. *Public Papers of the Presidents of the United States: William J. Clinton, 1993* (Washington, DC: Government Printing Office, 1994), 2.

33. "Address before a Joint Session of Congress on Administration Goals," 17 February 1993, ibid., 118.

34. "Remarks on Campaign Finance Reform," 7 May 1993, ibid., 584–86.

35. "Address before a Joint Session of Congress on the State of the Union," 4 February 1997, *Public Papers of the Presidents of the United States: William J. Clinton, 1997* (Washington, DC: Government Printing Office, 1998), 110.

36. Clawson et al., *Dollars and Votes*, 198–99.

37. 116 *Stat. at Large* 81 (2002).

38. American Enterprise Institute, the Brookings Institution, and the Campaign and Media Legal Center Press Briefing, "The Future of Campaign Finance Reform," Panel Discussion 1 March 2002, at www.brookings.org/comm/transcripts/20020301.htm, accessed 26 July 2003.

39. Public Citizen, "Bipartisan Campaign Reform Act of 2002," http://www.citizen.org/campaign/legislation/bcralaw/index.cfm, accessed 8 May 2004.

40. *Public Papers of the Presidents of the United States: George W. Bush: 1992–1993* (Washington, DC: Government Printing Office, 1993), 736.

41. "Bush Signs Reform Law," *Washington Post*, 27 March 2002. Nonetheless, Common Cause president Scott Harshbarger gave Bush credit for the measure's passage. Bush had changed his mind and told Congress he would not veto the law. Had he continued to oppose it, the Republican-controlled Congress would never have sent it to his desk.

42. Ibid., 27 March 2002.

43. The following section is based on Trevor Potter and Kirk L. Jowers, "Recent Developments in Campaign Finance Regulation," Brookings Institution, http://www.brook.edu/gs/cf/headlines/final approval.htm, accessed 10 May 2004, and the Federal Election Commission, *Record* 29 (January 2003), No. 1.

44. Clawson et al., *Dollars and Votes*, 204.

45. *Washington Post*, 28 March 2002.

46. Bopp had apparently been awaiting the call, because even as Congress approved BCRA and Bush signed it, he and Richard E. Coleson published a law review article that was in essence a brief attacking the law. Bopp and Coleson, "The First Amendment Needs No Reform: Protecting Liberty from Campaign Finance 'Reformers,'" *Catholic University Law Review* 51 (2002): 785. This article was summarized in a lengthy article in the BNA *Money and Politics Report*, 22 April 2002.

47. McConnell Press Releases, 21 and 27 March 2002, at http://mcconnell .senate.gov, accessed 11 May 2004.

48. Statement of 27 March 2002, http://stanford.edu/library/campaignfi-nance/NRAstatement.htm. The NRA statement also mentioned that during the course of the debate over BCRA, Senator Paul Wellstone (D-Minn.) claimed that the bill would silence the NRA.

49. McConnell Press Release, 7 May 2002, http://mcconnell.senate.gov.

50. ACLU Press Release, 21 March 2002.

51. McCain Press Release, 27 March 2002, http://mccain.senate.gov.

52. McCain Press Release, 2 April 2002, http://mccain.senate.gov.

Chapter 5

1. 531 U.S. 98 (2000).

2. Two years later, a Democratic senator from New Jersey, Robert Torri-celli, withdrew from his reelection race after charges of scandal. Although he did so after the deadline for parties to enter replacement candidates, the Democrats named the popular former governor and senator Frank Lautenburg to be their candidate, and agreed to pay any costs involved in reprinting ballots and other expenses. The New Jersey Supreme Court upheld the Democrats, and the Republicans immediately appealed to the Supreme Court on the basis of *Bush v. Gore*, but the High Court refused to hear the case.

3. 259 U.S. 45 (1935); *United States v. Classic*, 313 U.S. 299 (1941).

4. 321 U.S. 649 (1944).

5. 345 U.S. 461 (1953). For a good study of all the primary cases, see Darlene Clark Hines, *Black Victory: The Rise and Fall of the White Primary in Texas* (Millwood: KTO Press, 1979).

6. 78 *Stat.* 241 (1964).

7. 79 *Stat.* 437 (1965).

8. 383 U.S. 301 (1966), 324.

9. 383 U.S. 663 (1966). For more on the role of the Supreme Court in racial voting rights, see Steven F. Lawson, *Black Ballots: Voting Rights in the South, 1944–1969* (New York: Columbia University Press, 1976), and Ward Y. Elliott, *The Rise of Guardian Democracy: The Supreme Court's Role in Voting Rights Disputes, 1848–1969* (Cambridge, MA: Harvard University Press, 1974).

10. 364 U.S. 339 (1960).

11. *Easley v. Cromartie*, 532 U.S. 234 (2001). For the majority-minority cases, see Tinsley E. Yarbrough, *Race and Redistricting: The Shaw-Cromartie Cases* (Lawrence: University Press of Kansas, 2002).

12. *Colegrove v. Green*, 328 U.S. 549 (1946), 565. See Richard C. Cortner, *The Apportionment Cases* (New York: Norton, 1970), Chapter 1.

13. 369 U.S. 186 (1962).

14. *Reynolds v. Sims*, 377 U.S. 533, (1964), 567. See Cortner, *The Apportionment Cases*, and Robert McKay, "Reapportionment: The Success Story of the Warren Court," *Michigan Law Review* 67 (1968), 223.

15. Jack N. Rakove, *Original Meanings: Politics and Ideas in the Making of the Constitution* (New York: Vintage Books, 1996), 50–51.

16. Constitutional provisions include the power of Congress to impeach executive and judicial officers, internal regulation by each house of its members, prohibition of multiple office-holding, prohibition of titles, presents, and other emoluments, life tenure of judges, and jury trial in criminal and even minor civil matters.

17. Although it is not necessary for this study to look at each case, readers seeking a fuller list should consult Christopher P. Banks, "The United States Supreme Court's Response to American Political Corruption," Tables 2.2, "Cases Involving Allegations of Bribery" and 2.3, "Cases Involving Allegations of Conflict of Interest," in Christopher P. Banks and John C. Green, eds., *Superintending Democracy: The Courts and the Political Process* (Akron, OH: University of Akron Press, 2001), 19, 20.

18. 408 U.S. 501 (1972).

19. 383 U.S. 169 (1966).

20. *United States v. International Union of United Auto Workers*, 352 U.S. 567 (1957).

21. *Id.*, 570-77.

22. *United States v. Congress of Industrial Organizations*, 335 U.S. 106 (1948), 130 (Rutledge, J., dissenting).

23. *United States v. International Union of United Automobile, Aircraft, and Agricultural Implement Workers of America*, 352 U.S. 567 (1957), 579 (Douglas, J., dissenting).

24. *Pipefitters Local Union No. 562 v. United States*, 407 U.S. 385 (1972).

25. 279 U.S. 597 (1929).

26. *Burroughs and Cannon v. United States*, 290 U.S. 534 (1934), 545.

27. Ibid., 545–47.

28. *Buckley v. Valeo*, 424 U.S. 1 (1976), came down as a per curiam decision, i.e., as a memorandum expressing the opinion of the Court with no named author. Eight justices participated; only Brennan, Stewart, and Powell joined all eight holdings. Burger, White, Marshall, Blackmun, and Rehnquist filed separate opinions, concurring in part and dissenting in part. Justice Stevens, who had just joined the bench, did not participate.

29. Ibid., 19.

30. Ibid., 27.

31. Ibid., 39, citing *Williams v. Rhodes,* 393 U.S. 23 (1968), 32.
32. Ibid., 48–49, citing *Associated Press v. United States,* 326 U.S. 1 (1945), 20.
33. Ibid., 44n.52.
34. Ibid., 54.
35. Ibid., 286 (Marshall, J., dissenting). A noted *New York Times* Supreme Court reporter, Anthony Lewis, found this provision inexplicable. "In other words," he wrote, "the American system is absolutely powerless to prevent a Rockefeller from spending $4 million in family money to elect himself governor. . . . Does that make any sense? Does it make any constitutional sense? I think the American Constitution is not so simple-minded. . . . Of course money is a lot more than 'speech.' We know that money talks; but that is the problem, not the answer." *New York Times,* 5 February 1976.
36. 372 U.S. 539 (1963); 357 U.S. 449 (1958).
37. 424 U.S. at 66.
38. Ibid., 239 (Burger, C.J., dissenting).
39. *Brown v. Socialist Workers '74 Campaign Committee,* 459 U.S. 87 (1982), 94n.9.
40. 424 U.S. at 57n.65.
41. Ibid., 293.
42. Ibid., 241–42 (Burger, C.J., dissenting). Justice Blackmun in a separate opinion also could find no principled distinction between limits on contributions and expenditures, and would have struck both down (ibid., 290).
43. Ibid., 261–62 (White, J., dissenting).
44. Frank J. Sorauf, "Politics, Experience, and the First Amendment: The Case of American Campaign Finance," *Columbia Law Review* 94 (1994): 1348, 1349. The majority opinion, with an appendix, runs 229 pages; the partial dissents and concurrences add another 65 pages.
45. Darrell M. West, *Checkbook Democracy: How Money Corrupts Political Campaigns* (Boston: Northeastern University Press, 2000), 172.
46. Vincent A. Blasi, "Free Speech," *Columbia Law Review* 94 (1994) 1348, 1351.
47. Bradley A. Smith, *Unfree Speech: The Folly of Campaign Finance Reform* (Princeton, NJ: Princeton University Press, 2001), 110. Smith also argued that it is campaign finance reform, and not how the system currently works, that is the real problem in developing a more equitable system. "Faulty Assumptions and Undemocratic Consequences of Campaign Finance Reform," *Yale Law Journal* 105 (1996): 1049. Ironically, Smith became a member and was chairman of the FEC when the Supreme Court handed down its decision in *McConnell.*
48. 424 U.S. at 26–27.
49. Smith, *Unfree Speech,* 127.
50. David H. Strauss, "Corruption, Equality, and Campaign Finance," *Columbia Law Review* 94 (1994): 1369, 1370.
51. Lillian R. BeVier, "Campaign Finance Reform: Specious Arguments, Intractable Dilemmas," *Columbia Law Review* 94 (1994): 1258.

52. Lillian R. BeVier, "The Issue of Issue Advocacy: An Economic, Political, and Constitutional Analysis," *Virginia Law Review* 85 (1999): 1761.

53. 198 U.S. 45 (1905).

54. Cass Sunstein, "Free Speech Now," *University of Chicago Law Review* 59 (1992): 255.

55. Daniel R. Ortiz, "The Engaged and the Inert: Theorizing Political Personality under the First Amendment," *Virginia Law Review* 81 (1995): 1. For two well-reasoned economic analyses of the political system as a marketplace, see Martin H. Redish, *Money Talks: Speech, Economic Power, and the Values of Democracy* (New York: New York University Press, 2001), and Brian K. Pinaire, "A Funny Thing Happened on the Way to the Market: The Supreme Court and Political Speech in the Electoral Process," 18 *Journal of Law & Politics* 489 (2001).

56. 528 U.S. 377 (2000). A ballot initiative with even stricter contribution limits had been approved by 74 percent of Missouri voters, but it was then voided by the Court of Appeals for the Eighth Circuit, which nonetheless noted alleged improprieties with respect to contributions to Missouri political figures. *Carver v. Nixon*, 72 F.3d 633 (8th Cir. 1995), cert. denied, 518 U.S. 1033 (1996).

57. 528 U.S. at 397.

58. Ibid., 391.

59. Richard L. Hasen, "*Shrink Missouri*, Campaign Finance, and the 'Thing That Wouldn't Leave,'" *Constitutional Commentary* 17 (2000): 483, 484.

60. *New York Times*, 29 January 2000.

61. 528 U.S. at 406–407 (Kennedy, J., dissenting).

62. Ibid., 407 (Kennedy, J., dissenting).

63. Ibid., 420, 424 (Thomas, J., dissenting). In response to this charge, Justice Breyer, joined by Justice Ginsburg, wrote a concurrence arguing that in cases involving campaign finance limits, where there were competing constitutional interests, there was no place for a strong presumption against constitutionality, nor would a mechanical application of "strict scrutiny" (the normal First Amendment test) resolve the constitutional problem. The state statute was valid under the balance-of-interests approach, and if it ever turned out that *Buckley* denied the political branches sufficient leeway to enact appropriate regulations of campaign finance, then it should be reconsidered. Ibid. at 399 (Breyer, J., concurring).

64. This diversion of money into hidden channels is discussed in Samuel Issacharoff and Pamela S. Karlan, "The Hydraulics of Campaign Finance Reform," *Texas Law Review* 77 (1999): 1705.

65. 453 U.S. 182 (1981).

66. 2 USCS 441a(a)(1)(C) and 2 USCS 441a(f).

67. 453 U.S. at 197. Justice Brennan concurred in the result, but did not think a different constitutional test should apply to contributions and to expenditures. Justice Stewart, joined by Chief Justice Burger and Justices Powell and Rehnquist, dissented on jurisdictional grounds, believing that

the case had not been ripe when the district court certified it to the court of appeals, and that the matter should be returned there for a final decision prior to an appeal.

68. 470 U.S. 480 (1985).

69. Ibid., 519–521 (Marshall, J., dissenting).

70. 518 U.S. 604 (1996).

71. Ibid., 608–609, 618.

72. Ibid., 646 (Thomas, J., concurring in part and dissenting in part).

73. Ibid., 649 (Stevens, J., dissenting).

74. *FEC v. Colorado Republican Federal Campaign Committee*, 533 U.S. 431 (2001).

75. Ibid., 456.

76. Ibid., 457, 464–65.

77. *First National Bank of Boston v. Attorney General*, 371 Mass. 773 (1977).

78. 435 U.S. 765 (1978). Justice Powell wrote for himself and Justices Stewart, Blackmun, and Stevens; Chief Justice Burger concurred, making the fifth vote.

79. Ibid., 776, 777.

80. Ibid., 803–804 (White, J., dissenting). Justice Rehnquist also dissented, on grounds that the Fourteenth Amendment does not require a state to endow corporations with the same rights of free speech as an individual, and that he would uphold the law even if the legislature's purpose had been to muzzle the corporation's views. Ibid., 822 (Rehnquist, J., dissenting).

81. 459 U.S. 197 (1982).

82. Ibid., 207.

83. *FEC v. Massachusetts Citizens for Life*, 479 U.S. 238 (1986).

84. 494 U.S. 652 (1990).

85. Ibid., 664–65.

86. One critic of this decision claims that the Court missed the essential point. To require that campaign expenditures reflect existing public support is to ignore the primary function of expenditures—to persuade the public to support a particular viewpoint. Thus even if a majority of the public are at a given time opposed to a particular point of view, proponents of that viewpoint have a legitimate right to try to change minds, and this may require expenditures of money. Thomas Gais, *Improper Influence: Campaign Finance Law, Political Interest Groups, and the Problem of Equality* (Ann Arbor: University of Michigan Press, 1996), 174.

87. Ibid., 679–80 (Scalia, J., dissenting).

88. Ibid., 695, 704 (Kennedy, J., dissenting).

89. See, for example, Fisch, "Frankenstein's Monster Hits the Campaign Trail: An Approach to Regulation of Corporate Political Expenditures," *William and Mary Law Review* 32 (1991): 587, and Daniel Hays Lowenstein, "A Patternless Mosaic: Campaign Finance and the First Amendment after Austin," 21 *Capital Law Review* 381 (1992): 381.

90. 454 U.S. 290 (1981). Burger wrote for himself, Brennan, Powell, Rehnquist, and Stevens. Rehnquist, Marshall, and Blackmun (joined by O'Connor) concurred in separate opinions.

91. The Court dealt with these issues in other cases as well. See, for example, *Meyer v. Grant*, 486 U.S. 414 (1988), in which a unanimous Court struck down a Colorado law prohibiting the payment of people circulating petitions for ballot initiatives, and *Brown v. Hartlage*, 456 U.S. 45 (1982), which struck down a state law prohibiting certain types of campaign promises.

92. E. Joshua Rosenkranz, "Clean and Constitutional," in David Donnelly, Janice Fine, and Ellen S. Miller, eds., *Money and Politics: Financing Our Elections Democratically* (Boston: Beacon Press, 1999), 60, 61.

93. Redish, *Money Talks*, 115.

Chapter 6

1. The depositions and other materials presented by expert witnesses as well as members of Congress are gathered in edited form as part of the record and are available in Anthony Corrado, Thomas E. Mann, and Trevor Potter, eds., *Inside the Campaign Finance Battle: Testimony on the New Reform* (Washington, DC: Brookings Institution Press, 2003).

2. ACLU Press Release, 21 March 2002, at http://www.aclu.org/ FreeSpeech/ FreeSpeechcfm?ID=10057&c=20, accessed 15 May 2003.

3. *Washington Post*, 28 March 2002; BCRA specifically allowed members of Congress standing to participate in all legal challenges to the bill.

4. McConnell Press Releases, 21 and 27 March 2002, at http://mcconnell .senate.gov, accessed 11 May 2004.

5. NRA Statement of 27 March 2002, http://stanford.edu/library/campaignfinance/NRAstatement.htm. The statement also mentioned that during the course of the debate over BCRA, Senator Paul Wellstone (D-Minn.) claimed that the bill would silence the NRA.

6. McConnell Press Release, 7 May 2002, http://mcconnell.senate.gov.

7. Listed as *Senator Mitch McConnell et al. v. Federal Election Commission*, Civ. No. 02-582. It also included Alabama Attorney General Bill Pryor, the Libertarian National Committee, the Alabama Republican Executive Committee, the Libertarian Party of Illinois, the DuPage (Illinois) Political Action Council, the Jefferson County (Alabama) Republican Executive Committee, the American Civil Liberties Union, the Association of Builders and Contractors, the Association of Builders and its PAC, the Center for Individual Freedom, the Christian Coalition, the Club for Growth, the Indiana Family Institute, the National Right to Life Committee, the National Right to Life Educational Trust Fund, the National Right to Life PAC, the National Right to Work Committee, the 60 Plus Association, the Southeastern Legal Foundation, ProEnglish, Martin Connors, Thomas E. McInerney, Barrett Austin O'Brock, and Trevor M. Southerland.

The other litigant groups were the National Rifle Association and the NRA Political Victory Fund; Emily Echols, joined by Hannah McDow, Isaac McDow, Jessica Mitchell, Daniel Solid, and Zachary White, all minors who attacked the BCRA's provision against political contributions by minors; the National Association of Broadcasters; the Chamber of Commerce of the United States and its PAC, along with the National Association of Manufacturers, the National Association of Wholesaler Distributors; the American Federation of Labor and the Congress of Industrial Organizations (AFL-CIO) and its PAC; Congressman Ron Paul (R-Tex.), joined by the Gun Owners of America and its Political Victory Fund, Realcampaignreform.org, Citizens United and its Political Victory Fund, Michael Cloud and Carla Howell; the Republican National Committee, Michael Duncan (as a member and treasurer of the RNC), the Republican Parties of Colorado, Ohio. and New Mexico, and the Dallas County (Iowa) Republican County Central Committee; the California Democratic Party, joined by Art Torres, the Yolo County (California) Democratic Central Committee, the California Republican Party, Shawn Steel, Timothy Morgan, Barbara Alby, Douglas R. Boyd, Sr., and the Santa Cruz (California) Republican Central Committee; Victoria Jackson and Gray Adams, joined by Carrie Bolton, Cynthia Brown, Derek Cressman, Victoria Fitzgerald, Anurada Joshi, Peter Kostmayer, Nancy Russell, Kate Selly-Kirk, Rose Taylor, Stephanie Wilson, the Fannie Lou Hamer Project, and the Association of Community Organizers for Reform Now (ACORN); and finally, Representative Bennie G. Thompson (D-Miss.) and Rep. Earl F. Hilliard (D-Ala.).

8. Randolph Moss to author, e-mail, 2 August 2004.

9. Now Wilmer Cutler Pickering Hale and Dorr, LLP.

10. The witnesses would not testify at the trial, but would be deposed by one side, and then cross-examined by the other, with transcripts of the meetings submitted as part of the record.

11. The district court allocated a total of 355 pages for the consolidated brief, 335 to the McConnell group and 20 to the Thompson plaintiffs. Because plaintiffs within the McConnell Group differed in their interpretations and complaints, within each area of attack there would be a larger brief identified as "McConnell Omnibus," and then smaller sections attributed to the ACLU, NRA, or whatever group wanted to make separate points.

12. "Consolidated Brief for Plaintiffs in Support of Motion for Judgment," *Senator Mitch McConnell et al. v. Federal Election Commission et al.*, Civ. No. 02-0582, in the U.S. District Court for the District of Columbia, Redacted Version. The plaintiffs, especially the political parties and political action committees, claimed that some of the information they wished to present should not be made available to the public, since it would in effect provide data to their opponents that they otherwise would not have been able to access. This material would be akin to "trade secrets" that companies in civil suits may keep confidential because it is not normally available to the public, and would, if made public, work to the advantage of competitors. The court would see this confidential material, but it allowed plaintiffs the

opportunity to prepare a redacted version that would be available to the public. All references in this section are to this consolidated redacted plaintiffs'
brief.

13. "McConnell Omnibus," 2–3.

14. Ibid., 3–4.

15. Elizabeth Garrett to author, 6 September 2004.

16. RNC brief. Interestingly, the RNC had gathered such a large amount
of supporting material that rather than submit "volumes" of depositions and
other evidence, it submitted both a brief and the supporting record on an
interactive CD, allowing the court to jump back and forth from arguments
in the brief to corroborative material through hot links.

17. Ibid., 3–5.

18. California Democratic Party/California Republican Party, Redacted
Brief, 2.

19. Ibid., 2–3, citing Feingold deposition, 86–87.

20. Thompson, 2, citing *Hadnott v. Amos*, 394 U.S. 538 (1969)

21. Ibid., 5.

22. Ibid., 9.

23. Ibid., 11.

24. 79 Stat. 437 (1965).

25. *New York Times v. Sullivan*, 376 U.S. 254 (1964), 270.

26. "McConnell Omnibus," 47.

27. 424 U.S. at 14.

28. Ibid., 39.

29. "McConnell Omnibus," 49.

30. Ibid., citing Lillian R. BeVier, "The Issue of Issue Advocacy: An Economic, Political, and Constitutional Analysis," *Virginia Law Review* 85
(1999): 1761, 1769.

31. 494 U.S. 652 (1990).

32. See Samuel Walker, *In Defense of American Liberties: A History of
the ACLU* (New York: Oxford University Press, 1990).

33. ACLU brief, 4.

34. NRA Brief, 1.

35. Ibid.

36. Ibid., 2.

37. Ibid., 3.

38. Ibid., 5, quoting Harry Kalven, Jr., *A Worthy Tradition: Freedom of
Speech in America* (New York: Harper and Row, 1988), 63.

39. 376 U.S. 254 (1964), 276; *Brandenburg v. Ohio*, 395 U.S. 444 (1969).

40. 376 U.S. at 270.

41. NRA 7–8, quoting *Sullivan*, 376 U.S. at 272.

42. AFL-CIO Brief, 4

43. 47 U.S.C. §315(b).

44. "McConnell Omnibus," 90.

45. 2 U.S.C. §441f.

46. "McConnell Omnibus," 91.

47. Thompson Brief, 14.

48. Ibid., 15. The study indicating that infants and toddlers made contributions is from a *New York Times* article, citing a *Los Angeles Times* report, and entered at 148 *Congressional Record* S 2145 (20 March 2002).

49. "McConnell Omnibus," 97.

50. RNC Brief, 73–74.

51. Ibid., 74–75.

52. The plaintiffs did not challenge the constitutionality of Title IV, which involved a severability section; that is, if one part of the law were declared unconstitutional this would not affect the application of all other parts; §402 laid out dates when provisions of the law would go into effect; and §403 spelled out the means by which the case would be reviewed in district court and then taken directly to the Supreme Court, and gave members of Congress standing to intervene in any suit relating to the law's constitutionality.

53. "McConnell Omnibus," 98–99. The plaintiffs had little case law to rely upon in combating this provision, and relied upon an old Supreme Court decision, *Connally v. General Construction Company*, 269 U.S. 385 (1926), and a more recent circuit court opinion vacating the denial of a broadcast license because the denial had been based upon "confusing" and "unclear" regulations, *Trinity Broadcasting of Florida, Inc. v. Federal Communications Commission*, 211 F.3d 618 (D.C. Cir. 2000).

54. AFL-CIO Brief, 18.

55. *First National Bank of Boston v. Bellotti*, 435 U.S. 765 (1977).

56. *Consolidated Edison Co. v. Public Service Commission*, 447 U.S. 530 (1980).

57. *Austin v. Michigan Chamber of Commerce*, 494 U.S. 652 at 677 (Brennan, J., concurring).

58. 494 U.S. at 657; see Chamber/NAM Brief, 2–3.

59. Ibid., 5–6; Matheson won the election and was returned to his seat in 2002.

60. Randolph Moss to author, e-mail, 2 August 2004.

61. A list of the various studies as well as summaries of their findings can be accessed at http://www.pewtrusts.com, using the search function for connections to "Campaign Finance Reform." I am indebted to Elizabeth Garrett for alerting me to the role of the Pew Trusts.

62. "Serving the Public Interest," http://www.pewtrusts.com/udeas/ ideas _item.cfm?content_item_id=2046&content_type_I, accessed 17 November 2004.

63. Elizabeth Garrett to author, 6 September 2004. In addition, smaller think tanks also did particular studies for some of the affiliated defendant-interveners.

64. Brief for Defendants, *Senator Mitch McConnell et al. v. Federal Election Commission et al.*, Civ. No. 02-0582, All Consolidated Cases, in the U.S. District Court for the District of Columbia, Redacted Version, 32. All citations in this section refer to this brief.

65. *Investigation of Illegal or Improper Activities in Connection with 1996 Federal Election Campaigns,* Senate Report No. 105-167, 6 vols. (10 March 1998).

66. Defendants' Brief, 50–52.

67. Ibid., 59.

68. *Ibid.,* 62–63, and 66–86.

69. Ibid., 65, citing *Buckley,* 424 U.S. at 20–38, and *Shrink Missouri,* 528 U.S. at 387–88, 391–97.

70. Ibid., 22–36.

71. Ibid., I-42 (pages beginning with "I" represent interveners' brief.

72. Ibid., I-43.

73. Ibid., 133–46.

74. Ibid., 133–34.

75. Ibid., 163–64, emphasis included; the last quote refers to *Rostker v. Goldberg,* 453 U.S. 57 (1981), 64.

76. Ibid., I-68, citing *New York Trust Co. v. Eisner,* 256 U.S. 345 (1921) 349.

77. Ibid., I-68.

78. Ibid., I-69–I-78.

79. Ibid., I-80–I-83.

80. Ibid., 194, citing *Buckley,* 424 U.S. at 92–93.

81. Ibid., 208, I-152

82. Consolidated Brief, 211 ff.

83. Consolidated Reply Brief for Plaintiffs, "McConnell Omnibus," 1.

84. Ibid., citing Senator Snowe in 148 *Congressional Record* S2134 (20 March 2002).

85. Ibid., RNC 1.

86. Ibid., ACLU 1–2.

87. Reply Brief of Defendants, 43, 45.

88. Ibid., I-1.

89. Ibid.

90. *McConnell v. Federal Election Commission,* 251 F.Supp.2d 176, 209 (D.D.C. 2003).

Chapter 7

1. 251 F.Supp.2d 176 (D.D.C. 2003). Early news reports spoke about an opinion running 1,638 pages, referring to the initial decision sheets put out by the district court itself. Once typeset, however, it ran considerably fewer pages, but still ranks among the longest—and most confusing—cases ever reported.

2. Ibid., 187–88.

3. Tony Mauro, "Campaign Finance Ruling Gives No Satisfaction," *Legal Times,* 12 May 2003.

4. The following account is drawn from the *New York Times,* 5 and 6

December 2002; the *Washington Post,* 5 and 6 December 2002; and *U.S. Law Week* 71 (10 December 2002): 2375.

5. 251 F.Supp.2d, 184.

6. Ibid., 266, citing *New York Times Co. v. Sullivan,* 376 U.S. 254 (1964), 270. The only provision Henderson found to be constitutional was §323(e), which placed restrictions on federal candidates' use of soft money to assist candidates in local, state, or other federal elections.

7. Ibid., 435.

8. For a favorable analysis of her opinion, see Robert F. Bauer, "A Glimpse into the Future? Judge Kollar-Kotelly's View of Congressional Authority to Regulate Political Money," *University of Pennsylvania Journal of Constitutional Law* 6 (2003): 95.

9. Ibid., 757.

10. Richard Briffault, "What Did They Do and What Does It Mean? The Three-Judge Court's Decision in *McConnell v. FEC* and the Implications for the Supreme Court," *University of Pennsylvania Journal of Constitutional Law* 6: 58, 62–63. For whatever reasons—awareness that the Supreme Court would soon speak on the matter, the length and confusion of the opinion, or something else, the district court opinion received far less attention in the law journals than one might have expected. The best sustained analysis is the series of articles—of which this is one—that appeared in a symposium in this journal.

11. Ibid., 64. However, for a defense of the opinions, see Trevor Potter (general counsel for the Campaign Legal Center), who believes "the court has gotten a bad rap in its efforts to deal with an extremely complex matter." "Mc-Cain-Feingold and the D.C. District Court," *Journal of Constitutional Law* 6 (2003), 88; and Robert F. Bauer (chair of the political law group at the Washington, D.C., firm of Perkins Coie LLP), who "agree[s] with those who argue that the district court has been unfairly savaged for its decision," "A Glimpse into the Future," *Journal of Constitutional Law* 6 (2003): 95.

12. 251 F.Supp.2d, 761.

13. Ibid., 388ff; 651ff.

14. Ibid., 412.

15. Ibid., 412–17 (Henderson) and 790–91 (Leon); Kollar-Kotelly's view is on pages 705–07.

16. Briffault, "What Did They Do and What Does It Mean?" 72–73.

17. 116 *Statutes at Large* 81, 88–89.

18. 251 F.Supp.2d, 120.

19. Ibid., 266n1; see also Neely Tucker, "An Absence of Judicial Restraint?" *Washington Post,* 6 May 2003.

20. 251 F.Supp.2d, 296n5.

21. Ibid., 439n5.

22. *New York Times,* 3 May 2003.

23. ACLU Press Release, 2 May 2003, at http://www.aclu.org/news/NewsPrint.cfm?ID=12524&c=20, accessed 15 May 2003.

24. *Richmond Times-Dispatch*, 8 May 2003.
25. Daniel R. Otiz, "Drawing a Roadmap to Uphold BCRA," *University of Pennsylvania Journal of Constitutional Law* 6 (2003): 106–107.
26. ACLU Press Release, 9 May 2003, at http://www.aclu.org/news/NewsPrint.cfm?ID=12599&c=20, accessed 15 May 2003.
27. Tony Mauro, "Campaign Finance Ruling Gives No Satisfaction," *Legal Times*, 12 May 2003.
28. *McConnell et al. v. Federal Election Commission*, 253 F.Supp.2d 18 (D.D.C. 2003).
29. *McConnell et al. v. Federal Election Commission*, 539 U.S. 911 (2003).
30. There had been constant rumors in the spring that there would be one or more resignations from the Court. All rumors ceased immediately after the Court's announcement, since it was clear that all nine justices intended to stay on, not only for this case but until after the 2004 election. None of them, whatever their political leanings, wanted a nomination hearing for a successor to occur during the campaign.

Chapter 8

1. "McCain-Feingold Decision Appealed," *Washington Post*, 6 May 2003.
2. Anne Gearan, "Supreme Court to Review Campaign Finance Law in Special Session," Associated Press, 6 May 2003, www.law.com.
3. Associated Press dispatch, 13 May 2003.
4. "An Urgent Task for the Court," *New York Times*, 6 May 2003.
5. *McConnell v. Federal Election Commission*, 539 U.S. 911 (2003).
6. *Washington Post*, 6 May 2003.
7. One strange result of this situation is how the Court identified the parties. Normally, the party that appeals the lower court decision is known as the "appellant" and the other side as the "respondent." Since here both sides were appealing, the Court kept the original titles, naming the McConnell group as "plaintiffs" and the government as "defendant."
8. *Washington Post*, 5 June 2003.
9. Ibid.
10. 539 U.S. 146 (2003).
11. Ibid., 152.
12. *Nixon v. Shrink Missouri Government PAC*, 528 U.S. 377 (2000).
13. *Grutter v. Bollinger*, 539 U.S. 306 (2003).
14. *Easley v. Cromartie*, 532 U.S. 234 (2001).
15. Linda Greenhouse, "A Supreme Court Infused with Pragmatism," *New York Times*, 12 December 2003.
16. *Austin v. Michigan State Chamber of Commerce*, 494 U.S. 652 (1990).
17. *Federal Election Commission v. Massachusetts Citizens for Life, Inc.*, 479 U.S. 238 (1986), 266 (Rehnquist, J., dissenting in part and concurring in part).

18. *Federal Election Commission v. Colorado Republican Federal Campaign Committee,* 533 U.S. 431 (2001), 466, 473 (Thomas, J., dissenting).

19. *Washington Post,* 16 June 2003.

20. "A Trio of Good Rulings," *New York Times,* 17 June 2003.

21. Although no lawyer from the FEC was given time for oral argument, this was not a slap at the agency. Under law the solicitor general's office is responsible for the defense of all government laws that come up for review by the High Court.

22. Tony Mauro, "McCain-Feingold Plaintiffs Squabble over Argument Time," *Legal Times,* 21 July 2003.

23. See, for example, Tony Mauro, "High Court Hears Arguments on Campaign Finance Law," *Legal Times,* 9 September 2003; Linda Greenhouse, "Justices Hear Vigorous Attacks on New Campaign Finance Law," *New York Times,* 9 September 2003; and Charles Lane, "Justices Split on Campaign Finance," *Washington Post,* 9 September 2003. See also Jeffrey Rosen, "Magic Words," *New Republic,* 29 September 2003, 16–20.

24. *McConnell v. Federal Election Commission,* 124 S.Ct. 619 (2003), 656.

25. Ibid., 661.

26. As noted earlier, a facial challenge—that is a challenge to a law in general before it is actually applied—requires that the complaining parties present solid evidence that if the law were enforced it would surely deprive them of constitutional rights. Suppositions that it might do so are usually dismissed by courts with a proviso that if, in the future, the parties can show real evidence of harm, then they may return to court.

27. The Court did uphold the use of so-called Levin funds, which allowed state and local parties to use soft money for limited purposes.

28. 124 S.Ct. 619, 672–73.

29. Ibid., 678n.68.

30. *Printz v. United States,* 521 U.S. 898 (1997).

31. 124 S.Ct. 619, 686.

32. 479 U.S. 238 (1986). In this case, the Court declared that the same express advocacy standard of *Buckley's* "magic words" would be read into the federal statutory ban on the use of corporate and union treasury funds to pay for expenditures in connection with federal campaigns.

33. 124 S.Ct. 619, 688.

34. Ibid., 695–96.

35. Ibid., 695.

36. Ibid., 699.

37. Ibid., 701.

38. 424 U.S. at 47.

39. 124 S.Ct. 619, 705.

40. Citing *Burroughs v. United States,* 290 U.S. 534 (1934), 545.

41. Ibid., 706.

42. See next chapter.

43. 124 S.Ct. 619, 708. Justice Stevens, joined by Ginsburg and Breyer, dissented from the dismissal for lack of standing, and noted that they would have upheld §305 on its merits. Ibid., 784.

44. Ibid., at 709–10.

45. Ibid., 710.

46. Ibid., citing *Buckley*, 424 U.S. at 81.

47. In the lower court, Judge Kollar-Kotelly had listed some examples, 251 F.Supp.2d 176 (2003), 588–90, but in the briefings before the high court the government had produced no examples. The Court left open whether or not Congress could impose lower caps on contributions by minors, and whether, should actual abuse be shown, whether Congress could, with better factual justification, repass this section. 124 S.Ct. 619, 711.

48. Ibid.

49. Section 504 of BCRA amended the Communications Act of 1934, 47 USC §315(e), which, with many amendments, remained the controlling federal law regulating the broadcast media.

50. 124 S.Ct. 619, 713.

51. Ibid., 715.

52. Compare, for example, treatment of the print media in *New York Times v. Sullivan*, 376 U.S. 254 (1964), with that of the broadcast media in *Red Lion Broadcasting Co. v. FCC*, 395 U.S. 367 (1969).

53. 124 S.Ct. 619, 717.

54. Ibid., 783.

55. Ibid., 718, 719.

56. Ibid., 664, 666.

57. Ibid., 742.

58. Ibid., 746.

59. Ibid., 747.

60. Ibid., 746.

61. Ibid., 726.

62. Ibid., 735.

63. Ibid., 720.

64. Lillian R. Bevier, "*McConnell v. FEC*: Not Senator Buckley's First Amendment," *Election Law Journal* 3 (2004): 127. At the time of this writing, most law journals had not yet published any articles on the case. *Election Law Journal*, on the other hand, had arranged for a wide variety of academics and others to comment on the case and managed to get a full-scale symposium out by April 2004. This section is based primarily on that symposium.

65. Robert F. Bauer, "*McConnell*, Parties, and the Decline of the Right of Association," *Election Law Journal* 3: 199.

66. James Bopp, Jr., and Richard E. Coleson, "Electioneering Communication versus Abortion," *Election Law Journal* 3: 205, 209.

67. Charles J. Cooper and Derek L. Shaffer, "What Congress 'Shall Make' The Court Will Take: How *McConnell v. FEC* Betrays the First Amendment

in Upholding Incumbency Protection under the Banner of 'Campaign Finance Reform,'" *Election Law Journal* 3: 223.

68. Richard A. Epstein, *"McConnell v. Federal Election Commission:* A Deadly Dose of Double Deference," *Election Law Journal* 3: 231.

69. Elizabeth Garrett, *"McConnell v. FCC* and Disclosure," *Election Law Journal* 3: 237.

70. Samuel Issacharoff, "Throwing in the Towel: The Constitutional Morass of Campaign Finance," *Election Law Journal* 3: 259.

71. Quoted in Linda Greenhouse, "A Supreme Court Infused with Pragmatism," *New York Times,* 12 December 2003.

72. Thomas E. Mann and Norman J. Ornstein, "Separating Myth from Reality in *McConnell v. FCC*," *Election Law Journal* 3: 291.

73. 124 S.Ct. 619, 706.

Epilog

1. John McCain to author, 29 April 2004 (form letter); for a fuller elaboration of his views, see McCain, "Reclaiming Our Democracy: The Way Forward," 3 *Election Law Journal* 115 (2004).

2. Transcript, *Today* (NBC), 11 December 2003.

3. Helen Dewar, "McCain, Feingold and Co. Laugh Last," *Washington Post,* 11 December 2003.

4. *Washington Post,* 11 December 2003.

5. Public Citizen, Press Release, 10 December 2003, http://www.citizen .org/pressroom/release.cfm?ID=1064, visited 8 May 2004.

6. Common Cause, Press Release, 10 December 2003, http://common-cause.org/news/default.cfm?ArtID=258, visited 8 July 2004.

7. Pew Press Release, 10 December 2003, at http://www.pewtrusts.com/ ideas/ideas_item.cfm?content_id=2045&content_type_i visited 17 November 2004.

8. "Court's Ruling Validates Campaign Finance Reform" (editorial) *Alameda* (California) *Times-Star,* 14 December 2003.

9. *Boston Globe,* 12 December 2003.

10. *St. Louis Post-Dispatch,* 11 December 2003.

11. *Washington Post,* 11 December 2003.

12. ACLU Press Release, 10 December 2003, http://www.aclu.org/news/ NewsPrint.cfm?ID=14560&c=261, visited 8 July 2004.

13. *Washington Post,* 11 December 2003.

14. *Id.*

15. http://www.washingtonpost.com/ac2/wp-dyn/A52956-2003Dec10, visited 10 December 2003.

16. This section is based on news stories that appeared in the *New York Times* and *Washington Post* on 11 December 2003.

17. *Washington Post,* 27 August 2004.

18. *New York Times,* 26 October 2004.

19. Thomas B. Edsall, "Fundraising Specialists, Independent Groups Gain," *Washington Post,* 11 December 2003.

20. *New York Times,* 12 December 2003.

21. See above, pp. 78–83.

22. 124 S.Ct. at 522.

23. Edsall, "Fundraising Specialists," *Washington Post,* 11 December 2003.

24. *Washington Post,* 25 Aug. 2002.

25. *Id.,* 10 March 2004. Political Money Line, a Web site that tracks campaign money, reported that seven 527's had raised more than $50 million by the end of March 2004.

26. *Id.,* 2 March 2004.

27. Chellie Pingree, president of Common Cause, to Mai T. Dinh, acting assistant general counsel, FEC, 9 April 2004, on http://www.commoncause .org/news/printable.cfm?ArtID=92, visited 8 July 2004. Common Cause submitted its letter in conjunction with the Brennan Center for Justice at NYU Law School.

28. See, for example, *Washington Post,* 11 March 2004, and Bradley A. Smith, "*McConnell v. Federal Election Commission:* Ideology Trumps Reality, Pragmatism," 3 *Election Law Journal* 345 (2004). Smith, a former academic, had in his university years written opposing campaign finance reform. See his *Unfree Speech: The Folly of Campaign Finance Reform* (Princeton University Press, 2001)

29. *Washington Post,* 16 Feb. 2004.

30. *Id.,* 19 Feb. 2004.

31. *Id.,* 13 May 2004.

32. *Id.,* 15 September 2004. Interestingly, Robertson, appointed to the bench by President Clinton, noted that he was rejecting Bush's request based on "an impeccable decision by Judge Kenneth Starr . . . decided, figuratively speaking, when the shoe was on the other foot." Starr, when on the federal appeals court, had ruled in 1985 that the courts could not order the FEC to act more quickly on a Democratic congressman's complaint of campaign violations.

33. *Shays and Meehan v. Federal Election Commission,* 337 F.Supp.2d 28 (DC Dist. of Columbia, 2004).

34. *Washington Post,* 13 May 2004.

35. Political Money Line, http://www.tray.com/fecinfo/, visited 28 July 2004.

36. *Washington Post,* 11 June 2004.

37. *Id.,* 6 November 2004, citing a study by the Center for Public Integrity.

38. http://actforvictory.org, visited 28 July 2004.

39. For the success, and failures, of this campaign, see Matt Bai, "Who Lost Ohio?" *New York Times Magazine,* 21 November 2004, 66–74.

40. Kirsten Mitchel, Keith Epstein and Ted Byrd, "527 Groups Gain Political Clout," Media General News Service, 14 June 2004, http://info .mgnetwork.com, visited 18 July 2004.

41. Transcript of "Marketplace" (NPR news show), 7 July 2004; on the Club for Growth, see also *New York Times*, 20 December 2003.

42. *New York Times*, 20 October 2004.

43. Apparently the Bush campaign came perilously near crossing the line in its relation to the Swift Boat veterans, in that a former member of the Bush campaign organization helped direct the 527's activity; see "Can Kerry Make a Case that Bush Broke the Law?" MSNBC, 20 August 2004, http://www.msnbc.com/id/5772722/print/1/displaymode/1098/ visited 22 August 2004.

44. *New York Times*, 18 June 2004.

45. *Washington Post*, 27 August and 3 December 2004; Political Money Line, http://www.fecinfo.com, visited 21 November 2004.

46. *Washington Post*, 3 June 2004.

47. Thomas E.. Mann and Norman Orenstein, "So Far, So Good on Campaign Finance Reform," *id.*, 29 February 2004.

48. *Richmond Times-Dispatch*, 6 November 2004.

49. Certainly the airwaves in northern Virginia carried many of the old-style issue ads attacking various candidates right up to the day of the election, a situation apparently widespread throughout the country and unaddressed by the FEC.

50. *New York Times*, 16 June 2004.

51. *Buckley v. Valeo*, 424 U.S. 1, 17–18 (1976), quoting *United States v. O'Brien*, 391 U.S. 367, 382 (1968).

Appendixes

1. P.L. 92-225, 86 *Stat.* 3 (1972). Although Congress did not actually finish passage of the bill until January 1972, it continues to be known as the act of 1971. It is codified at 2 U.S.C. §§431–455.

2. 88 *Stat.* 1263 (1974), codified at 2 U.S.C. 432 et seq. and 18 U.S.C. 591 et seq. The public financing provisions are amendments to the 1954 Internal Revenue Code, Subtitle H, and are codified at 26 U.S.C. 9001 et seq.

3. P.L. 94-283, 90 Stat. 475.

4. P.L. 96-187, 93 Stat. 1339.

Index